LITERACY AS TRANSLINGUAL PRACTICE

"To me, this is a dream collection that I cannot wait to own and read! .... It includes most of the major players working on translingualism today."

Patricia Bizzell, Reverend John E. Brooks S.J.
Professor of Humanities and Professor of English,
College of the Holy Cross, USA

"Timely, of the highest scholarly caliber, and needed. Scholars will learn from this book. It will inspire rich discussion."

Catherine Prendergast, Professor of English, University Scholar
and Director of the First Year Rhetoric Program,
University of Illinois at Urbana-Champaign, USA

The term *translingual* highlights the reality that people always shuttle across languages, communicate in hybrid languages and, thus, enjoy multilingual competence. In the context of migration, transnational economic and cultural relations, digital communication, and globalism, increasing contact is taking place between languages and communities. In these contact zones new genres of writing and new textual conventions are emerging that go beyond traditional dichotomies that treat languages as separated from each other, and texts and writers as determined by one language or the other.

Pushing forward a translingual orientation to writing—one that is in tune with the new literacies and communicative practices flowing into writing classrooms and demanding new pedagogies and policies—this volume is structured around five concerns: refining the theoretical premises, learning from community practices, debating the role of code meshed products, identifying new research directions, and developing sound pedagogical applications. These themes are explored by leading scholars from L1 and L2 composition, rhetoric and applied linguistics, education theory and classroom practice, and diverse ethnic rhetorics. Timely and much needed, *Literacy as Translingual Practice* is essential reading for students, researchers, and practitioners across these fields.

A. Suresh Canagarajah is Erle Sparks Professor and Director of the Migration Studies Project at Pennsylvania State University.

LITERACY AS TRANSLINGUAL PRACTICE

Between Communities and Classrooms

Edited by A. Suresh Canagarajah

Routledge
Taylor & Francis Group

NEW YORK AND LONDON

First published 2013
by Routledge
711 Third Avenue, New York, NY 10017

Simultaneously published in the UK
by Routledge
2 Park Square, Milton Park, Abingdon, Oxon OX14 4RN

Routledge is an imprint of the Taylor & Francis Group, an informa business

© 2013 Taylor & Francis

Library of Congress Cataloging in Publication Data
    Literacy as translingual practice : between communities and
    classrooms / edited by A. Suresh Canagarajah.
    p. cm.
    Includes bibliographical references and index.
    1. Multilingualism—Social aspects. 2. Literacy—Social aspects.
    3. English language—Globalization. 4. Intercultural communication.
    5. Second language acquisition. 6. Sociolinguistics.
    I. Canagarajah, A. Suresh. II. Title.
    P115.45.L58 2013
    306.44'6—dc23
    2012037796

ISBN: 978–0–415–52466–7 (hbk)
ISBN: 978–0–415–52467–4 (pbk)
ISBN: 978–0–203–12029–3 (ebk)

Typeset in Bembo
by Swales & Willis Ltd, Exeter, Devon

CV 07.03.2019 1647

CONTENTS

ACKNOWLEDGMENTS

Many of the chapters in this book emerged out of the conversations and interactions in the 22nd Penn State Conference on Rhetoric and Composition in July 2011. I thank Dean Susan Welch, Jack Selzer and the College of Liberal Arts for the resources made available for this conference. I am also indebted to the scholars of national and international prominence who attended the conference and contributed to the intellectual synergy generated in Happy Valley.

The authors of the chapters in this book have to be thanked for working with me diligently and patiently over the several rounds of revision and editing.

Dorothy Worden, graduate student in applied linguistics and instructor in second language writing, helped organize the conference with great success. She went on to assist me in putting this book together, playing an important role in the editorial work.

Finally, I thank Naomi Silverman of Routledge for being supportive of this book project and giving me useful suggestions.

1

INTRODUCTION

A. Suresh Canagarajah

The best way to understand the term *translingual* is by focusing on the prefix. What does "trans" do to language? Firstly, the term moves us beyond a consideration of individual or monolithic languages to life between and across languages. Sociolinguists might go to the extent of defining "language" itself as constituting hybrid and fluid codes that earn their labels only in the context of ownership ideologies (see Blommaert, 2010). Despite such labels and ideologies, language resources always come into contact in actual use and shape each other. From this perspective, we have to consider all acts of communication and literacy as involving a shuttling between languages and a negotiation of diverse linguistic resources for situated construction of meaning. Secondly, the prefix encourages us to treat acts of communication as involving more than words. We have to treat communication as an alignment of words with many other semiotic resources involving different symbol systems (i.e., icons, images), modalities of communication (i.e., aural, oral, visual, and tactile channels), and ecologies (i.e., social and material contexts of communication).

There are good reasons why scholars are currently re-envisioning writing and literacy through the translingual lens. Before I articulate the shifts involved for literacy, and the new research challenges and pedagogical implications they raise, I must emphasize that the neologism "translingual" is indeed needed. Existing terms like *multilingual* or *plurilingual* keep languages somewhat separated even as they address the co-existence of multiple languages. From their point of view, competence involves distinct compartments for each language one uses. Similarly, in literacy, different languages may occupy different spaces in texts. However, the term translingual enables a consideration of communicative competence as not restricted to predefined meanings of individual languages, but the ability to merge different language resources in situated interactions for new meaning construction. Competence is not an arithmetical addition of the resources of different languages, but the transformative capacity to mesh their resources for creative new forms and meanings. Similarly, the term translingual treats textual practices as hybridizing and emergent, facilitating creative tensions between languages. The term also helps us go beyond the dichotomy mono/multi or uni/pluri. These binaries may give the impression that cross-language relations and practices matter only to a specific group of people, i.e., those considered multilingual. However, the term translingual enables us to treat cross-language interactions and contact relationships as fundamental to all acts of communication and relevant for all of us. In this sense, the shift in literacy is not relevant for traditionally multilingual students/subjects alone, but for "native" speakers of English and "monolinguals" as well.

Despite the novelty of the term, we mustn't think of the types of competence and practices implied by the term translingual as having merely pedantic or academic interest. The urgency for scholars to address translingual practices in literacy derives from the fact that they are widely practiced in communities and everyday communicative contexts, though ignored or suppressed in classrooms. Social relations and communicative practices in the context of late modernity—featuring migration, transnational economic and production relationships, digital media, and online communication—facilitate a meshing of languages and semiotic resources. Bazerman's chapter (ch. 2) outlines the social conditions which call for a literacy beyond separate languages and communities. However, we must remember that these practices are not new or recent. Translingual literacies have always characterized the practices of diverse communities in the past. Mao (ch. 5) and Morris Young (ch. 6) define the indigenous or the local as always creolized. Reyhner (ch. 7) and Cushman (ch. 8) show how different Native American communities have developed traditions of education and literacy that involve a meshing of language and cultural resources, including those of the colonizer. This orientation is backed by historiographical research on precolonial practices in South Asia (Khubchandani, 1997) and Africa (Makoni, 2002). Postcolonial communities such as Lebanon (Bou Ayash, ch. 9) and Kenya (Milu, ch. 10) are drawing from local translingual traditions to absorb colonizing languages and fashion creative literate and communicative practices. The objective of this book is to learn from these community practices—whether the late modern West or precolonial orient, and many traditions and places in between—to enhance literacy education in pedagogical contexts. Translingual literacies are not about fashioning a new kind of literacy. It is about understanding the practices and processes that already characterize communicative activity in diverse communities to both affirm them and develop them further through an informed pedagogy.

It is not surprising, however, that scholars are still struggling to define these literacies and implement relevant pedagogies. Having defined literacy according to monolingual ideologies since modernity, they have to now revise their understanding to conceive of literacy as translingual. With hindsight, scholars have now started analyzing how ideologies that territorialized, essentialized, and circum-scribed languages came into prominence around the enlightenment and romanti-cism, especially in the thinking of those like Johannes Herder and John Locke (see Bauman & Briggs, 2000; Blommaert & Verscheuren, 1992). With the colonial enterprise, these ideologies have also migrated to other parts of the world, often imposed as literacies more conducive to science, rationality, development, and civilization, threatening diverse local translingual practices. This ideological work of monolingualism is still unfinished, displaying feverish and concerted efforts in countries like the United States, as linguist Michael Silverstein (1996) has shown. With the monolingualist paradigm becoming difficult to sustain under the fasci-nating technological developments and irrepressible social mobility which engen-der different communicative practices, we are now ready to travel back in time or to other places to reconstruct new scholarly constructs.

Compositionists started theorizing these literacies from a product-oriented per-spective earlier. The hybridity of texts in community and student writing under-standably attracted their attention and called for a different explanation. Labels like ALT DIS (Schroeder, Fox, & Bizzell, 2002), hybridity (Bizzell, 1999), and code-meshing (Young, 2004) that dominated discussion in composition circles were an attempt to understand the politics and poetics of such texts. Though these textual products still have a lot of resonance to certain communities (i.e., African American, Hispanic, and postcolonial), there has also been some questioning as to the extent to which they are desirable for others. Some communities fear that such hybridization of codes will lead to the dilution of their language resources and identity and threaten their sovereignty (as Lyons, 2009 has argued on behalf of Native American communities). Some argue that the values attached to the ver-nacular and the dominant languages are different in their communities, and express a desire to reserve different codes for different functions, rather than meshing them (as Milson-Whyte argues in ch. 11). More importantly, valorizing difference in texts has created the impression among students and scholars from dominant com-munities (Anglo-American, in the U.S. context) that a text in standard English lacks creativity or voice (as addressed in Lu and Horner (ch. 3) and Bou Ayash (ch. 9) in this volume). Minority students might also go away with the impression that something approximating dominant conventions are disempowering.

While code-meshing will remain important for certain students and commu-nities for voice (and the chapters by Milu (ch. 10) and Bou Ayash (ch. 9) show that it will continue to be practiced in postcolonial communities and character-ize popular media such as hiphop and social networking sites) and will generate more debates on its politics and pragmatics (as we feature in Part III of this book, with a spirited defense of code-meshing by Vershawn Young (ch. 13)), some scholars feel motivated to develop a paradigm of translingual relations that moves beyond valorizing hybrid texts. A translingual orientation emphasizes that what we treat as "standard English" or "monolingual" texts are themselves hybrid. These labels are ideological constructs that mask the diversity inherent in all acts of writing and communication. Consider that in each act of communication the semiotic resources we use are recontextualized for the purposes and participants in that activity, with their own resonance. If code-meshing draws attention to difference, the translingual orientation also emphasizes difference-in-similarity. That is, it makes us sensitive to the creativity and situatedness of every act of communication, even in seemingly normative textual products. In this sense, "translingual practice" is emerging as a term that accommodates hybrid practices without ignoring the inherent hybridity in products that appear on the surface to approximate dominant conventions. The orientation thus enables us to discern agency and voice of both multilingual and monolingual writers in textual products that have varying relationships to the norm.

However, there are different facets to the term translingual that need to be unpacked. Initially, some scholars presented the term translingual as an *orientation* to writing and literacy (see Horner et al., 2011; and Lu & Horner, ch. 3 this volume). From this perspective, it is not a text but an approach to texts. This definition is sufficiently broad as to accommodate the metalinguistic and cognitive awarenesses involved in such literacy. It emphasizes the attitudes and perspectives that need to be cultivated toward cross-language relations in literacy. For teachers, it encourages a way of looking at the implications for writing and teaching from an awareness that languages are always in contact and complement each other in communication.

As we proceed to narrow down this orientation, we have started focusing on the practices that constitute translingual literacies. We have started asking what strategies characterize the construction and negotiation of meaning in such forms of literacy. Monolingual ideologies have relied on form, grammar, and system for meaning-making, motivating teachers and scholars to either ignore strategies and practices or give them secondary importance. A translingual orientation requires an important shift to treating practices as primary and emergent, as form is so diverse, fluid, and changing that it cannot guarantee meaning by itself. The focus is now on social agents who give meaning to language resources (of course, building on the traces of meanings they bring from their prior use) in situated literacy practices. Such meaning has to be constructed and negotiated through strategic practices, as intelligibility and success depend a lot on collaboration. Many of these practices are developed through socialization and are often intuitive to all of us. Hanson (ch. 19) develops a pedagogy to tap into these intuitive strategies by encouraging her "native speaker" students to decode multilingual websites for their research. Strategies such as guessing the meaning from contexts and other semiotic cues (such as fonts and images) reflect those that multilinguals use in other contact situations (see Canagarajah, 2007). Lorimer (ch. 15) and Wible (ch. 4) discuss other such strategies from their research. We have only scratched the surface in understanding the practices of trilingual literacy. More progress in this front will help us devise practice-based pedagogies that don't focus on codes and norms, but strategies of production and reception of texts.

We need to focus on practices rather than forms because the translingual orientation treats heterogeneity as the norm rather than the exception. In monolingual ideologies, meaning is guaranteed by the uniform codes and conventions a homogeneous community shares. When we move beyond bounded communities and consider communication at the contact zone (whether in precolonial multilingual communities or postmodern social media spaces), we are unable to rely on sharedness for meaning. It is practices that help people negotiate difference and achieve shared understanding. Practices therefore have an important place in translingual literacy. Ratcliffe's (1999) notion of rhetorical listening is an insightful articulation of the listening/reading strategies one has to adopt in order to communicate across difference. We need more knowledge on the speaking/writing strategies to facilitate such negotiation.

Just as these negotiation strategies are developed through socialization in contact zones and multilingual communities, we are also finding that people are bringing certain *dispositions* that favor translingual communication and literacy. These dispositions—similar to Bourdieu's (1977) concept of *habitus*—constitute assumptions of language, attitudes toward social diversity, and tacit skills of communication and learning. Examples of such dispositions include an awareness of language as constituting diverse norms; a willingness to negotiate with diversity in social interactions; attitudes such as openness to difference, patience to co-construct meaning, and an acceptance of negotiated outcomes in interactions; and the ability to learn through practice and critical self-reflection. Lorimer uses the term "rhetorical attunement" (ch. 15) to describe such dispositions among her multilingual subjects. Wible also shows how a different set of attitudes and orientations comes into play in the World Social Forum where people can simultaneously use their own languages and still achieve semantic and social understanding. Pedagogical reports of others like Lu and Horner (ch. 3), Hanson (ch. 19), and Krall-Lanoue (ch. 21) also demonstrate how these dispositions help their students to negotiate cross-language relations without teachers having to instruct them on such negotiation strategies. What we are finding is that even native/monolingual students are socialized into such dispositions in networking sites and online interactions which compel them to negotiate language diversity effectively (see Williams, 2009). As we discover more of these dispositions and formulate them in a systematic manner, we may gain new insights into pedagogical possibilities. Teachers don't have to assume that translingual literacy has to be taught afresh to their students. They can tap into the dispositions of their students for such interactions and explore ways to scaffold them for further development. Among students who lack adequate socialization into multilingual and contact zones encounters, teachers may consider working at the level of attitudinal shifts and language awareness to prepare them for such interactions.

Another direction in the effort to unpack the translingual orientation is the realization that this kind of literacy is intrinsically rhetorical. Multilingual words gain their logic and uptake in relation to the rhetorical objectives, participants, setting, and interests concerned. In fact, uptake is primarily about persuasion—i.e., persuading listeners/readers on the appropriateness of one's semiotic choices for one's purposes. Wible (ch. 4), Mao (ch. 5), and Morris Young (ch. 6) consider how we can better understand the rhetoric of translingual communication. Such a rhetoric involves certain ethical values suitable for negotiating difference (not dissimilar to the notion of dispositions introduced above) and certain negotiation strategies (also discussed earlier) for reception and interpretation. In terms of production, this rhetoric involves processes such as recontextualization, whereby semiotic resources from diverse languages and cultures are reconfigured for one's purposes. As these are rhetorical processes, we are compelled to treat translingual literacy beyond the narrow bounds of language norms or textual structures and situate them in larger contexts of history, culture, and social relations.

A particularly important construct such rhetorical considerations are developing for translingual literacy is the constitutive and emergent role of place/space. Place is important in a definition of translingual literacy, for several reasons. As we move away from considering literacy as shaped by grammatical norms and formal considerations, with their own intrinsic logic or meanings guaranteed by an autonomous structure, we have to ask what we can ground such forms of communication and literacy on. In this exploration, we are now beginning to see the material context that was earlier bracketed off as insignificant emerging as constitutive of meaning. The material context shapes literacy and communication in profound ways. While geographical/physical *place* contextualizes literacy, even more influential are the social negotiations and rhetorical encounters that create alternative *spaces* for creativity and understanding. Wible (ch. 4), Mao (ch. 5), and Morris Young (ch. 6) treat these spaces as characterized by recontextualization, co-construction, and creolization, as people from subjugated backgrounds find voice through an appropriation and reconfiguration of conflicting norms and values. The fact that certain places are colonized doesn't prevent social agents from constructing rhetorical and translingual spaces for renegotiating power relationships.

In defining the semiotics and rhetoric of translingual literacy, there is still room to understand the multimodality of texts. Applied linguists have coined the term *alignment* to characterize the manner in which diverse communicative ecologies, modalities, and symbol systems are configured by multilinguals in meaning-making activity (see Atkinson Churchill, Nishino, & Okada, 2007). Alignment draws attention away from grammar or language system as the locus of meaning, and points to the activity of social agents in putting together diverse semiotic resources for meaning. Hanson (ch. 19) suggests the value of this approach by unveiling the strategies students (surprisingly, "native" speakers in this case) adopt to align different modalities and symbols to guess the meaning of multilingual websites for their research. The many studies in this volume from communicative domains such as hiphop (Milu, ch. 10), folk songs (Mao, ch. 5; Morris Young, ch. 6), public signs (Milson-Whyte, ch. 11), urban interactions (Bou Ayash, ch. 9), graffiti (Morris Young, ch. 6), and digital communication (Hanson, ch. 19; Scenters-Zapico, ch. 17) have the potential for further interpretation beyond language for the way in which diverse modalities and semiotics contribute to both the production and reception of texts.

While our efforts in defining translingual literacy and understanding its communicative potential will continue at the theoretical level, such an orientation also offers new directions for research. The value of this shift in orientation is that even traditional research methods can be revised to yield new findings. Donahue (ch. 14) discusses how she revised a study she undertook from a comparative perspective on student writers from different communities with new outcomes. The translingual orientation makes her look at her research subjects from France and the United States as not compartmentalized into their different language and cultural backgrounds, but inhabiting contact zones that show the mediation and reconstruction of their texts. Since it is the compartmentalization of disciplines in modernity that led to the definition of language and literacy in monolingual, formalist, and autonomous terms, we can understand why the translingual orientation is bringing disciplines together for new research. The translingual orientation has motivated scholars to merge resources not only from different disciplines but also from different academic communities. We find that the dominance of occidental communities in modernist knowledge construction has led to a reductive perspective on literacy and communication. The rediscovery of vibrant traditions of translingual practices outside the West—in East Asian, Caribbean, African, and Mediterranean communities, with knowledge relating to them (as represented in the chapters in this volume)—can help us immensely in our theorization of literacy and communication in the global contact zones. Bazerman (ch. 2) outlines the motivations for such merging of knowledge from diverse literacy traditions and identifies the efforts already underway in this direction.

There are also new pedagogical possibilities coming into prominence as we research a translingual orientation to literacy. Socialization is emerging as an important means for people to learn these new literacies and develop the necessary dispositions and strategies for their negotiation in the global contact zones. Product-oriented, monolingual, and norm-based teaching can often stifle these complex dispositions and strategies students bring from outside the classroom. However, classroom and educational ethnography shows that behind the backs of their teachers, students are turning pedagogical sites as spaces for socialization, tapping into the rich communicative ecologies found therein (see Creese & Blackledge, 2010). Learners are collaborating with their peers and mentors, and shuttling between different languages, literacies, and communities, as they develop translingual competence. Poe reports on such as an experience (ch. 16). She shows how an international graduate student drew from the affordances in the graduate program and the disciplinary community for effective academic literacy development. Such a socialization orientation is also revealing that literacy is a collaborative and social enterprise. Literacy brokers and literacy sponsors play an important role in developing translingual literacy competence. No longer is literacy or communication perceived as an isolated or individual activity. Scenters-Zapico (ch. 17) and Jerskey (ch. 18) continue this line of exploration and show the roles diverse sponsors and brokers can play in the development of translingual literacy.

Pedagogical implications deriving from such an orientation still need imaginative rethinking and creative design. Though teachers might feel helpless in relation to such new definitions of literacy and the need to rethink their practices, students don't feel lost. This is because, as I pointed out earlier, people are developing relevant strategies and dispositions for translingual literacies in the contact zones outside the classroom. It is possible to make the classroom a safe house for such practices and facilitate such interactions for further development of these competencies. This is exactly what Jerskey (ch. 18) does in her institution. Going beyond the native/nonnative divide, she encourages both groups to broker each other's literacy products in the safe learning spaces she constructs. Similarly, Hanson (ch. 19) allows her native speaker students to tap into their intuitive strategies to gather research information from multilingual sources. Pandey (ch. 20) devises a strategy to help students analyze literate products from a more holistic perspective, treating languages and cultures as mediating such products.

It is important to emphasize that we cannot ignore the implications for form and micro-level language features in translingual literacy or pedagogy. The position that translingual literacy treats place and rhetorical practice as more primary shouldn't be interpreted to mean that form is irrelevant. It is simply that form is shaped for meaning in relation to these ecological, social, and contextual factors. In fact, this perspective makes us even more sensitive to form than in the traditional approaches. In monolingual orientations, form could be taken for granted as it came with readymade meanings and values which ensured communicative success. If form doesn't hold shared meanings in the contact zone, participants have to be sensitive to co-constructing meanings. In this regard, we may have to reorient to traditional constructs such as *error* in our teaching. Error is what fails to gain uptake in situated interactions, not those which deviate from an abstract predefined norm. This orientation encourages a pedagogy that values students' choices and helps teachers think along with the rhetorical intentions of the students to find their meanings. There is responsibility on both sides of the production/reception divide here. Just as readers have to collaborate in co-constructing meaning, writers have to adopt suitable strategies to populate words with their intentions and convey those intentions appropriately. Krall-Lanoue (ch. 21) demonstrates the value of such a pedagogy in the penultimate chapter of the book.

The purpose of this book is not to provide a definitive statement on translingual literacy. It is too early for that kind of book. Besides, knowledge making doesn't work that way. We construct paradigms in relation to changing social conditions and new communicative realities that demand suitable alternatives. In this sense, Matsuda's chapter (ch. 12) on the changing currents of composition scholarship and the resulting imprecision of terminological usage needs to be understood differently. Though we do have to be careful about romanticizing new theories and constructs for the sake of academic merit, as Matsuda rightly points out, we also have to be flexible enough to change our paradigms when experiences dictate otherwise. Sometimes dominant paradigms can be discriminatory to certain communities and student groups, not to mention irrelevant to certain community experiences. Furthermore, we have to be open to traveling theories being taken up in new ways in different communities and disciplines. The way the term *code switching* has been taken up in composition is such an example. Though it is used in ways different from applied linguistics, it brings a special resonance that is lacking in the former field (as I argue in Canagarajah, 2009). Compositionists have brought out the conservative and rhetorically limited ways code switching is used by linguists. There could be power inequalities in the codes switched. Also, those who switch the codes do not need equal or advanced proficiency in both languages. They can switch for performative reasons, representing subtle identities and values beyond the broad social functions studied in linguistics. To capture the fascinating ways in which the meshing of codes can achieve performative meanings and voice that defies the more structured ways in which linguists perceive switching, compositionists adopt the term *code-meshing* (see Young, 2004). Such migrations and reappropriations of theories can therefore be healthy and open up new perspectives.

This tentativeness in knowledge claims in this book doesn't have to mean that teachers and students are totally helpless. What we find is that people have engaged in such forms of communication and literacy at the level of *practice* for quite a long time in history, with even more creative performances demonstrated in technological developments in late modernity. It is at the level of scholarship and knowledge that we are limited. What this means is that the classroom/community connection, highlighted in the title of the book, can come to the rescue of teachers. By allowing community practices into the classroom, teachers can study the strategies and dispositions students have already developed elsewhere. Building on these resources rather than imposing their own understanding of literacy, teachers can also facilitate spaces for voice for students. However, this is not a one way relationship of schools learning from communities. It is also important for communities and students to be mindful of the power of educational institutions. They reproduce monolingualist language ideologies and dominant norms in society and institutions. However unfair and limited they may be, these norms and ideologies have to be taken seriously. Social and educational success means *engaging* with these norms, though this doesn't mean uncritical acceptance or conformity. As many of the chapters in this book show, the translingual practices of local communities already show such critical engagement and appropriation. Teachers can help students develop the dispositions and strategies they bring with them in more critical, reflective, and informed ways by engaging with the dominant norms and ideologies. As the chapters by Milson-Whyte (ch. 11) and Reyhner (ch. 7) show, minority communities are always looking up to the school to provide spaces and resources for such engagement. It is such critical educational engagement that can also lead to the pluralization of norms and the construction of more democratic social spaces. Classrooms can facilitate new community relationships.

References

Atkinson, D., Churchill, E., Nishino, T., & Okada, H. (2007). Alignment and interaction in a sociocognitive approach in second language acquisition. *Modern Language Journal, 91*, 169–188.

Bauman, R., & Briggs, C. L. (2000). Language philosophy as language ideology: John Locke and Johann Gottfried Herder. In P. V. Kroskrity (Ed.), *Regimes of language: Ideologies, polities, and identities* (pp. 139–204). Oxford, UK: James Currey.

Bizzell, P. (1999). Hybrid forms of academic discourse: What, why, how. *Composition Studies, 27*, 7–21.

Blommaert, J. (2010). *The sociolinguistics of globalization*. Cambridge, UK: Cambridge University Press.

Blommaert, J., & Verschueren, J. (1992). The role of language in European nationalist ideologies. *Pragmatics 2*(3), 355–376.

Bourdieu, P. (1977). *Outline of a theory of practice*. Cambridge, UK: Cambridge University Press.

Canagarajah, A. S. (2007). Lingua franca English, multilingual communities, and language acquisition. *Modern Language Journal, 91*(5), 921–937.

Canagarajah, A. S. (2009). Multilingual strategies of negotiating English: From conversation to writing. *Journal of Advanced Composition, 29*, 711–743.

Creese, A., & Blackledge, A. (2010). Translanguaging in the bilingual classroom: A pedagogy for learning and teaching? *Modern Language Journal, 94*(1), 103–115.

Horner, B., Lu, M.-Z., Royster, J. J., & Trimbur, J. (2011). Language difference in writing: Toward a translingual approach. *College English,* 73 (3), 303–321.

Khubchandani, L. M. (1997). *Revisualizing boundaries: A plurilingual ethos*. New Delhi, India: Sage.

Lyons, S. (2009). The fine art of fencing: Nationalism, hybridity, and the search for a Native American writing pedagogy. *Journal of Advanced Composition, 29*, 77–106.

Makoni, S. (2002). From misinvention to disinvention: An approach to multilingualism. In G. Smitherman, A. Spear, & A. Ball (Eds.), *Black linguistics: Language, society and politics in Africa and the Americas* (pp. 132–153). London, UK: Routledge.

Ratcliffe, K. (1999). Rhetorical listening: A trope for interpretive invention and a "Code of Cross-Cultural Conduct." *College Composition and Communication, 51*, 195–224.

Schroeder, C., Fox, H., & Bizzell, P. (Eds.). (2002). *ALT DIS: Alternative discourses and the academy*. Portsmouth, NH: Boynton/Cook.

Silverstein, M. (1996). Monoglot 'standard' in America: Standardization and metaphors of linguistic hegemony. In D. Brenneis and R. Macaulay (Eds.). *The matrix of language: Contemporary linguistic anthropology* (pp. 284–306). Boulder, CO: Westview Press.

Williams, B. (2009). Multilingual literacy strategies in online worlds. *Journal of Advanced Composition,* 29, 255–258.

Young, V. (2004). Your average Nigga. *College Composition and Communication, 55*, 693–715.

PART I
Premises

2

GLOBAL AND LOCAL COMMUNICATIVE NETWORKS AND IMPLICATIONS FOR LITERACY

Charles Bazerman

So there is this story going around that the world is flat (Friedman, 2005), such that all knowledge, all finances, all communication can flow everywhere to result in a thin shallow sheet of water, maybe just thick enough to drown us all. If all were flat our educational mission would be a lot simpler. Somebody needs to give these people 3D glasses.

For millennia humans have been developing structures of communication, knowledge, and institutions that provide the spaces within which we play our lives. Knowledge, in particular, is created, inscribed and stored, calculated upon, accessed and applied from particular kinds of documents, or genres, which then circulate in specific activity systems within particular languages (Bazerman & Rogers, 2008a, 2008b). As literacy becomes the knowledge and calculative infrastructure of social institutions, relationships, and actions, we come to live our lives in a built symbolic environment (Bazerman, 2011).

The activity systems within which knowledge flows are complexly organized, finely structured, and deeply varied (Bazerman, 1994; Russell, 1997). The meaning and functions of knowledge even within a single system vary depending on participant interests, roles, and positions. Movement of knowledge across systems, such as from science to law, is far from automatic, requiring translation and repurposing. Language, social, and national differences increase variety and add barriers to common knowledge.

The broad spread of knowledge and common orientations to that knowledge are a result of active communicative work by groups and individuals with interests in extended activity systems and shared knowledge. These range from scientists with a variety of first languages seeking to engage in common inquiries to entertainment and tourist industries wanting to extend markets, from governmental agencies and NGOs attempting to solve regional and global problems, to investment bankers wanting to coordinate and profit from increasingly integrated economies. These networks continue to grow denser, larger, more complex, with higher entry barriers, even though the balance and relationship of some of the more obvious components are shifting.

A Short History of Literacy and Society

Literacy and communication at a distance have at each juncture in their history been associated with changing social arrangements, sometimes reinforcing existing relations and institutions, but more often putting power in new hands and building new forms of organization that are larger, deeper and more complex. Let me cite some episodes.

In the ancient fertile crescent, the introduction of literacy helped farmers to keep track of produce, amass larger holdings than they could directly keep watch over, and transmit property without immediate physical transfer. It allowed traders to make deals over wider areas, make contracts, and amass great wealth. It facilitated governments spreading and coordinating power over larger domains, subordinating other kingdoms and tribes, gathering taxes, establishing uniform laws, and organizing and controlling large military forces and bureaucracies. Belief, as well, could become organized and disseminated through scriptures, creating modern religions, with literate clerical bureaucracies that could interpret and apply divine writ, administer, collect gifts, gather holdings, and regulate followers (Goody, 1986).

The Chinese empire showed the power of the unification of all these literate systems—government, law, finances, belief, and knowledge—across a wide domain. The invention of the printing press served to reinforce the organizational structures already in place, as it quickly came under imperial control to produce documents for government use or to reproduce the classical canon—which reinforced the centralized culture and provided texts for students taking the imperial exams (Bodde, 1991; Carter, 1955; Lee, 2000; Luo, 1998). This containment by the central authority and use to intensify central control was facilitated by a common literate language, purchased at great cost in blood and book burning. As a result, for two thousand years there was a highly developed literacy in Mandarin among the elites, but they were largely isolated from L2 books. Further, few speakers of other languages could effectively read Chinese texts, let alone participate in the Chinese literate world (Needham, 1970). About a century ago a series of changes in China began transforming these literate communicative dynamics, with the process still ongoing (Chen, 2010).

In Europe the printing press arrived about five centuries after it did so in China, at a time of religious and political fracturing, and served to further that fracturing—along with establishing institutions and communities that escaped national, religious, and cultural borders. Literacy, printing, and participation in transnational networks of commerce, science, technology, belief, and philosophic inquiry became assets to many of the emerging nations in their struggles. Thus some states sponsored more open inquiries and communications (Eisenstein, 1979).

One final example—in the United States the coordinated introduction of telegraphy and railroads facilitated the transformation from local agrarian economies with limited small-scale manufactures to a national corporate economy and a national market (Yates, 1989).

The Nation State and the Organization of Literate Activity Systems

By the 19th century such dynamics had left the nation state as a central organizing principle in much of the developed world. Laws, economies, corporations, governance mechanisms, transportation systems, education, languages, politics, and even newspapers were organized and regulated largely within national boundaries and carried out within national languages (Anderson, 1983). Less developed countries that wanted to enter as players into the global system needed to develop those nationally bounded systems of internal governance, economy, and culture in order to take their place among nations, as occurred in Mexico in the 1920s and thereafter (De los Santos, 2007).

Prior to the 20th century there was, of course, transregional communication. Trade routes and interregional dissemination of texts go back to antiquity, but they were limited arrangements (e.g., Frank, 1998). Also, the fluid history of European royal families and borders had created a transnational European commerce and culture, though the effect was mostly limited to the elites. Imperialism was the primary mechanism by which the scope of nationally organized systems spread beyond primary borders. Imperialism also led to the development of communicative systems, whether the large correspondence and archive networks centered in Seville and London or technological advances such as foreign postal systems and telegraphy. Imperialism also led to global distribution of selected European languages and a limited and asymmetric intermingling of cultures.

In the post World War II period, European-wide institutions of security, governance and economics have also emerged and gained strength, overlaying national bureaucracies and institutions, resulting in a flourishing translation industry. Recently, movement of students and employees has increased multilingual competence. Yet, *de facto*, this may mean that the working language of most institutions winds up being English, as it is the language that Finns, Rumanians, Spaniards, and Czechs have in common with some degree of fluency.

Globally, international cooperation after World War II seeking peace and security have resulted in such institutions as the United Nations, but also realized through many NGOs and regional organizations. The great divisions of the Cold War, and now the turmoil in the Islamic world, have also fostered a global orientation. These, in turn, foster an ideology of international curiosity, influencing the education and entertainment industries. International tourism, including its ideological themes of culture, environmentalism, and service, has coordinately increased as transportation has become easier and affluence has grown in some parts.

Science, from its early years, had been an international endeavor, relying on the printing press for its global reach (Eisenstein, 1979)—but in the 20th century it grew rapidly, transforming higher education.

All these domains, however, have become pervaded by economic development and the growth of corporations that became large powers within states and the vehicles for cooperation, until the corporations themselves escaped the bounds of the nations. I can hardly begin to unpack this complex story of economic growth, corporatism, and capitalism, and the formation of entities of sufficient power and wealth to dominate nations. Nor can I unpack the intertwining of economic interests, scientific growth, rise of global entertainment industries, the formation of global news, and new cooperations among nations.

Immigration also has changed. It was initially fostered by imperialism which brought imperial nationals to rule over foreign lands. As land and property was taken from indigenous peoples, many of whom perished, immigrants from other regions were also encouraged or forced by slavery to come to the newly opened lands, bringing their heritage languages within them—particularly in the Americas after independence. Up to World War I in the United States, Scandinavian and German immigrant communities continued to use and school in their heritage languages, and New York City maintained multiple linguistically insulated communities. Brazil, Chile, and Argentina have many European speaking enclaves, and some even had monolingual heritage language schools until recently. But throughout the 20th century the pressures for national loyalty, identity, and economic integration have demoted heritage languages to a marginal cultural practice. L1 public education grew in the USA and elsewhere.

However, in recent decades indigenous communities have been gaining rights, more immigrants are arriving as fully educated, and the rise of multinational companies has created an international group of managers, diverse within their corporations and moving about the world. Immigrants are likely to visit homelands and maintain business relations, supporting multiple identities and languages. All these changes have gone hand in hand with changing ideologies of diversity and complex identities within immigrant countries. Many countries, nonetheless, still resist immigration or impose large nationalizing pressures on immigrants.

Whatever these observations add up to, this is now the world we must help our students thrive in. This does not mean we have to approve of all the elements of it. The fact that the strongest institutions globally are now becoming financial and corporate, able to trump the interests and needs of nation states and other institutions, I find deeply troubling. But if there are strong networks to counterbalance them, it may not be the older institutions of the nation state that can do it, and we need to facilitate our students to contribute to building other communicative social systems with global force to assert other interests on the transnational level.

In particular I want to follow through on several implications.

Changing Immigration and Changing Students

Among our students we may find students whose heritage language has more vitality and a greater role in their lives than previously, who have strong connections with relatives in other regions (supported by communicative technologies), and who have substantial international experience. This will impact the ideas, goals, and knowledge they bring to their writing tasks, as well as their knowledge of and attitude toward language.

Changing Career Paths of Students

Students' careers are likely to involve large institutions with complex communicative environments which they will need to understand in order to participate effectively. They will need to understand the complex, multiple, and segmented audiences of their writing, particularly as framed by organizational roles. They will need to understand the distributed and collaborative processes and how to contribute effectively within them. They will need to understand the genres, their purposes, their circulation paths, and the actions they need to accomplish within the complex activity system of the organization. If students enter the riskier world of the professions, emergent organizations, journalism, or public sphere activity, they will need even more subtle knowledge of the communicative systems they are going up against and how they can create counter-discourses and communicative institutions that will project other interests forcefully and that will create thoughtful judgments.

Further, in all careers, to communicate effectively people will need to be able to consider the role of data and knowledge appropriate to each domain, and wield that knowledge intelligently and analytically, relying on theoretical orientations. In many academic, industrial, governance, and activist roles, they will need to be able to collect data, find new knowledge, and develop powerful theory and ideas as the basis for action. This brings us to universities.

How Universities Stand With Respect to Other Institutions

Universities first developed in Europe as a response to the influx of manuscripts into Europe through Muslim Spain during the wars of rechristianization and Constantinople (Makdisi, 1981; Ridder-Symoens, 1991). The guilds of students and scholars that formed came under the control of the church, and the teachings were limited to a limited canon that remained largely fixed even after the religious proliferation of the Reformation. Rote learning of texts with authoritative interpretation from the professor became entrenched as the educational model. The sciences only gained a substantial place in the 19th century after the French and German reforms of the university (Ruegg, 2004), with engineering, social sciences, and business only gaining major university place in the 20th century (Porter & Ross, 2003). With the reforms and changing knowledges within the university, national differences proliferated, but rote learning of authoritatively presented canonical texts remained the dominant educational mode in much of the world. Examination often remained oral but, even when written, writing skills needed to reproduce preformulated knowledge were limited. Major exceptions were the German seminar model and the Oxbridge tutorial model.

The United States was the other major exception, because of the need from the beginning to create social elites in a land without a longstanding elite class, and after the revolution to create citizen leaders for democracy. Rhetorical training was at first central to the curriculum and then the USA modified the German disciplinary specialization model by keeping two years of general education, within which the writing requirement emerged (under the auspices of literature departments). This unique history has meant that there has been a much stronger emphasis on meaning, expression, idea development, analysis, agency, and identity than elsewhere. As other nations now are finding a need to provide more support for advanced academic writing, they are needing to find institutional space for it to happen, but there is typically no department that has it in their economic interest to mount courses, and intellectual leadership tends to come either from within the disciplines or, more often, from applied linguists or educational psychologists. Each of these sponsoring locations has its own perception and priorities.

Another key issue for universities is who pays the bills and who calls the shots. For centuries, the universities were church institutions, fostering elites for church-dominated societies. In the United States, beginning with Jefferson's plan for the University of Virginia, and the later the Morrill Act, the state asserted for public universities an interest in creating an educated citizenry, developing regional economies, and advancing knowledge, fostered by free inquiry and broad freedom of expression, within American rights ideology and within the separation of church and state, with little specific immediate accountability (Veysey, 1965). Through the middle of the 20th century, however, even as public support for higher education expanded, government saw more direct interest in academic knowledge, beginning with the Manhattan project and reflected in current high levels of Department of Defense research funding (Van Nostrand, 1997). In addition, in recent decades industry has begun to assert its authority over university priorities. Further, as the power of academic inquiry to influence an educated citizenry and foster social change began to be realized, some political forces became suspicious of and attempted to limit university autonomy. Particularly relevant to writing is the increasing research orientation of universities that has heightened the focus both on graduate education and on the undergraduate major as a preparation for graduate education and research careers.

The Increasing Role for Writing Education in the USA and Globally

In both the developed and developing world, expectations of participation of faculty in international research and scholarship and the growth of advanced degree programs are increasing, often tied to governmental funding models, as in England, Spain, Hong Kong, Mexico, Brazil, and Chile. This pressure on graduate students and faculty has required higher degrees of more tightly focused and evidenced original arguments tied to disciplinary contributions. In addition, needs to have professionals at the highest international level to address pressing problems in health, environment, and other issues requiring scientific knowledge have required full participation in global academic and governance communications. Local economic interests are, as well, being tied into global financial and corporate organizations.

The problem is often first recognized at the end of the educational process, when graduate students need to write theses and dissertations, or researchers need to publish. Often the first writing support offered is at the Masters and Doctoral level, but in some cases this is starting to wash back to the undergraduate and secondary level. Of course, having highly skilled academic writers at the graduate level requires continuous attention and support from the earliest years of schooling onward. As writing support seeps downward it raises tensions with whatever local traditions and beliefs about literacy and writing have been forming the curricula at lower levels, because the higher end needs or professionals, business, and researchers are shaped by contemporary international standards.

The Issue of English and Multilingualism

Writing at the higher end of professionalism, scientific and medical research, multinational corporate and financial organizations, international activism, government cooperation, and so on, means that writing is directed towards the international languages of cooperation—which currently is predominantly English, although in evolving forms to reflect its new global status (Crystal, 2003).

Earlier colonialism, recent corporate neocolonialism, the Cold War, and US military dominance are no doubt important forces in this linguistic spread, along with media and popular culture from films to the internet. But also are the dominance of US and British science and academic research in the latter half of the 20th century. The expansion and reputation of US universities and the attractiveness of the elite British universities has meant that many leading scholars, professionals, and government and corporate leaders received undergraduate or graduate educations in the United States. Because of this academic dominance, in a number of countries the medium of instruction shifts from local languages to English as students move from secondary to higher education and postgraduate education, particularly in scientific disciplines.

Whatever the forces that have led to the situation, there is no doubt English is the dominant global language and becomes more important as one moves into elite or leadership professions, though elite British and US dialects no longer set absolute standards. English has escaped the English-speaking nations so that now there are about twice as many people who speak English as an additional language than do so as a first language. Of the estimated billion and a half English speakers in the world, half are from not from English-speaking countries or the former colonial empires of the USA and Britain (Crystal, 2003, pp. 68–69). If we stratified English speaking in those countries by education, wealth, or position, we might have even more striking results. Further, English as a language has escaped the control of dominant dialects from England and the USA, as new dialects have developed and are gaining recognition in different regions, though the weight of propriety, and education still tilts towards Anglo-American prestige dialects (Kachru, 1990).

The international role of English carries the ideological baggage of the events that fostered its growth. Equally, the growing dominance of English exerts unfortunate pressures on local languages, as many of the more sophisticated and/or power-related functions migrate to the international language. Yet global cooperation requires some ability to communicate with each other in a common language. In the past, the emergence of international languages of cooperation was accompanied and maintained by the governmental and religious institutions, often at the cost of violence. The rise of English certainly followed this pattern, but it is not clear that this will be the case in the future, as many of the interests and activities supporting global English are no longer tied so directly and exclusively in the interests of the English-speaking nations. For example, the default language on the websites of both Unilever and Phillips is English, not Dutch, as are all the major company documents available there, despite the history and corporate homes of each being in The Netherlands. We will see what the future holds, and also whether communication technology cements this global presence of English, or whether improvement of translation technologies will allow more symmetricality among languages. Nonetheless, in the interim, there seems a real global need for English, and knowledge of English creates inequities not just between nations but within non-English-speaking nations, between those who can write fluently and precisely participate in international activities and those who cannot. As language and literacy educators this is an issue of vital concern, defining our role.

The Increase in Diverse Forms of Writing Research

All the concerns I have spoken about to this point have eventuated in an increase internationally in research on writing, writing processes, how people develop as writers, how education can support writing development, and other related issues. This has happened in each region, but has also led to international communication and support.

In the United States, while there was some movement to advance research on the teaching of writing since the 1960s with linguistically based work, and peaking in the mid-1980s with cognitive psychological research, this effort remained small compared to the large endeavor of the teaching of writing and the growth of practice-based institutions like the National Writing Project, the Conference on College Composition and Communication, and the Council of Writing Program Administrators. In the 1990s this psychological work diminished, but work on rhetorical history and the history of the profession continued and there were regular conferences. Student- and community-based ethnography grew, as did studies of specialized forms of writing in science, technology, and industry, but largely meeting at the periphery of practice-based meetings. As Haswell (2005) documented, National Council of Teachers of English based institutions were not centrally focused on research, though a few independent research journals thrived.

I must qualify this characterization in one way. The opportunities of the new communicative technologies, changing the economies and dynamics of publishing and expanding the possibilities of student expression, were rapidly taken up in college composition and in the new literacies movement elsewhere.

In any event, out of caution, when we first started running regional conferences in Santa Barbara in 2002, we framed the topic to straddle practice and research, but to our surprise our first iteration in 2002 turned out to draw nationally and doubled our attendance expectation at around 150. So, in 2005 we framed the conference nationally and on writing research, though modestly as "Writing Research in the Making." Again we doubled expectation, at around 350, and drew internationally. This suggested to us that there was something serious going on, as there was, and so in 2008 we created an international conference, inviting interest in all age levels and all methods. We drew around 600, representing over 30 nations. In 2011 we drew around 700 from over 40 nations to the conference at George Mason University, and founded the International Society for the Advancement of Writing Research in order to carry on the conference under global societal auspices and to carry on other activities. Membership now numbers close to a 1000. Through this and other conferences that are mentioned below, I have become aware of the variety of work going on globally. What follows is my idiosyncratic impressions of what is going on in different regions. I am sure there are many counter-examples to be cited.

For a half a century, a strong applied linguistic research tradition has emanated from the Britain and Australia, in large part motivated by the teaching of English as an additional language and English for Specific Purposes (ESP). This work has been global in its influence, and research along these lines has been done in many regions and many different languages have been studied. This strain of work has looked at linguistic forms, from the micro to the macro level, from a functionalist perspective, as resources for expression.

In Europe, writing research started to heat up in the 1990s, with the first meeting of SIG Writing in 1988 in Padova, Italy, and its 13th conference in 2012 in

Porto, Portugal. In recent years this organization has brought together a stable core of around 150 to 200 researchers from across Europe, with growing numbers from elsewhere. The organization is a special interest group of the European Association for Research on Learning and Instruction (EARLI), and the traditions it draws on have been focused on psychology and education, but include higher education as well as primary and secondary education. The psychological work done in North America has had some influence on European activities, but European workers also have their own traditions that have grow out of phenomenography, emergent literacy, linguistic cognition, and other educational and psychological traditions.

During the last decade, research in writing in Brazil has centered on the concept of genre, and the biannual International Symposium on Genre Studies (SIGET) has become the main site for presenting writing research, though this subject also receives some attention at applied linguistics meetings. Genre is identified as an educational priority in the Brazilian national curricular parameters for elementary and secondary schools, but the concept has also gained force in higher education and has come to stand for the kinds of things students should be writing. The genre and applied linguistics worlds are quite eclectic, drawing on multiple traditions, including Anglo-Australian applied linguistics and ESP and North American genre theory—but also Swiss French educational investigations of genre, drawing on Vygotsky, other European educational traditions, and French literary theory. One of the leading approaches is grounded in the philosophy of language (Marcuschi, 2001). But all of these are bound together in a uniquely Latin American Frierian interest in the everyday world and power relations, with a concern for social justice (Freire, 1970). Elsewhere in Latin America there is emerging interest in higher education writing, with a focus on graduate student and research writing, to support the development of intellectual leaders and international scholars, but again with a continuing concern for social justice and the needs of minority and poor populations. Argentina, Colombia, Chile, and Mexico are at the forefront of this work.

In China there are two separate writing worlds that are just becoming aware of each other. One of these is English, based on English as a Foreign Language (EFL), with a strong interest in ESP (academic and scientific writing), and drawing on applied linguistics, but with an expanding view into social context and purpose. The other is L1 Chinese writing, which still draws heavily on the ancient literary canon and standards of style. Interest in genres, functions, and situations of writing is also divided by language, with a special focus on English language in scientific and technical writing.

This interest in research writing (often associated with English) seems to motivate much research in many parts of the world, often starting with applied linguistic investigations with an expansion of perspective as issues of context and communicative expression grow. It is curious that much of writing research globally is focused on higher education, except primarily in Europe where there is a good spread across all age groups. In the USA, given the large higher education world of practice, one would expect much research at that level. Less research at the lower grades may have to do with the conflation of literacy with reading and with the development of what practice there is through the National Writing Project being largely outside the world of research. The recent addition of writing in school assessment has motivated some research, but much of it is limited and focused by the particular terms of assessment. There is, nonetheless, some strong ethnographic work in the primary and secondary world.

In the rest of the world where there are few sites of higher education writing support and few teachers of writing in higher education, the focus on higher education writing is indeed worth noting. The focus on higher education, particularly in an EFL context, speaks to the large perceived need, plus the neglect of attempting to develop a deep and principled understanding of writing beyond the development of basic transcription skills, which often relies on traditional methods and beliefs. The one bright spot in early childhood and early education research for more than three decades has been the emergent literacy tradition. This has been truly an international movement, with major research produced in Latin America, North America, Europe, and the Middle East.

These various traditions are now becoming more aware of each other through conferences and publications, particularly handbooks that have appeared in the past five years. Whereas six years ago there were no handbooks or reference books devoted exclusively to writing research, today there are at least four published, some with a deeply international perspective, and several more on the way. The journals and books also are becoming more international, as publications in Europe, Latin America, and North America are soliciting and receiving more international submissions. There are also several major initiatives that are expanding capacity in Europe and Latin America.

Final Comments

As educators we work within national educational systems within the national language of schooling, yet our students are increasingly international and multilingual in complex ways, as are their likely careers and the forces that will affect their lives. These complexities intersect local and global institutions and activity systems, through media that permeate national barriers—and create the locales at which people now write. This is the world we are educating for. The richness of institutions depends on maintaining multiple complex strands of communicative activity that move across languages, with institutions able to counterpoise each other. The real danger of flatness is that the financially motivated communicative systems in a single disciplinary and national language will wash over all other systems and languages. Money and finances are strong motivators and create the resources for strong action. But if money talking overwhelms all other discourses, leaving the rest of the world flat, guided by the mountains of wealth, then we really are in trouble. Governance in a democratic spirit without the dominance of strong imperial nations is a complex affair, requiring communication, cooperation, and coordination at many levels and in many venues. It is our rewarding and challenging task to help people learn to express and recognize in their writing the great complexity of humanity, with all its desires, needs, knowledge, and visions carried in the many languages of the world.

References

Anderson, B. (1983). *Forms of nationhood*. London, UK: Verso.

Bazerman, C. (1994). Systems of genre and the enactment of social intentions. In A. Freedman & P. Medway (Eds.), *Genre and the new rhetoric* (pp. 79–101). London, UK: Taylor & Francis.

Bazerman, C. (2011). Electrons are cheap; society is dear. In D. Starke Meyeering, A. Paré, N. Artemeva, M. Horne, & L. Yousoubova (Eds.), *Writing in the knowledge society* (pp. 75–84). Anderson, SC: Parlor Press/WAC Clearinghouse.

Bazerman, C., & Rogers, P. (2008a). Writing and secular knowledge apart from modern European institutions. In C. Bazerman (Ed.), *Handbook of research on writing* (pp. 143–156). New York, NY: Routledge.

Bazerman, C., & Rogers, P. (2008b). Writing and secular knowledge within modern European institutions. In C. Bazerman (Ed.). *Handbook of research on writing* (pp. 157–176). New York, NY: Routledge.

Bodde, D. (1991). *Chinese thought, society, and science: The intellectual and social background of science and technology in pre-modern China*. Honolulu, HI: University of Hawaii Press.

Carter, T. F. (1955). In L. C. Goodrich (Ed.), *The invention of printing in China and its spread westward* (2nd ed.). New York, NY: Ronald Press.

Chen, H. (2010). Modern "writingology" in China. In C. Bazerman, R. Krut, K. Lunsford, S. McCleod, S. Null, P. Rogers, & A. Stansell (Eds.), *Traditions of writing research*. New York, NY: Routledge.

Crystal, D. (2003). *English as a global language* (2nd ed.). Cambridge, UK: Cambridge University Press.

De los Santos, R. (2007). Nation Building as Rhetoric and Socio-cultural Activity: Two Institutional Moments in Post-revolutionary Mexico, 1928–1940 (unpublished doctoral dissertation). Santa Barbara, CA: University of California Santa Barbara.

Eisenstein, E. L. (1979). *The printing press as an agent of change*. Cambridge, UK: Cambridge University Press.

Friedman, T. (2005). *The world is flat*. New York, NY: Farrar, Straus and Giroux.

Frank, A.G. (1998). *Reorient: Global economy in the Asian age*. Berkeley, CA: University of California Press.

Freire, P. (1970). *Pedagogy of the oppressed*. New York, NY: Continuum.

Goody, J. (1986). *The logic of writing and the organization of society*. Cambridge, UK: Cambridge University Press.

Haswell, R. (2005). NCTE/CCCC's recent war on scholarship, *Written Communication, 22*(2), 198–223. doi:10.1177/0741088305275367.

Kachru, B. (1990). *The alchemy of English: The spread, functions, and models of non-native Englishes*. Champaign, IL: University of Illinois Press.

Lee, T. H. C. (2000). *Education in traditional China, a history*. Leiden, Netherlands: Brill.

Luo, S. (1998). *An illustrated history of printing in ancient China.* Hong Kong: City University Press.

Makdisi, G. (1981). *The rise of colleges: Institutions of learning in Islam and the West.* Edinburgh: Edinburgh University Press.

Marcuschi, L. A. (2001). *Da fala para a escrita: Atividades de retextualização.* São Paulo: Editora Cortez.

Needham, J. (Ed.). (1970). *Clerks and craftsmen in China and the West.* Cambridge, UK: Cambridge University Press.

Porter, T. M., & Ross, D. (Eds.) (2003) *The modern social sciences* (Vol. 7). Cambridge, UK: Cambridge University Press.

Ridder-Symoens, H. (Ed.). (1991). *A history of the university* (Vol. 1). Cambridge, UK: Cambridge University Press.

Ruegg, W. (Ed.) (2004). *A history of the university* (Vol. 3). Cambridge, UK: Cambridge University Press.

Russell, D. R. (1997). Rethinking genre in school and society: An activity theory analysis. *Written Communication, 14*(4), 504–554. doi:10.1177/0741088397014004004.

Van Nostrand, A. D. (1997). *Fundable knowledge: The marketing of defense technology.* Mahwah, NJ: Erlbaum.

Veysey, L. R. (1965). *The emergence of the American university.* Chicago, IL: University of Chicago Press.

Yates, J. (1989). *Control through communication.* Baltimore, MD: Johns Hopkins University Press.

3

TRANSLINGUAL LITERACY AND MATTERS OF AGENCY

Min-Zhan Lu and Bruce Horner

In this chapter we examine how a "translingual" approach to the teaching of writing would address matters of agency in all writing, including not only writing that appears to deviate from language norms, but also writing that appears simply to reproduce language norms. For a variety of reasons, those arguing for a translingual approach have been concerned primarily with the agency of those producing writing that appears to deviate from language norms.[1] For example, the call Horner, Lu, Royster and Trimbur (2011) made recently for taking a translingual approach to writing is framed not in terms of language in writing but "language *difference* in writing." And some approaches aligned with the translingual approach have argued that we should not require students to "code-switch"—that is, to use only the code deemed appropriate to a particular situation—but instead to "code-mesh"—that is, to mix codes within individual utterances (Canagarajah, 2006; Young, 2009; Young & Martinez, 2011).[2]

These efforts have developed as a response to dominant tendencies to reject any writing that appears to deviate from conventional language use. Those tendencies assume such deviations to represent writer deficit—a sign that the writers lack linguistic, cognitive, or even moral competence. Against such assumptions, scholars have demonstrated the legitimacy of deviations as evidence of writers' linguistic capacity, intelligence, effort, and agency. However, in defending the production of recognizable difference in writing, these efforts have inadvertently led to identification of writerly agency only with the production of recognizably different writing.

To disrupt this identification of agency only with production of recognizably different writing, we first outline a translingual framework for grasping the agency in all language use. This framework sees writing, writer identity, language forms used, and writer competence as always emergent, and hence writer agency as both always in operation and always in development as writers shape themselves and language forms through recontextualization. This framework enables us to recognize writer agency in writing that reiterates standardized forms as well as in writing that deviates from such forms: both, we argue, can be understood as involving choices made in particular situations and in light of particular purposes. Rather than asking whether writers should code-switch or code-mesh, a translingual approach asks us to consider how, when, where, and why specific language strategies might be deployed. This approach thus offers a more promising avenue for pedagogies aimed at helping writers to respond to what appear to be reader expectations and demands.

Defining a Translingual Approach

For the purposes of our argument, the following tenets are key to grasping a translingual approach:

* language as a dynamic process of structuration
* reading–writing as integrally related acts of translation–transformation
* relations between language, language users, and the temporal–spatial contexts and consequences of language acts as co-constitutive.

A translingual approach treats language as a dynamic process of "structuration"—the term social theorist Giddens uses to mark the mutually dependent and co-constitutive relationship between structure and agency. As Giddens (1979) states, "The structural properties of social systems are both the medium and the outcome of the practices that constitute those systems" (p. 69).

Following Giddens' theory of structuration, a translingual approach locates language codes or structures temporally, in history, and hence understands these as always emergent, in process. Adopting a frame that is temporal–spatial, rather than just spatial, counters the long-standing tendency to treat languages as discrete, self-evident entities belonging to set territories, such as the nation, school, or home. That tendency, we argue, leads to impoverished debates aimed at pinning down the structure of individual languages and the social boundaries for their use (Pennycook, 2010, p. 82; cf. François, 2009). That tendency is manifested in such concepts as "variety," "code," "bilingualism," "mother tongue," "borrowing," and "appropriate." By contrast, a translingual approach defines languages not as something we have or have access to but as something we do. It centers attention on languaging: how we do language and why.

At the same time, however, this approach insists on locating language use in the material social realm. Reading and writing, for example, are understood as social, economic, geopolitical, and cultural, as well as linguistic transactions across asymmetrical relations of power. In such transactions, meaning is necessarily and always the product of translation across differences, even in ostensibly monolingual settings. And because these rewritings involve relations of power, individual language practices are understood as negotiations that have the effect of forming and transforming their contexts, the identities of the participants, and their relations with each other, others, and the world. The relations between language, language users, and the contexts of language acts are thus seen as co-constitutive. Just as language is seen as always emerging from interactions rather than preceding these, in a translingual approach, contexts are likewise understood as always emergent, exerting pressure on but also being actively shaped and reshaped by individual language practices. Writers can thus be seen not as writing *in* a language or context but always writing, or rewriting, language and context with each writing. And thus, from a translingual perspective, those whose utterances are commonly recognized as either "code-meshing" or "code-switching" are not so much writing within, switching between, or mixing pre-existing "codes." Instead, they are seen as bringing these, and the contexts of their use, into being through their utterances. Culture, ethnicity, nationality, race, geography, and environments are likewise seen as emerging in performance, informing and informed by individual acts of speaking–listening, reading–writing. In a translingual approach, reading and writing are understood as actively producing texts—worlds and the very languages employed—and asymmetrical relations of power are understood as both mediated by as well as mediating—transformed by and transforming—individual instances of languaging.

By foregrounding the mutual interdependence of structure and language practices, a translingual approach shifts attention to matters of agency—the ways in which individual language users fashion and re-fashion standardized norms, identity, the world, and their relation to others and the world. And by foregrounding the specificity of the temporal context of individual instances of language practice from moment to moment, writers are seen not in terms of their degree of proximity, mastery, or adjustment to dominant definitions of exigent, feasible, appropriate, and stable "contexts" or "codes," but as always responding to and shaping these.

In response to calls for taking such a translingual approach, we have persistently encountered two vocal concerns: First, what about students' desire and need to know how to produce grammatically correct texts? The assumption appears to be that acknowledging student writers' agency in shaping language inevitably means dismissing dominant expectations that they produce something understood as "standard English," the need and desire of students to meet these expectations, and the responsibility of teachers to help them do so. Thus, it appears to threaten students' potential academic and socio-economic success. This is a threat that seems especially troublesome when directed at socially and academically marginalized students. Second, and conversely, teachers question whether a translingual approach to language is relevant for those students who appear to fit cultural norms of language, race, class, ethnicity, and so on. While a translingual approach to language might be interesting, and even useful, for students not fitting these norms, it can seem to have little to do with the abilities, needs, and desires of students identified as mainstream, native-English speaking monolinguals. Hence both the approach and the students for whom it appears likely to be relevant are dismissed as simultaneously exotic and unimportant, and in either case peripheral to the mainstream of the work of writing programs and their constituents.

In response to these concerns, we argue that, while the need of students to meet readers' expectations and the responsibility of teachers to help them do so are legitimate, the sense that a translingual approach would interfere with these is misguided, based on the false assumption that agency manifests itself only in recognized deviations from the norm rather than in all language acts. For example, some writers appear to assume that taking a translingual approach to language would require that students engage in code-meshing, and that they avoid code-switching, in their writing, and that they avoid producing writing that appears to simply reproduce standardized conventions of syntax, notation, register, and organization. In other words, they assume that writers exercise agency only by code-meshing.

However, from our perspective, taking a translingual approach does not prescribe the forms of writing that students are to produce. Instead, it calls on students (and their teachers) to develop specific dispositions toward languages, language users, contexts and consequences of language use, and the relations between all these, and to do so in all their engagements with reading and writing. By recognizing writers' agency in and responsibility for all their language productions, whether these seem to reproduce standardized forms of writing or deviate from them, it is applicable and of benefit to all students (and all writers), including those deemed mainstream monolinguals and those deemed multilinguals.

To foreground the agency and responsibility of writers in all acts of composition, those taking a translingual approach need to accompany work that foregrounds the agency operating in deviations from the norm with work that foregrounds the agency operating in seeming reproductions of the norm. As we have already suggested, a rich body of scholarship and teaching has developed out of the need to demonstrate the logic and legitimacy of language practices deviating from what is thought to be Standard Written English and to defend the rights and intelligence of the groups affiliated with those practices against charges that their writing shows their cognitive immaturity, ignorance, and laziness.[3] Those involved in these efforts include teacher-scholars of students identified as "basic writers" and speakers of varieties of English deemed non-standard, teacher-scholars of second-language writing and ESL, and teacher-scholars concerned with programs advancing multilingualism (García, 2009; Kramsch, 1998; Makoni & Pennycook, 2007; Pennycook, 2008) and the use of world Englishes and English as a global "lingua franca" (Canagarajah, 2006; Jenkins, 2006; Kirkpatrick, 2007; Seidlhofer, 2004).[4]

These efforts are still ongoing and are still necessary, especially at a time in the United States when language difference has become a proxy target for discrimination against subordinated populations. However, the focus of much of this work on language uses perceived to be different, and of the agency of those engaging in such uses, has had the unintended consequence of leaving the impression that writers' production of conventional language shows a lack of agency—the subordination of the individual will to institutional demands, say, or unwitting, unagentive mechanical reproduction of language "norms."

To counter this impression, we need a fully articulated account of agency in writing that seems to merely repeat or imitate standardized forms and meanings. To develop such an account, we turn to Pennycook's (2010) notion of the sedimentation of language. In his book *Language as a Local Practice* and elsewhere, Pennycook has argued for the need to treat language not as a set of pre-existing rules but as an achieved outcome of the everyday doing of language by ordinary people (2010, p. 115). To account for the *appearance* of language as a set of fixed forms and rules, he has introduced the notion of the sedimentation of language. That process of language sedimentation—of building up, over time—produces the appearance of language stability (Pennycook, 2010, p. 125). For example, in this view, "grammar" is the name for certain categories of observed repetitions in language practices (Pennycook, 2010, p. 46).

The imagery of sedimentation highlights the temporal dimension of context, language, and identity, recognizing their character as emergent products of movement and memory rather than being timeless systems and structures (Pennycook, 2010, p. 125). Invoking the proverb that we never step into the same river twice, Pennycook has asked us to consider the possibility of simultaneous sameness and difference, or what, borrowing from Homi Bhabba, is termed "fertile mimesis" (Pennycook, 2010, p. 35). From this perspective we can recognize that what is commonly viewed as doing the same thing again in fact represents doing something different. That which we do is both the "same" and "different," just as the river is and is not the same, and just as we ourselves and our actions are and are not the same when we step, seemingly again, into a river.[5]

Key to grasping the process of fertile mimesis is the notion of recontextualization. It is that recontextualization that makes it possible for ostensibly identical utterances to carry significantly different meanings and significance in different contexts. These include differences, or changes, in meaning (semio-diversity), and differences in the meaning and order of power relations as we recontextualize linguistic patterns such as a standardized lexico-grammatical code across time and space. As post-colonial theories have taught us, mimicry of dominant powers, arts, discourses, and colonizers by the subordinate creates new meanings and new relationships between colonized and colonizer, with the potential to undermine the status and distinction of the dominant (Pennycook, 2010, p. 44; cf. Bhabha, 1985; Pratt, 1991).

The notion of the inevitable recontextualization of ostensibly the same brings out the degree to which every instance of the use of language, including what is recognized as repetition, represents an exercise of agency, a choice, whatever the level of consciousness in the making of it. As Giddens (1979) puts it, "Every instance of the use of language is a potential modification of that language at the same time as it acts to reproduce it" (p. 220). The specific differences between temporal–spatial and macro–micro contexts of individual instances of imitation recontextualize—and hence re-form—the very feature or meaning we appear to borrow from (our own and others') previous instances of language use, which themselves represent socially and historically sedimented patterns of linguistic resources (Pennycook, 2010, p. 45).[6] In this sense, the apparent regularity of language and grammar is the achievement of recontextualization or re-forming that participates in the ongoing sedimentation of language practices. Furthermore, as Pennycook (2010) observes, we "can make intentional changes to what we do, and these changes may [themselves] become sedimented over time" (p. 49). Even "small, unintentional slippages, changes to the ways we do and say things," may start to be repeated and become sedimented practices when social, cultural, and economic reasons for change recur as demands to be addressed in instances of language acts (Pennycook, 2010, p. 49). And this sedimentation as a result of fertile mimesis affects the formation of not only language but also our subjectivities, life trajectories, the world we live in, and our relations with others and that world.

The theory of agency in iteration outlined above suggests ways by which we might refine dominant frameworks for understanding and responding to student writing. Adopting a temporal–spatial frame for understanding discourse enables us to recognize writers' participation in the ongoing sedimentation of ways of thinking, talking, reading, writing, acting, and relating in all their discourse productions. Within such a framework, iterations of discourse can be recognized as acts of fertile mimesis that (inevitably) produce semio-diversity through recontextualization. Such recognition enables teachers and students to use iterations of discourse as sites for probing options and making decisions on how to recontextualize existing norms and why, and to do so in light of the specificity of the temporal–spatial and micro–macro contexts of their writing.

Adopting a translingual approach enables us to recognize agency even in the production of the most seemingly clichéd, resolutely conventional writing. Traditional spatial frameworks give teachers few options for responding to such writing. If we understand such writing as mechanical reproduction, we appear to have little to do except attempt to cajole students to do something different, or wait for them to develop cognitively to the point at which they can do something different—here something understood as doing more than reproduce the conventional. Paradoxically, those frameworks perpetuate the before–after model that also supports dismissing the agency of student writers whose writing seems to deviate significantly from conventionalized discourse: Either persuade the students to do something different (conform to norms), or wait for them to develop, cognitively or linguistically, to the point where they are able to do something different—in their case, however, something more, rather than less, conventional.

Thus a purely spatial conceptual framework, in which each language has a central core belonging to a social space or people, with peripheral deviations, seems to doom both those barricaded in the center and those consigned to the periphery. By contrast, the temporal–spatial framework of a translingual approach identifies both apparently all too conventional writing as well as unconventional writing as acts contributing to the ongoing sedimentation of language. By recognizing the agency exhibited in the production of what seems to be the "same," this approach can help students recognize and exercise their agency in how they do and might actively recontextualize sedimented features of English in ways that help them better grasp, respond to, and reshape the temporal–spatial, macro–micro contexts of their past, current, and future lives. By asking students to explore not what to do and not do, but how they are doing English and why, we put them in a position to probe their responsibility in using the linguistic "commons" that currently constitutes English as a putative global link across different peoples, cultures, and languages. In doing so, we can engage the agency of not just students and writing designated "mainstream," and not just those designated as outside that "mainstream," but both.

Engaging All Forms of Agency

To further illustrate what engaging the agency of all student writers might entail, we turn to an early example of what we would identify as translingual pedagogy and its critical reception: Lu's 1994 article "Professing Multiculturalism," and Canagarajah's discussion of Lu's article in his own, 2006 article "The Place of World Englishes in Composition: Pluralization Continued," both appearing in the journal *College Composition and Communication*. Lu's article described a class discussion in which she asked students to perform a "close reading" of several papers written by a first-year undergraduate writing student from Malaysia whose native language is Chinese (p. 451). We'll refer to this student as Writer M. In her papers, Writer M had used the construction "can able to" to bring out the difference in definitions of *can* to mean "having the ability to" and "having permission to," a difference she felt was overlooked in idiomatic use of "can" to signify both. During the discussion of Writer M's papers, students were asked to consider ways to make sense of "can able to" against the grain of their trained disposition to dismiss the construction as a grammatical error resulting from Writer M's unfamiliarity with idiomatic English, and to consider whether and how they would revise "can able to" in light of Writer M's critique of dominant beliefs in the transcendental power of the individual, and in light of the specific contexts of each student's life.

As argued by both Lu and, subsequently, Canagarajah in his comments, what seems key about the production of constructions such as "can able to" is not the construction itself, but whether or not students engage in a process of negotiation and deliberation in deciding whether or not to produce such a construction or a more conventional construction. However, because both Lu and Canagarajah's *[handwritten annotation at top: "Talk w/ students about popular coinages; 'Because'; turning nouns into verbs ('adulting')"]*

essays foregrounded writer agency operating in the production of writing that appears to deviate from the norms of Standard Written English, their attention to agency operating in the iteration of standardized forms of writing is likely to be glossed over. Conversely, the notion of language sedimentation and recontextualization can help us recognize such agency, as when a student of Lu's, identified as Vietnamese American, decided to opt for the idiomatic convention of using "can" and "be able to" interchangeably. Lu has defended this decision not as a submission to demands of the dominant, but rather in terms of the "connotations of agency" associated with such treatment of *can* and *able to*, connotations that "inspired modes of resistance and individual empowerment against the fatalism of the student's own community" (pp. 454–455). Canagarajah has likewise emphasized the legitimacy of this student's decision to choose a "standard" grammar structure, arguing that such a decision can "become an ideologically favored option for a minority student" (2006, p. 610). Thus, Canagarajah has joined Lu in affirming the agency operating in all the decisions different students arrived at, including decisions to follow conventional usage.

To these arguments, Canagarajah (2006) has made the further point that there are additional pedagogical benefits to all students of discussing grammatical deviations like "can able to," including (1) helping students to "develop a metalinguistic awareness of the values and interests motivating grammar rules and decisions on how to use them," and (2) "enabl[ing] students to use grammar meaningfully, rather than opting for stereotypical choices" (p. 610). To this point, we would add that the goal of enabling students to use grammar meaningfully can also be achieved by discussing seeming iterations of conventional discourse. For example, in the class discussion Lu described, we can see students, both monolingual and multilingual, exhibiting agency and an interest as well as know-how in exercising that agency through their labor as writers in their suggestions about ways to revise Writer M's idiosyncratic construction. Some of these students suggested adding an "if" clause to "be able to," as in "If the person is able to." Likewise, when, as Lu recounted, the phrase "can able to" "became a newly coined phrase she and the students shared throughout the term" (1994, p. 454), we see both the exercise of agency and, as Canagarajah (2006) has observed, a dramatization of "the process by which ... certain cases of peculiar usage become 'standardized'"—or, in terms of our argument, sedimented—"once their meanings and purposes are socially shared" (p. 610). This example of the students' active recontextualization of a feature in a previous instance of language practice by Writer M indicates all writers' agency in iteration, not just those labeled "minority" and "multilingual."

In short, the metaphor of emerging sedimentation and the notion of fertile mimesis can help translingual research and pedagogy take seriously the political and rhetorical agency of repetition, identification, mimicry, and reproduction (Pennycook, 2010, p. 36), enabling teachers to complement their honoring of the agency exhibited in utterances recognizably "different" and "transformative" with an honoring of agency exhibited in students' production of what is recognized as conventional, or "the same." Thus, our engagement with students' efforts to meet reader expectations for standardized forms of writing can work in tandem, rather than at odds, with engagement in pursuing the possibility of transforming forms of writing and readers' expectations and demands.

The translingual approach's recognition of agency in iteration also provides a more useful perspective on efforts to help members of subordinated groups produce texts that meet expectations for standardized English. While these efforts are typically defended as a means of ensuring the survival of at-risk populations through submission to the demands of dominant groups, the translingual approach justifies and suggests a pedagogically more productive way to teach minority and multilingual students to produce standardized forms of English. Instead of asking them to engage in mechanical reproduction of forms the boundaries and stability of which are in fact questionable, it would ask students to explore ways by which they might engage in fertile mimesis and critical agency in recontextualizing all forms of English, including those recognized by some as standard and those not. For example, we can find ways to identify the semio-diversity that producing standardized forms yields as a consequence of who is using what language forms when and how: its recontextualization, and the potential that recontextualization has for transforming the conditions in which the writers live.

Likewise, rather than present the iteration of standardized forms as simply the default or required code to which writers must submit, we can explore how both iterations of ostensibly the same and deviations from conventional usage can and need to be cued textually. In her 1994 essay, Lu noted (p. 454) that some students suggested using "can able to" with a parenthetical explanation or a footnote about the need for this unusual usage—a strategy, Canagarajah (2006) subsequently observed, that represents "a form of compromise as it acknowledges that the writer is aware of using the structure in a peculiar way for a unique rhetorical purpose" and that iterates "a valued convention of academic writing" (p. 610), namely the footnote. We can help students develop these and other strategies by which to persuade readers to respond with more tolerance to their texts as well as to imagine readers' anticipated difficulties with their writing. As we have suggested elsewhere (Horner & Lu, 2008), this involves teaching students not simply to identify expectations of their anticipated audience but also to propose alternative ways of reading for their readers to adopt.

The standard pedagogical repertoire of many writing instructors already addresses ways of anticipating readers' expectations and responding to them: Helping writers develop the habit of imagining, as they write and revise, the kinds of questions and difficulties various readers might have in responding to their work, and of deciding whether and how to accommodate these as they write by such means as addressing imagined questions, say, or adding explanations, or defining their terms, offering alternative phrasings, and contextualizing their arguments—all while recognizing the likelihood of remaining disagreements and confusion over meaning (see Kaur, 2009, on ELF strategies of "repair"; Canagarajah, 2011). Part of this work will entail helping writers learn to monitor the forms and conventions they encounter in the discourse of others, to assume their meaningfulness, and to consider ways in which they might adapt and adopt them in their own writing (see Canagarajah, 2007, p. 927). And, part of this work will involve finding ways for writers to persuade readers to adopt more open, patient, and inquiring attitudes towards one's writing. If we accept that reading and writing are integrally related acts of translation–transformation, then taking a translingual approach must involve finding ways for teachers as well as students to "listen" against the grain of systems of reading privileging dominant groups and to explore alternative ways of reading (see Royster, 1996).

We have argued that a translingual approach identifies the issue we face not as a question of whether to teach standardized forms and meanings but, rather, the need for all of us, in our reading and writing, to deliberate over how and why to do what with language in light of emergent and mutually constitutive relations of language, context, identity, and power relations. This requires a more fully articulated approach to the agency of acts of seeming repetition, one that recognizes the production of difference through temporal–spatial recontextualization of what might pass as "the same." That is, we need to learn to recognize, and help students learn to recognize, the production of the same in what appears to be different, the production of difference in what appears to be the same, and the agency operating in both. Adopting such an approach to agency can help teachers to address whatever positions students adopt, offering an alternative perspective on current disputes about the kind of language education we need. In short, a translingual approach to agency brings to the fore the ways in which all writing involves re-writing language, with all the possibilities and responsibilities that such rewriting entails.

Notes

1 The meaning of "translingual" (and variations such as "translingualism") remains contested and competes with such terms as *interculturalité*, multilingualism, plurilingualism, translanguaging, transculturation, *creolité*, and *diversalité*, whose meanings are likewise contested. Our concern here is not with sorting through all the nuances of these terms and their relations to one another. Rather, following Horner et al.'s (2011) concluding caution in their call for a "translingual approach" that "we are still at the beginning stages of our learning efforts in this project, which by definition will require the ideas and energy of many" (p. 310), we aim to address what seem common concerns expressed in the responses prompted by such an approach, by whatever name. For a sampling of discussions forwarding these terms, see, for example: Bernabé, Chamoiseau, & Confiant, 1990; Blanchet & Coste, 2010; Canagarajah, 2011; Candelier, Ioannitou, Omer, & Vasseur, 2008; Confiant, 2007; Council of Europe/ Conseil de l/Europe, 2001; Gilyard, 1997; Guerra, 1997, 2008; Horner et al., 2011; Khubchandani, 1998; Kramsch, 1998; Pennycook, 2008; Severino, Guerra, & Butler, 1997; Zamel, 1997; Zarate, Lévy, & Kramsch, 2008.

2 The term "code-switching" is used in such arguments to refer to what applied linguists

traditionally term "code-shifting," and what applied linguists term "code-switching" would, in these arguments, represent a form of what is meant by "code-mixing."

3 See, for example, Bartholomae, 1980, 1985, 1993; Canagarajah, 1999; Fox, 1990a, 1990b; Grego & Thompson, 2008; Horner & Lu, 1999; Hull & Rose, 1990; Hull, Rose, Fraser, & Castellano, 1991; Kells, Balester, & Villanueva, 2004; Lees, 1989; Lu, 2004, 2006; Shaughnessy, 1977; Slevin, 2001; Smitherman & Villanueva, 2003; Spack, 1997; Valdés, 1992; Young, 2009; Young & Martinez, 2011.

4 This is not to say that all those involved in combating monolingualist approaches would see themselves as advancing a "translingualist" approach. Rather, we see a translingualist approach emerging out of the body of scholarship and teaching produced by those involved in these efforts, who are diverse in their assumptions and approaches, however aligned in combating a view equating language difference in student work with deficit and defect.

5 See F. François's concept (1999) of *reprise–modification*, leading to his argument that "il y a toujours de la différence dans la relation de ressemblance" (p. 217 and *passim*).

6 Or if, in Bakhtin's (1981) well-worn phrase, "every utterance is always half someone else's," then, conversely, any re-iteration of that utterance is also simultaneously always half one's own. The utterance reconstructs the very contexts shaping and shaped by our recontextualization of such linguistic resources.

References

Bakhtin, M. (1981). *The dialogic imagination: Four essays* (M. Holquist Ed., C. Emerson & M. Holquist, Trans.). Austin, TX: University of Texas Press.

Bartholomae, D. (1980). The study of error. *College Composition and Communication, 31*, 253–269. doi:10.2307/356486.

Bartholomae, D. (1985). Inventing the university. In M. Rose (Ed.), *When a writer can't write: Studies in writer's block and other composing problems* (pp. 134–165). New York, NY: Guildford.

Bartholomae, D. (1993). The tidy house: Basic writing in the American curriculum. *Journal of Basic Writing, 12*(1), 4–21.

Bernabé, J., Chamoiseau, P., & Confiant, R. (1990). *Éloge de la créolité*. Paris, France/Baltimore, OH: Gallimard/Johns Hopkins University Press.

Bhabha, H. (1985). Of mimicry and man: The ambivalence of colonial discourse. *October, 34*, 126–133.

Blanchet, P., & Coste, D. (2010). *Regards critiques sur la notion d' "interculturalité": Pour une didactique de la pluralité linguistique et culturelle*. Paris, France: L'Harmattan.

Canagarajah, A. S. (1999). *Resisting linguistic imperialism in English teaching*. Oxford, UK: Oxford University Press.

Canagarajah, A. S. (2006). The place of world Englishes in composition: Pluralization continued. *College Composition and Communication, 57*(4), 586–619.

Canagarajah, A. S. (2007). Lingua franca English, multilingual communities, and language acquisition. *Modern Language Journal, 91*, 923–939. doi:10.1111/j.1540-4781.2007.00678.x.

Canagarajah, A. S. (2011). World Englishes as code-meshing. In V. A. Young & A. Martinez (Eds.), *Code meshing as World English: Policy, pedagogy, performance* (pp. 273–281). Urbana, IL: National Council of Teachers of English.

Candelier, M., Ioannitou, G., Omer, D., & Vasseur, M. (Eds.) (2008). *Conscience du plurilinguisme: Pratiques, représentations et interventions*. Rennes, France : Presses universitaires de Rennes.

Confiant, R. (2007). Créolité et francophonie: un éloge de la diversalité. Retrieved from http://www.potomitan.info/articles/diversalite.htm (accessed Nov. 15, 2012).

Council of Europe/Conseil de l'Europe. (2001). *Common European framework of reference for languages: Learning, teaching, assessment.* Cambridge, UK: Cambridge University Press.

Fox, T. (1990a). Basic writing as cultural conflict. *Journal of Education, 172*(1), 65–83.

Fox, T. (1990b). *The social uses of writing: Politics and pedagogy.* Norwood, NJ: Ablex.

François, F. (1999). *Le discours et ses entours: Essai sur l'interprétation.* Paris, France: L'Harmattan.

García, O. (2009). *Bilingual education in the 21st century: A global perspective.* Oxford, UK: Wiley-Blackwell.

Giddens, A. (1979). *Central problems in social theory: Action, structure and contradiction in social analysis.* Berkeley, CA: University of California Press.

Gilyard, K. (1997). Cross-talk: Toward transcultural writing classrooms. In C. Severino, J. C. Guerra, & J. E. Butler (Eds.), *Writing in multicultural settings* (pp. 325–331). New York, NY: Modern Language Association of America.

Grego, R., & Thompson, N. S. (2008). *Teaching/writing in third spaces: The studio approach.* Carbondale, IL: Southern Illinois University Press.

Guerra, J. C. (1997). The place of intercultural literacy. In C. Severino, J. C. Guerra, & J. E. Butler (Eds.), *Writing in multicultural settings* (pp. 248–260). New York, NY: Modern Language Association of America.

Guerra, J. C. (2008). Writing for transcultural citizenship: A cultural ecology model. *Language Arts, 85*(4), 296–304.

Horner, B., & Lu, M. Z. (1999). *Representing the "other": Basic writers and the teaching of basic writing.* Urbana, IL: National Council of Teachers of English.

Horner, B., & Lu, M. Z. (2008). *Writing conventions.* New York, NY: Pearson Longman/Penguin Academics.

Horner, B., Lu, M. Z., Royster J. J., & Trimbur, J. (2011). Language difference in writing: Toward a translingual approach. *College English, 73*(3), 303–321.

Hull, G., & Rose, M. (1990). "This wooden shack place": The logic of an unconventional reading. *College Composition and Communication, 41,* 287–298. doi:10.2307/357656.

Hull, G., Rose, M., Fraser, K. L., & Castellano, M. (1991). Remediation as social construct: Perspectives from an analysis of classroom discourse. *College Composition and Communication, 42,* 299–329. doi:10.2307/358073.

Jenkins, J. (2006). Current perspectives on teaching World Englishes and English as a lingua franca. *TESOL Quarterly, 40*(1), 157–181. doi:10.2307/40264515.

Kaur, J. (2009). Pre-empting problems of understanding in English as a lingua franca. In A. Mauranen & E. Ranta (Eds.), *English as a lingua franca: Studies and findings* (pp. 107–123). Newcastle-upon-Tyne, UK: Cambridge Scholars Publishing.

Kells, M., Balester, V. M., & Villanueva, V. (Eds.) (2004). *Latino/a discourses: On language, identity, and literacy education.* Portsmouth, NH: Boynton/Cook Heinemann.

Khubchandani, L. M. (1998). A plurilingual ethos: A peep into the sociology of language. *Indian Journal of Applied Linguistics, 24*(1), 5–37.

Kirkpatrick, A. (2007). *World Englishes: Implications for international communication and English language teaching.* Cambridge, UK: Cambridge University Press.

Kramsch, C. (1998). The privilege of the intercultural speaker. In M. Byram and M. Fleming (Eds.), *Language learning in intercultural perspective: Approaches through drama and ethnography* (pp. 16–31). Cambridge, UK: Cambridge University Press.

Lees, E. O. (1989). "The exceptable way of the society": Stanley Fish's theory of reading and the task of the teacher of editing. In P. Donahue and E. Quandahl (Eds.), *Reclaiming pedagogy: The rhetoric of the classroom* (pp. 144–163). Carbondale, IL: Southern Illinois University Press.

Lu, M. (1994). Professing multiculturalism: The politics of style in the contact zone. *College Composition and Communication, 45*(4), 442–458. doi:10.2307/358759.

Lu, M. (2004). An essay on the work of composition: Composing English against the order of fast capitalism. *College Composition and Communication, 56*(1), 16–50. doi:10.2307/4140679.

Lu, M. (2006). Living-English work. *College English, 68*(6), 605–618. doi:10.2307/25472178.

Makoni, S., & Pennycook, A. (Eds.) (2007). *Disinventing and reconstituting languages.* Clevedon UK: Buffalo.

Pennycook, A. (2008). English as a language always in translation. *European Journal of English Studies, 12*(1), 33–47. doi:10.1080/13825570801900521.

Pennycook, A. (2010). *Language as a local practice.* London, UK: Routledge.

Pratt, M. L. (1991). Arts of the contact zone. *Profession, 91,* 33–40.

Royster, J. J. (1996). When the first voice you hear is not your own. *College Composition and Communication, 47,* 29–40. doi:10.2307/358272.

Seidlhofer, B. (2004). Research perspectives on teaching English as a lingua franca. *Annual Review of Applied Linguistics, 24,* 209–239. doi:10.1017/S0267190504000145.

Severino, C., Guerra. J. C., & Butler, J. E. (Eds.) (1997). *Writing in multicultural settings.* New York, NY: Modern Language Association.

Shaughnessy, M. P. (1977). *Errors and expectations: A guide for the teacher of basic writing.* New York, NY: Oxford University Press.

Slevin, J. F. (2001). *Introducing English: Essays in the intellectual work of composition.* Pittsburgh, PA: University of Pittsburgh Press.

Smitherman, G., & Villanueva, V. (Eds.) (2003). *Language diversity in the classroom: From intention to practice.* Carbondale, IL: Southern Illinois University Press.

Spack, R. (1997). The rhetorical construction of multilingual students. *TESOL Quarterly, 31,* 765–774. doi:10.2307/3587759.

Valdès, G. (1992). Bilingual minorities and language issues in writing. *Written Communication, 9*(1), 85–136.

Young, V. A. (2009). "Nah, we straight": An argument against code switching. *JAC: A Journal of Composition Theory, 29*(1–2), 49–76.

Young, V. A., & Martinez, A. (Eds.). (2011). *Code meshing as World English: Policy, pedagogy, performance.* Urbana, IL: National Council of Teachers of English.

Zamel, V. (1997). Toward a model of transculturation. *TESOL Quarterly, 31*(2): 341–352. doi:10.2307/3588050.

Zarate, G., Lévy, D., & Kramsch, C. (Eds.). (2008). *Précis du plurilinguisme et du pluriculturalisme.* Paris, France: Editions des archives contemporaines.

4

RHETORICAL ACTIVITIES OF GLOBAL CITIZENS

Scott Wible

Dating back to at least ancient Greece, rhetoric scholars and teachers have sought, in the words of Isocrates, to develop in students the skills and knowledges that will enable them "to govern wisely both [their] own households and the commonwealth" (as cited in Atwill, 1998, p. 132). Such an education would help students to obtain a deep understanding of subjects related to civic life, such as the law, political philosophy, and ethics. Equally as important, this rhetorical education would give students practice in a broad range of strategies for deliberating with other citizens about public matters. And, finally, through such rhetorical education students ideally would be exposed to and learn to inhabit the culture's values, commonplaces, and worldviews. While there have been many notable exceptions throughout history for racialized, gendered, and disabled minorities, rhetorical education has, in short, aimed to prepare students to participate fully in public political life.

These latter two aspects of rhetorical education—teaching a common set of communication strategies and fostering or preserving a sense of a common culture—draws on a political philosophy expressed most recently by philosophy scholar Kymlicka (2001). While speaking specifically about democracies, Kymlicka stresses that "a system of collective deliberation and legitimation" demands that "participants understand and trust one another" (p. 212). Kymlicka suggests that such mutual understanding and trust "requires some underlying commonalities," the two most important of which he believes to be sharing a common language and a common culture (p. 212). This political philosophy highlights two important, yet often implicit, assumptions underlying many theories and practices of rhetorical education. First, rhetorical education commonly orients itself toward public affairs conducted within a distinct political boundary, such as the commonwealth of Isocrates' time or, in more recent centuries, the nation state. Second, rhetorical education often reinforces a belief that the success of the culture resides in a common language, as the use of a single language would seem to enable public deliberations to proceed as clearly and efficiently as possible.

This chapter extends and complicates such an understanding of rhetorical education by investigating the rhetorical practices that have developed within one group, the World Social Forum, to enable its participants to govern more wisely the affairs of contemporary globalization. For the past decade, the World Social Forum has arranged international and regional meetings to create space for social movements and activists from around the world to come together and deliberate collectively. Participants reflect on the causes and consequences of neoliberal globalization, share experiences of local challenges to present forms of globalization, develop and debate alternative proposals for global policies, and coordinate political actions across nation-state boundaries. The World Social Forum's participants maintain that another type of global world is possible, one created by and for the benefit of more than just the world's financial, political, and cultural leaders.

A Different Rhetorical Education

What is compelling about this group in terms of rhetorical education is that it strives to educate people from various linguistic and cultural communities to participate in global discussion. Traditional conceptions of public deliberation would suggest that such discussions would not be effective because the participants do not share a common culture or language. Structures have been created within the World Social Forum and its regional meetings, however, to enable people from a variety of language communities to participate in deliberations about globalization. These efforts to promote multilingual dialogue can serve as heuristics for thinking about what rhetorical education might look like when viewed through the lens of globalization. The social forum's practices prompts amendments, in the name of attending more closely to linguistic diversity, to central questions that have concerned scholars of rhetorical education: What language and rhetorical strategies do citizen-activists promote to engage global and transnational conversations? What attitudes and values do individuals and groups develop through such engagement? What knowledge gets created through cross-cultural and cross-language deliberations, and toward what ends might this knowledge be used? This chapter aims to begin thinking through these questions about rhetorical education and the linguistic dimensions of global citizenship.

Before turning to these two examples, a brief explanation is in order of the rationale for thinking about citizenship in relation to the global or transnational sphere, not just the commonwealth or nation state. This rationale draws primarily on rhetoric scholar Asen's (2004) discourse theory of citizenship. Asen argues that it is limiting to view citizenship as an identity simply granted to people by a nation state. This perspective leads scholars to focus only on identifying what does and does not "count" as a civic act—voting, for example, or joining politically affiliated organizations—rather than also considering the contexts within which some-one pursues a public activity and the dispositions of the person performing the act (pp. 190–191). Asen maintains that it is the person's attitudes and aims that mark a public act as "civic." Specifically, he suggests that acts of citizenship are marked by a person's desire to "wide[n] public agendas and invit[e] greater participation" (p. 199); to "risk thinking differently" and "putting [one's] beliefs in the open, subject to criticism and revision" (pp. 199–200); to commit to interaction that "privileg[es] norms of inclusion and fairness" (p. 201); to express oneself in crea-tive ways (p. 201); and to be mindful of one's positioning and perspectives rela-tive to people situated differently (pp. 202–203). Civic acts, then, are the means people use to forge connections with other individuals and groups in public, no matter the geographic or political scale. It is in this sense that one can think of the World Social Forum's *multilingual* activities as forms of global citizenship.

This desire to expand participation and to recognize the perspectives of others lies at the heart of the World Social Forum's international and regional meetings. The World Social Forum was first held in Porto Allegre, Brazil, in April 2001, as an emergence from the anti-neoliberal globalization movement. Since that time, the Forum's annual meetings have brought together activists and civil society organizations concerned with issues such as women's rights, agriculture and natu-ral resources, global warming, HIV/AIDS, independent media, and economic equality. The Forum is not a deliberative body; its participants do not debate and vote on policies that would be binding for all participating organizations and individuals. Instead, as the first principle of the World Social Forum's Charter of Principles (2001) explains, the Forum serves as "an open meeting *place* for reflec-tive thinking, democratic debate of ideas, formulation of proposals, free exchange of experiences, and interlinking for effective action" (emphasis added). While Principle 1 defines the Forum as a "place," however, Principles 2 and 3 describe the Forum as becoming "a permanent *process* of seeking and building alternatives" and "a world *process*" (emphasis added). This emphasis on "process" is significant. It encourages one to read the Forum's motto, "Another world is possible," not only in terms of the alternative models for global development and anti-global activism that might emerge from the World Social Forum meetings but also the alternative processes of deliberation and decision-making enacted through the Forum meetings themselves.

Central to this process is the structure that has been created to enable face-to-face multilingual dialogue at the World Social Forum, as well as regional social forum meetings. In many sessions at the various social forum meetings, the floor is open for all participating groups to raise concerns and present ideas that they feel others need to give greater attention. Quite significantly, the participants in World Social Forum and regional social forum meetings are given the opportu-nity to speak in local languages, rather than one of the dominant international languages, should they choose to do so. What enables this multilingual dialogue to work are the efforts of volunteer networks of translators, such as the group

Babels, along with a radio-based digital interpretation technology developed by the media activist network Alternative Interpretation System. The participants in the regional preparatory meetings are given the opportunity to speak in local languages, rather than one of the dominant international languages, should they choose to do so. The World Social Forum has created this unique multilingual structure to promote values of fairness and equality. This policy ensures that people who have less experience in formal democratic dialogue, as well as people from historically marginalized groups and language backgrounds, have just as much opportunity as anyone else to contribute to the deliberations.

Compared to monolingual political debates, these multilingual dialogues do not measure up by traditional evaluative criteria. The normal conception of political debate gives primacy to actions such as delivering messages as clearly and efficiently as possible, controlling how others receive and interpret messages, and promptly drawing dialogue to a conclusion so that "real action" can take place. The World Social Forum, however, aims to bring into being alternative forms of global citizenship and political deliberation, and citizen-activists' participation in this multilingual, translated dialogue illustrates what these alternative forms might entail. Sociologist Doerr (2009) suggests, "[T]he need to translate discussions into different languages at meetings had the effect of *lengthening discussions* and *increasing the effort* required by participants *to listen* to each other" (p. 154, emphasis added). She also notes, though, that while some social forum participants described the translation process as "time consuming," most did not consider the need for translations to be a problem, and instead thought of the slowness as a positive (as cited in Doerr, 2009, p. 155). As one European Social Forum participant explained to Doerr, when things slow down, "then it gets more politically balanced" (as cited in Doerr, 2009, p. 155). The slow pace of dialoguing with translators seems to prompt valuable rhetorical work. It allows more time for participants to listen to, reflect on, and discover new ways to work with others' expressed ideas. This inventional activity in turn performs global citizenship as it broadens the public agenda and enacts more pluralistic processes of creating knowledge.

The translators who enable this multilingual dialogue highlight another important aspect of global civic activity. Central to the World Social Forum and regional social forums are the efforts of a volunteer network of translators coordinated by the group Babels. Significantly, Babels volunteers see themselves as something other than passive conduits that simply translate what they hear others say. Instead, they approach translation work as "opportunities to create political spaces" at the intersections of language and cultural difference, and they identify themselves as "political partners within the social forums" (Babels, 2005). At the organization's international conferences and within its online forums, Babels volunteers learn and teach each other translation techniques that allow them to adapt to and work with the widely diverse participant communities, subject matter, and presentation formats within the social forum meetings. For Babels translators, the acts of translating the languages and negotiating the cultural differences unique to each social forum are part of the larger "comprehensive experiential approach of alterglobalist practices" (Babels, 2005). In other words, Babels volunteers see alternative social arrangements being created through their translation work as well as the broad cross-cultural and cross-language dialogue it enables. This "experiential approach" toward creating alternative global societies underscores the potential for cross-language work to be an important means of enacting global citizenship. In terms of Asen's definition of citizenship activity, translation can be a means of risk-taking necessary to create new transnational communities; it can be a means of widening public agendas, as it fosters greater participation and reinforces norms of inclusiveness and fairness in public debate.

Given this collection's investment in rhetoric and writing across language boundaries, it is also important to note another result of the World Social Forum's multilingual dialogue. Just as the Babels volunteers continue to refine their translation techniques, many activists who participate in these translated meetings have learned to experiment with language and have built a diverse set of linguistic strategies to communicate with activists from other language groups. Doerr (2009) reports that activists have adopted new words into their lexicons and reached consensus on the meanings of translated words (pp. 155–156). They have also learned to move between languages where it seemed beneficial to do so, and mixed the languages at other times. As one European Social Forum participant explained, "we invent a special type of language here, our own one, and we invent a culture of communication" (as cited in Doerr, 2009, p. 155). This linguistic inventiveness highlights an important idea for rhetorical education and global citizenship. This rhetorical education must aim not simply to teach students how to master skills and knowledges in a single language or even in multiple, yet discrete, languages. Rather, this rhetorical education should also develop in students the willingness to try as best they can to collaborate in creating mutual understanding with people speaking and writing in other languages. As rhetoric scholar Beale (1990) contends, rhetorical education is a means of developing an individual's character. In this sense, a rhetorical education for global citizenship would in part develop students who welcome and take risks in cross-language settings, all as a means to heighten their powers of flexibility and creativity in communication.

A Different Communication Strategy

In addition to this structure for creating multilingual meetings, the World Social Forum community also provides an important lesson for global citizenship in terms of deploying language diversity within transnational information campaigns. Since 2003, the Panos Institute West Africa (PIWA) has created the *Flame of Africa* print newspaper to provide African perspectives on the World Social Forum meetings. More recently, PIWA (2005), with its mission to create "democratic and open African societies based on public space that promotes change and social justice" (PANOS), expanded *Flame of Africa* to an online edition and a radio production. In the lead-up to the World Social Forum meeting held in February 2011 in Dakar, Senegal, however, the African Social Forum solicited PIWA's help in creating an extensive communications strategy to ensure both that an African perspective on global issues could be heard by people throughout Africa and also be transmitted to the wider world.

The African Social Forum's communication strategy was diverse. The texts at the heart of this communication strategy ranged from traditional mass media forms such as radio programs, videos, and printed newspapers and newsletters to a host of non-mass mediated modes of communication, such as local music, art, and handicrafts (African Social Forum, "African Communications," 2010, pp. 4–6, 8–9). More important for the present reader's concerns, these texts, depending on each one's specific rhetorical situation, were produced in a number of local languages that are used transnationally throughout Africa, such as Swahili, Fulani, Malinke, and Bambara, with some also being translated into international languages such as English, French, and Arabic (5). As the languages and audiences for each text varied, so did the specific topics, so that readers could see how neoliberal globalization policies affected their local communities, often in negative ways. Significantly, however, every piece of this communications campaign also highlighted how African citizens are challenging these policies and inventing alternative responses to them.

The African Social Forum's multilingual communication strategy was enacted via a networked authoring process rather than a centralized one. The strategy relied on building new and leveraging existing networks with individuals and groups who are positioned in different geographic, cultural, and linguistic communities (African Social Forum, 2010). It included mobilizing the ever growing number of citizen media outlets throughout Africa, connecting with independent media networks of global scope, and linking with local and international broadcast and print media professionals who have attended to social issues in their work. Each person in this network shared a similar vision about what the aims of the communication ought to be, but then each person worked to document different aspects of the relationship between global economics and local politics and cultures. Just as important, the authors in the network decided what languages and what locally relevant rhetorical strategies to use in developing their texts, and then the African Social Forum provided the resources to help participants compose and distribute their texts.

The use of local languages was vitally important to the African Social Forum's communications strategy for both pragmatic *and* symbolic reasons. These social activists see Western languages such as English and French as the languages that policy-makers and journalists have used to compose the image of Africans as lazy, dependent victims unable to help themselves (African Social Forum, 2010). This image, African activists maintain, has worked to sustain a global policy-making process in which non-Western perspectives and cultural logics are often absent, ignored, or misrepresented. By building a network of people working in local languages, generating local content for publications, and highlighting local activities that resist neoliberal globalization policies, the African Social Forum hoped to assert an image of Africans as "resilient and inventive," as agents who work together—rather than relying on outside help—to create positive social change (African Social Forum, 2010).

The African Social Forum's communications strategy is compelling in a few ways when considering how to reimagine the concerns of rhetorical education in an era of globalization. This strategy explicitly builds on the African Social Forum's Charter of Principles, which emphasizes not only "stimulat[ing] reflection" but also "the maximum transparent circulation of the results of this reflection" (African Social Forum, 2003). In other words, the communication strategy partly involved creating insightful analysis of how local African communities were challenging neoliberal globalization. Just as important, however, the strategy also entailed circulating this analysis transnationally throughout Africa and the wider world and creating opportunities for Africans from many different language communities to join the dialogue on global policies. The emphasis here on both invention *and* delivery—on prompting reflection and on circulating the knowledge that emerges from it—highlights the need for rhetors to design strategies for reaching multilingual audiences. As Asen suggests, enacting citizenship in part entails putting one's beliefs into the open and inviting greater public participation. In today's globalizing world, and in today's increasingly multilingual U.S., efforts to foster broader public dialogue demand an attention to language diversity and the need for translation. Putting one's beliefs into the open means delivering them in relevant linguistic forms to forums in which stakeholders from different language groups can read them and respond to them.

Significantly, however, the African Social Forum's communication strategy challenges the notion that a single rhetor must necessarily possess some sort of cosmopolitan ideal of fluent multilingualism in a host of languages. That is, the forum's strategy emphasizes collaborating and networking with people in different political, cultural, and linguistic communities rather than solitary composing. The idea here is that rhetorical education for global citizenship should prompt reflection on the limits of a monolingual communication strategy, limits in terms of both to whom texts might circulate and from whom texts invite response. This rhetorical education would also help people begin to generate a range of strategies for building a multilingual network through which to develop and circulate ideas, strategies ranging from securing volunteer or professional translation and localization services to learning to develop creativity—not perfection—in language use. Rhetorical education would put less emphasis on efficiency in communication and grant more value to patience. It would give more attention to learning how to listen in cross-cultural and cross-language contexts. Students would learn how to work at the borders of language well enough to forge relationships with similarly invested citizens.

Implications

These examples from the World Social Forum's deliberative practices and public information campaigns suggest that—to loosely paraphrase the forum's motto—another means of communicating is possible. As Isocrates reminds us, rhetorical education scholars have long been concerned with the skills and knowledges that students need to govern the affairs of the household and the commonwealth. Participants in the World Social Forum enact global citizenship in part by listening to people from other regions and other cultures analyze how global policies affect their local activities. Equally as important, their global citizenship practices also underscore the benefits of learning to work with or across the borders of language diversity. Rhetorical education for global citizenship is about cultivating an attitude that leads students to listen to people from many different language groups and to share their experiences of inventing local solutions to manage global problems. This multilingual political communication can enable global citizens to develop a broader base of knowledge about how to define global problems and how to create strategies for resolving them. Another world is possible, and cross-language practices are an important means for global citizens to bring that world into being.

References

African Social Forum. (2003, July). Charter of Principles and Values of the African Social Forum. Retrieved from http://www.africansocialforum.org/english/charter.htm (accessed Dec. 3, 2012).

African Social Forum. (2010, July). African Communications Strategy for the 2011 WSF. Retrieved from http://fsm2011.org/en/news/the-african-communication-strategy-for-the-2011-wsf (accessed Dec. 3, 2012).

Asen, R. (2004). A discourse theory of citizenship. *Quarterly Journal of Speech, 90*(2), 189–211. doi:10.1080/0033563042000227436.

Atwill, J. M. (1998). *Rhetoric reclaimed: Aristotle and the liberal arts tradition.* Ithaca, NY: Cornell University Press.

Babels. (2005, Nov. 6). Call to other Babels projects. Retrieved from http://www.babels.org (accessed Nov. 15, 2012).

Beale, W. H. (1990). Richard M. Weaver: Philosophical rhetoric, cultural criticism, and the first rhetorical awakening. *College English, 52*(6), 626–640.

Doerr, N. (2009). Language and democracy "in movement": Multilingualism and the case of the European Social Forum process. *Social Movement Studies, 8*(2), 149–165.

Kymlicka, W. (2001). *Politics in the vernacular: Nationalism, multiculturalism, and citizenship.* Oxford, UK: Oxford University Press.

PANOS Institute West Africa (PIWA). (2005, June 22). Mission. Retrieved from http://www.panos-ao.org/ipao/spip.php?article3231&lang=fr (accessed Nov. 15, 2012).

World Social Forum. (2001, April 9). Charter of Principles. Retrieved from http://www.fsm2013.org/en/node/204 (accessed Nov. 15, 2012).

5

REDEFINING INDIGENOUS RHETORIC:[1] FROM PLACES OF ORIGIN TO TRANSLINGUAL SPACES OF INTERDEPENDENCE-IN-DIFFERENCE

LuMing Mao

Introduction: Two Competing Motives and One Shared Discourse

Lately China has witnessed a feverish revival of "Red culture"—the Maoist-era songs—as part of the campaign led by the Communist Party to celebrate the 90th anniversary of its founding on July 1, 2011. Schools, state-owned companies, and neighborhood committees have been asked to organize choirs to stage musical numbers and sing what has now been referred to as "Red songs." Maoist classics, including "The East is Red," "Sailing the Sea Depends on the Helmsman," and "Without the Communist Party There Would Be No New China," have returned to the airways with a vengeance. Hundreds of millions of schoolchildren, teachers, officials, and retirees have been organized to lend their voices to these Red songs, and they apparently have embraced them with genuine interest (Beech, 2011).

In the city of Chongqing, for example, even prisons are holding sing-alongs, and one psychiatric hospital has prescribed Red songs for patients. In initiatives reminiscent of the Cultural Revolution, the local government has ordered each cadre to live with a family in the countryside for a month, transmitted Maoist slogans to residents via text messages, and told television stations to fill prime-time hours with educational Red programming and cut all commercial advertising (E. Wang, 2011).

What do we make of all this? Does this campaign signal that the Party is attempting to reverse course and to take China back to the revolutionary era again, however expedient or temporary it might be? Or, if these Red songs are indeed being brought back for the sole purpose of commemorating the founding of the Chinese Communist Party, then how do we reconcile this apparent contradiction between the revival of a "retro-Red" ideology (E. Wang, 2011) and the ongoing social and economic reforms whose underlying values are anything but Red?

The Party's motive in launching this Red-culture revival is perhaps easy to ferret out.[2] By way of reviving these revolutionary songs, the Party seems to be interested in connecting ordinary Chinese to a recent past when love for the country and loyalty to the Party apparently reigned supreme, and when the gap of the present time between the rich and the poor was nowhere to be seen. The invocation of such a past serves as a timely response to the widespread apathy and distrust among the population, and it aims to rekindle their patriotism toward the country and restore their confidence in the Party. In fact, I want to suggest that this campaign represents an integral part of the Party's ongoing effort to construct a new rhetoric or to rebrand an existing or almost forgotten one that can best promote cultural nationalism and protect its hold on power. Appealing to its own revolutionary heritage lends this new rhetoric native legitimacy and authority, both of which are slipping away from the Party in the face of globalizing capitalism and its attending ideology.

The response so far exhibited by hundreds of millions of ordinary Chinese, on the other hand, comes as a bit of a surprise to many Chinese liberal elites (Beech, 2011; E. Wang, 2011). Not only because these Red songs have been associated with the era of radicalism, hysteria, and zealotry, but also because ordinary Chinese generally have shown cynicism in the recent past toward any Party-led campaign that smells of politics, let alone Red politics. However, their willingness to sing along may very well betray a competing motive—one that is not so much about joining the Party in its campaign to instill patriotism and loyalty as about reclaiming their own sense of moral belonging and agency which has been severely undermined by the ongoing economic and social reforms and by the increasing wealth and power gap. It is also more about trying to reconcile their lived experiences with the import of these Red songs. Like the Party, they must also develop a new rhetoric or rebrand an existing or almost forgotten one that can mobilize and empower them. A rebranded revolutionary discourse, which preaches harmony and loyalty, and which yields new discursive alignments, seems to offer an efficacious native medicine for the ills ordinary Chinese are experiencing. To draw from Bourdieu (1977), what they are singing then is neither the lyrics, nor the music *per se*, but their entire social personhood and its attending social and cultural conditions (pp. 653–655). Singing these Red songs, therefore, becomes their way of searching for a meaningful rhetoric.

In spite of their varying motives, and in spite of their different positions of power, both the Party and ordinary Chinese appear to be reconstructing and embracing the same rhetoric—one that is indigenous to them and unsullied by globalizing capitalism of the present time. Such a rhetoric can then accord them the necessary agency with which to speak to or stand up to the dominant discourses on the Chinese discursive terrain.

What, then, exactly are these Red songs if they can be claimed as examples of Chinese indigenous rhetoric? More generally, what are examples of indigenous rhetoric of the 21st century? Under what conditions do they arise? Can indigenous rhetoric remain tethered to its place of origin even as it is entering and claiming new spaces where the *modus operandi* is the establishment not of provenance but of interdependence-in-difference in the making? What is the relationship between indigenous rhetoric and translingual practices?[3] It is to these questions that I now turn.

From the Almost Forgotten to the Importantly Present: The Rise of Red Songs as Chinese Indigenous Rhetoric

To characterize any given rhetoric as indigenous is to highlight the fact that it originated from the place where its participants continue to live, and that its history has been marked by rejection, subordination, and/or exploitation, as the case might be. Since any indigenous rhetoric in the 21st century is bound to dialogue with or speak back to other discourses in search for its rightful place on the global discursive terrain, I suggest that we characterize indigenous rhetoric as rhetoric of hybridity borne of a creative process where the indigenous and the exogenous engage with each other, and where the discursive past of the indigenous makes its presence felt in the global present. Indigenous rhetoric is further informed by a recovery and reclaiming imperative—an all-out effort to recover and reconstitute a native past that has been ignored, ill-regarded, or altogether erased by an exogenous power. Moreover, what in large part shapes this recovery and reclaiming imperative is likely the project of cultural nationalism, of asserting a claim on the larger national and cultural imaginary, which "gives rise to collective identity, community, and a sense of 'peoplehood'" (Omi & Winant, 1994, p. 40).

For example, these Maoist-era songs could be said to have provided their promoters and followers with a much needed sense of indigeneity and ownership. As signifiers of a retro-Red ideology, they cannot help but forge ideological bonds and stir up national pride among the population because their lyrics portray a new China that is created and nurtured by the supreme leadership of Chairman Mao, and its people whose love for the Party and the Motherland is unparalleled. Many ordinary Chinese have participated in the experiences portrayed by these songs. By embracing these songs, both the Party and ordinary Chinese are able not only to cultivate nostalgia for a recent past, the utopian ideals of which seem to be gaining favor as the gap between the haves and have-nots in the present time keeps widening, but also to contest the globalizing liberal ideologies whose presence in China has taken center stage.

Here is the first stanza of the lyrics to "There Will Be No New China Without the Community Party," one of many Red songs that have been brought back in this revival campaign:

There will be no new China without the Community Party.
There will be no new China without the Community Party.
The Community Party has shed blood and sweat for the nation,
It has devoted itself to the cause of liberating China.
It has opened the path for liberation for its people,
It has led China to a bright future.
It has fought the Japanese for eight years;
It has improved people's lives;
It has opened up revolutionary bases;
And it has practiced democracy.
There will be no new China without the Community Party.
There will be no new China without the Community Party.[4]

(X. Wang, 2001, p. 164)

A panegyric through and through, these, and indeed the rest of the lyrics in the song lend the Party the necessary rhetoric with which to reclaim its revolutionary heritage and, more importantly, to reestablish its lost credibility and authority. At the same time, they also allow ordinary Chinese to use this rebranded revolutionary past as their own rhetorical antidote to the dizzying capitalist present so that the path for social and economic liberation will be open to them, and so that they can still be part of this new China.

As these Red songs are being rebranded as a viable alternative to the ideological challenges brought on by the ongoing social and economic reforms, they are beginning to construct a new order on the Chinese discursive terrain. This new order is to redefine and reshape the relationship between what is "importantly present" and what is "merely present" or, better still, between what is "importantly present" and what is "almost forgotten."

By "importantly present" I draw upon Hall and Ames (1995) to mean that the importance of any particular belief or any set of ideologies in a culture depends not on its mere presence or its past presence, but on whether it is importantly present "in such a way that it significantly qualifies, defines, or otherwise shapes the culture" (p. xv). Prior to this revival campaign orchestrated by the Party, these Red songs had almost been left in the dustbin of history. Since their revival, they have begun to make their presence felt, transforming themselves from the almost forgotten to the importantly present as they help restore creditability for the Party, and relevance and agency for ordinary Chinese. Of course, what must be emphasized is that the emerging status of the importantly present is anything but secure because other competing rhetorics are bound to contest its newly acquired status and to compete for the right to control and dominate the same space.

The question now becomes this: Can these Red songs remain tied to their place of origin, to their revolutionary past? Are they not already weakening, if not severing altogether, the link to such a past by their rebranded presence or by what they are enacting in the present time?

Indigenous rhetoric in the 21st century, I suggest, can no longer remain tethered to its place of origin and that our conceptualization of it must be based on the larger context to which they are inextricably connected, and with which they are invariably expected to dialogue. According to Mignolo (1998), the current stage of globalization—transnational corporations and technoglobalism—is "creating the condition for and enacting the relocation of languages and the fracture of culture," thus engineering "the uncoupling of the 'natural' link between languages and nations, languages and national memories, languages and national literature" (p. 42).

Indigenous rhetoric undergoes a similar decoupling process. That is, it disassociates itself from a place defined by physical boundaries and moves into a space populated by discursive practices and ideological exigencies. In the process it establishes new connections that cross traditional boundaries and defies the existing hierarchies that privilege one ideology over other competing or emerging ideology or ideologies. Whatever the original link, natural or otherwise, it ties any given indigenous rhetoric to its place of origin, and dissolves under the weight of porous boundaries and fractured cultures.

Therefore, what makes these revolutionary songs indigenous is not about a revolutionary past marked by borders and chronological timelines, or about how such a past makes its origin claim through these "origin identity-markers." Rather, what makes them indigenous is the borderless space these songs have entered where they claim their unique link, however weakened or even imagined, to a utopian past and accord the Party and ordinary Chinese the authority and legitimacy for their respective positions in the present time. In addition, as indigenous rhetoric, these Red songs are always in the process of being constituted and reconstituted in a multi-authored act of representation, re-representation, or even counter-representation, forever preparing for new relationships and new alignments to emerge without forgetting "the inherent right and ability of *peoples* to determine their own communicative needs and desires" (Lyons, 2000, p. 449; emphasis in original). Consequently, (the rebranding of) these Red songs can lead to some (unintended) incongruities between, for example, their retro-Red ideology and the ideology of globalizing capitalism, and between what they were created to accomplish then (to incite revolution) and what they are being primed to perform now (to cultivate harmony and unity).

The most extreme incongruity can be seen or experienced in these Red songs when they become "flipped"—that is, when their meanings become completely reversed, giving rise to an example of counter-representation. A case in point is the Red song "There Will Be No New China Without the Community Party." Its complete reverse has appeared on the virtual space. Titled "A New China Without the Party" (2009), its lyrics begin and conclude with the line: "Only without the Communist Party will there be a new China." And stanza after stanza, the new lyrics negate and make a total mockery of the original ones, and together they turn into a scathing rebuke and condemnation of the Party and of what it has done since it seized power in 1949.

There is one more dimension that deserves our attention regarding these Red songs. As Chinese indigenous rhetoric, they reshape and redefine the relationship between what is importantly present and what is merely present or what is almost forgotten from within. At the same time, they cannot help but speak to and interact with what is importantly present, merely present, or almost forgotten from without. To be more specific, while these Red songs are intended to help legitimize a new cultural and national order in China, their revival has to be understood within the overall global context. That is, the relevance and importance of the rebranded Red songs is being made possible both by the internal nostalgia for a mythical past of innocence, equality and harmony and by the external ideology of capitalist globalization. These songs thus move, to quote cultural theorist Liu Kang (1998), "between historically changing fields of struggle and *habitus* of discrete dispositions" (p. 169)—out of which their significance and cultural capital are being legitimated, recognized, and experienced.

This kind of movement or interaction from both within and without brings together and re-engages different discourses (importantly present, merely present, and almost forgotten). Further, it enables them to enter and influence one another's discursive fields. By "discursive fields" I mean textual spaces where related terms and concepts form clusters to speak to one another, and where semantic alignments and subject positions take shape and acquire authority and legitimacy. As they become connected to one another, these discourses will vie for audience and dominance amidst tension, indeterminacy, and even contradiction. While it does not resolve or dissolve tension or difference, togetherness of this kind calls on us to reconsider or recalibrate such perennial binaries as being and becoming, permanence and process, self and other, and inside and outside, for example. Togetherness of this kind further transforms and solidifies these interwoven and interconnected relationships, creating translingual spaces of interdependence-in-difference in the making.

For example, below are the lyrics of "The East Is Red," one of the Red songs that is perhaps the most well-known:

> The East is red, the sun rises.
> China has produced a Mao Zedong.
> He seeks happiness for people,
> And he is our great savior.
>
> Chairman Mao loves people.
> He is our leader.
> To build a new China
> He is guiding us forward.
>
> The Communist Party is like the sun.
> Wherever it shines it has light.
> Wherever the Party goes,
> The people become liberated.

(Eulogy of Mao Zedong, 1978, pp. 1–9)

These lyrics worship and eulogize Chairman Mao and the Party to an unprecedented degree, affirming them as saviors and elevating them to the status of sainthood. As this and other Red songs are being sung on a mass scale, they inevitably mark a disturbingly jarring presence punctuating this euphoria for market economy and Western liberal individualism. They jostle with other discourses for audience and uptake, since their own meanings are anything but secure. For example, "happiness," "liberation," and "democracy" could connote very different implications to different audiences. For those ordinary Chinese, whose economic fortunes have not benefited from the ongoing economic and social reforms, these words become either completely empty or quite ironic because of an inescapable contradiction between what these words are saying and what is taking place on the ground. And for those who have "made it," they may very well attribute their happiness, liberation, and democracy not to the Party, but to capitalist and other Western ideologies. And still for many other Chinese, these Red songs have enabled them to reconnect to a past of which they were an integral part, and their happiness, liberation, and democracy depend on this nostalgia for a past, not on renewed love and loyalty for the Party in the present time.

Yet, amid this kind of cacophony and incongruity, further fueled by a combination of folk melodies and features characteristic of Western mass songs,[5] these Red songs become Chinese indigenous rhetoric in the 21st century. The louder or more important they grow, the more varied their uptake may become. Not only can individual Chinese deploy these Red songs to address their different rhetorical exigencies as they try to make sense of the clashes or conflicts between the retro-Red ideology and discourses of global capitalism in their daily lives, but also groups and institutions are likely to claim these Red songs as their very own, as representing or validating their own voice and vision for a new China. Even Western liberal discourses may jump on the bandwagon as they fend off serious challenges on the ground and as they try to hold onto their positions of influence and dominance. There is simply no shortage of efforts being expended to utilize these songs to suit one's own ideological needs or to advance one's own political agendas. The more these efforts are being put forth, the more translingual these Red songs will become. It is this kind of interdependence-in-difference in the making that may best characterize Chinese indigenous rhetoric or, for that matter, indigenous rhetoric in general right now.

Conclusion: A Few Implications

Discourses travel. As they do, they mingle, negotiate, and further contend with other discourses in search of new homes. Along the way they experience adulation, comprehension, miscomprehension, apprehension, and/or rejection amidst some highly asymmetrical structures of power. They participate in a transformative process in which, to paraphrase L. Liu (1995), discursive differences are being fought out, authorities invoked and challenged, ambiguities dissolved or created, until new words and meanings emerge (p. 26) or, I might add, until old words and meanings become rebranded or reconstituted. Indigenous rhetoric is no exception. While the place of origin will always attend indigenous rhetoric wherever it travels, its values and significances will be more dependent on the new home it has found, and, to adapt a famous expression of Lévi-Strauss, on how good it is being made there to think with (Lloyd, 1996, p. 122).

My characterization of these Maoist-era songs as rhetorical is not necessarily new. It has long been noted that songs are often rhetorical, and they often convey powerful messages, address exigencies, arouse emotions, and carry out ideological agendas (Lu, 2004, p. 100). However, in calling our attention to these Red songs that are now being revived in China, I am interested in not only spelling out the particularizing conditions under which they have arisen, but also articulating the rhetorical use they now have been deployed to perform. Moreover, I see these Red songs as a form of Chinese indigenous rhetoric, as part of a new discourse the ownership of which is being contested and reconstituted at the present moment.

As should be made evident by now, to characterize these revolutionary songs as indigenous rhetoric is to challenge, and to break away from, the "tyranny" of place that has influenced our understanding of indigenous rhetoric. It is further to put more emphasis on the new discursive space, and on how it redefines and reshapes indigenous rhetoric. Perhaps more important, as the new kid on the (discursive) block, these Red songs provide us a compelling example of how meanings get made and remade in close relationship to their varying attending circumstances, and of how the relationship between the importantly present, the merely present, and the almost forgotten undergo the process of realignment, reformation, and reconstitution. In short, as these Red songs travel from their place of origin to the new space, their indigeneity is not so much transformed when they travel from one place to the other as invented within this new translingual space where the primary mode of representation becomes interdependence-in-difference in the making, and where new subject positions arise to acquire agency and legitimacy.

To study the revival of Red songs and its rhetorical significances also has immediate implications for our writing classrooms and pedagogies. For example, we writing teachers now can use the revival of Red songs to illustrate how meaning gets made or remade and how discourses find their new homes. We can help our students better appreciate this dynamic, transformative meaning-making process that is fraught with uncertainty, incongruity, and possibility. Equally important, as the field of composition moves more decisively toward what Horner, NeCamp, and Donahue have recently called "a translingual norm" (2011, pp. 286–287), we can invite our students to engage these Red songs as an example of moving between discourses in a global context and of developing a critical understanding of how appropriateness and rhetorical importance are both tied to histories of ideas and to local or immediate occasions of use. Just as the Party and ordinary Chinese can deploy these same Red songs to enact their different agencies and to realize their different ideological agendas, so our students can learn to imagine their own context where the use of these Red songs becomes rhetorically effective and appropriate to *them*. In addition, as we embrace a multimodal approach to the teaching of writing, we can stage (the singing of) Red songs, as well as other songs, to demonstrate the multiple ways in which meaning can be composed and communicated and embodied performance can be valued and validated. Only by promoting all available means of communication across language and culture can we truly prepare our students for this new translingual space constituted by multilingualism, multimodality, and multiple forms of interdependence-in-difference.

Notes

1   The use of the singular, rather than the plural, noun "rhetoric" in "indigenous rhetoric" here, and elsewhere in this chapter, aims to contest the dominance of European American rhetoric and its exclusionary biases. It does not mean or imply at all that indigenous rhetoric is monolithic, homogeneous, or unaffected by shifting political, social, and cultural forces. For more on this point, and on its underlying paradox, see Mao and Young (2008, pp. 8–11). And I define "rhetoric" as the systematic, effective use of language and other symbolic resources in political, social, and cultural contexts to respond to discursive patterns and crises at a given point in time in society and to construct new discursive orders and material conditions.
2   The revival of Red culture was initially launched by the now deposed Chinese leader Bo Xilan, who became party secretary in Chongqing in 2007. The revival campaign was greeted enthusiastically by China's "New Left" movement, but viewed with suspicion and distrust by Chinese reformers, including President Hu Jintao. One wonders whether the downfall of its creator would put an end to this revival of Red culture or whether the latter would be co-opted by the discourse of the reformers.
3   I define "translingual practices" as discourses and modes of representation that arise out of the dynamic engagement of two or more discursive and cultural practices against a global communicative context that is regularly marked by power asymmetry and filled with histories of incomprehension, miscomprehension, and/or total silence.
4   Unless otherwise noted, all English translations in this chapter are mine.
5   Mass singing was a Western practice introduced to China by Protestant missionaries in the 19th century, and subsequently reinforced by German military instructors in training Chinese troops. For more on this point, see Lu (2004, pp. 97–99).

References

A new China without the Party (2009) [Video file]. Retrieved from http://www.youtube.com/watch?v=cINx1-gVxAU (accessed Nov. 15, 2012).

Beech, H. (2011, July). Red state. *Time*. Retrieved from http://www.time.com (accessed Nov. 15, 2012).

Bourdieu, P. (1977). The economics of linguistic exchanges. *Social Science Information, 16*, 645–668. doi:10.1177/053901847701600307.

Eulogy of Mao Zedong: Collection of 500 Songs (毛泽东颂：歌曲集500首). (1978). Shanghai: Art Press.

Hall, D. L., & Ames, R. T. (1995). *Anticipating China: Thinking through the narratives of Chinese and Western culture*. Albany, NY: SUNY Press.

Horner, B., NeCamp, S., & Donahue, C. (2011). Toward a multilingual composition scholarship: From English only to a translingual norm. *College Composition and Communication, 63*(2), 269–300.

Liu, K. (1998). Is there an alternative to (capitalist) globalization? The debate about modernity in China. In F. Jameson & M. Miyoshi (Eds.), *The cultures of globalization* (pp. 164–188). Durham, NC: Duke University Press.

Liu, L. (1995). *Translingual practice: Literature, national culture, and translated modernity—China, 1900–1937.* Stanford, CA: Stanford University Press.

Lloyd, G. E. R. (1996). *Adversaries and authorities: Investigations into ancient Greek and Chinese science.* Cambridge: Cambridge University Press.

Lu, X. (2004). *Rhetoric of the Chinese cultural revolution: The impact on Chinese thought, culture, and communication.* Colombia, SC: University of South Carolina Press.

Lyons, S. R. (2000). Rhetorical sovereignty: What do American Indians want from writing? *College Composition and Communication, 51*(3), 447–468.

Mao, L., & Young, M. (2008). Introduction: Performing Asian American rhetoric in the American imaginary. In L. Mao, & M. Young (Eds.), *Representations: Doing Asian American rhetoric* (pp. 1–22). Logan, UT: Utah State University Press.

Mignolo, W. (1998). Globalization, civilization processes, and the relocation of languages and culture. In F. Jameson & M. Miyoshi (Eds.), *The cultures of globalization* (pp. 32–53). Durham, NC: Duke University Press.

Omi, M., & Winant, H. (1994). *Racial formation in the United States: From the 1960s to the 1990s* (2nd ed.). New York: Routledge.

Wang, E. (2011, June 29). Repackaging the revolutionary classics of China. *The New York Times.* Retrieved from http://www.nytimes.com/2011/06/30/world/asia/30redsong.html?pagewanted=all (accessed Nov. 15, 2012).

Wang, X. (Ed.) (2001). *Hongqi piaopiao: hongse jingdian gequji* 红旗飘飘：红色经典歌曲集 [*Red Flag Waving: Songs of Red Classics*]. Beijing: Heichao Press.

PART II
Community Practices

6

NEITHER ASIAN NOR AMERICAN: THE CREOLIZATION OF ASIAN AMERICAN RHETORIC

Morris Young

The emergence of Asian American rhetoric as an area of study remains one of contestation and collaboration. In this era of "individual rights" and uncivic discourse, scholarship that focuses on the rhetorical practices of a specific community shaped by experiences such as racism, linguistic discrimination, anti-immigrant policies, or even the denial of U.S. citizenship is contested, even dismissed, for its seeming inability to contribute to color-blind truth and knowledge. However, understood as part of a collaboration among the range of American, even global, communities, a theory of Asian American rhetoric can contribute to understanding how a people is both producer of and produced by rhetoric.

In this chapter, I will reflect on the development of Asian American rhetoric and look toward the connections that may be made with existing rhetorical traditions and emerging rhetorical theory. In this sense, Asian American rhetoric might be understood as a creole discourse, informed by diverse and multiple rhetorical theories and practices, but situated in the exigencies of protest or resistance required in a moment of crisis and moving toward the sustained and stable critique of injury to Asian Americans. To illustrate, I'll turn to two examples of Asian American rhetoric and discuss its development and function as a creole discourse.

Spaces for Rhetoric

This chapter is one component of a larger project that examines the possibility of Asian American rhetorical space. While my thinking has been informed by recent composition and rhetoric scholarship that takes up the spatial turn, recalling work by people such as Ralph Cintron, Jeff Grabill, Nan Johnson, Richard Marback, and Nedra Reynolds, I have relied on Mountford's (2001) definition of "rhetorical space" as "the geography of a communicative event [that] may include both the cultural and material arrangement, whether intended or fortuitous, of space" (p. 41). In particular, Mountford's suggestion that "rhetorical spaces carry the residue of history upon them, but perhaps, something else: a physical representation of relationships and ideas" (p. 42) is especially useful for people whose histories are often unfamiliar or even unknown, as is often the case with Asian Americans.

When describing Asian American rhetoric previously, I have suggested that this rhetoric is generated within and from the specific spaces that Asian Americans inhabit, acknowledging and reflecting their identities without being essentialist, and acknowledging and responding to the particular conditions—the actions within their specific places—in which they find themselves (Young, 2011). Thus Asian American rhetorical space may be illustrated in specific material sites; and Asian American rhetoric is generated within these material sites to respond to specific occasions. For example, while the Japanese American internment camps of World War II held Japanese and Japanese Americans as threats to the nation without any other evidence than their race, these internees produced petitions and letters protesting their condition and composed *tanka* poetry expressing their frustration. I have also argued that spatial metaphors are especially important in Asian American rhetoric as Asian Americans address travel and mobility, containment and community, and imagined or real geographies (Young, 2011). For example, the discursively constructed Asiatic Barred Zone of the early 20th century acted both metaphorically and materially because it generated constituent acts and practices that, on the one hand, reinforced "Yellow Peril" discourse by constructing Asians as foreign others and materially excluding Asians from immigration to the United States and naturalization as U.S. citizens; and, on the other hand, the Asiatic Barred Zone provided an opportunity for Asians to enter the United States national discourse as they addressed these bars placed against them through legal challenges that ultimately were arbitrated in the U.S. Supreme Court.

Given these conditions, we might consider the rhetoric produced in these spaces as indigenous or vernacular, the "native" rhetoric of an emerging or transforming people, neither simply Asian nor considered fully American, who when finding themselves in a new locale must develop tactics for communication and expression in order to respond to the strategic and hegemonic forces of languages already in place. However, to understand an indigenous rhetoric in this sense is fraught with problems and politics, since this confuses indigeneity and colonialism, erases natives, and extols settlers. Instead we can see these rhetorical spaces as sites where pidgin or emergent cultures interact with and resist dominant culture, often creating new rhetorical practices to express new or creole cultural identities. In the context of Asian American rhetoric, Mao (2005) has described these spaces as rhetorical borderlands where Asian American (or, in his argument, Chinese American) rhetoric because of its hybridity remains an "ongoing representation and negotiation of both traditions, of their complex interrelationships … that seeks not uniqueness qua coherence from within, but complexity and complementarity from both within and without" (p. 433). I want to suggest that we think of Asian American rhetoric as a creole discourse, a practice that is not simply a rudimentary or novel expression due to necessity for immediate communication, but rather a native, systematic, and effective use by Asian Americans of symbolic resources (which may indeed be multilingual) in social, cultural, and political contexts (Mao & Young, 2008a, p. 3).

While the work in *Representations: Doing Asian American Rhetoric* (Mao & Young, 2008b) has described what Asian American rhetoric might look or act like, I think it is less important to identify or even reproduce formal features or practices that might be more akin to a grammar. In some ways an expectation of formal properties becomes limiting, installing generic or strategic practices that structure communication rather than creating the conditions for efficacious, and sometimes improvised, action. Thus, while there is always a need to understand how language is being used—as an oppositional discourse, as a means of maintaining ideological positions, or simply an expression of cultural identification—I want to suggest that place, history, and experience create the exigency—an exigency that crosses time and space—for an Asian American rhetorical act.

Writing and Walls: Spatial and Material Rhetoric

To illustrate how place, history, and experience create an exigency, I'd like to examine two examples where Asian Americans or Asians in U.S. contexts have developed and performed rhetorical work. First, I will discuss the early 20th-century immigration center, Angel Island, and the poems composed there by Chinese immigrants waiting to enter the United States Then I will consider Japanese immigrants to Hawai'i who, facing difficult labor and social conditions on the plantations, created and sang field songs, *hole hole bushi*, critiquing their field bosses literally under their watch.

Angel Island served as the immigration detention center primarily for immigrant Chinese between 1910 and 1940. Situated in San Francisco Bay, Angel Island in some cases has been constructed as analogous to Ellis Island in New York Harbor. However, while Ellis Island is often romanticized as the gateway for European immigration, where many entered under the watchful gaze of the Statue of Liberty, Angel Island has not captured the American imagination nor been part of the grand narrative of immigration in the same way. The dreams of the "Gold Mountain" for many Chinese immigrants never materialized, as those who successfully made it to the mainland often found poor-paying, hard-labor jobs, while others remained detained only to be returned to China.

The "need" for Angel Island was created in part by the passage of the Chinese Exclusion Act of 1882 and subsequent legislation that severely restricted Chinese immigration. Chinese who had satisfactory documentation—papers that allowed them to leave and return to the United States—were allowed to proceed to the mainland. Others who were seeking entry to the United States for the first time were subject to medical exams, hearings to review their applications, and interrogation to determine their identities. The material space of Angel Island functions to contain these Chinese immigrants. While not "prisoners," the Chinese certainly faced many restrictions. Men and women were separated, even if they were husband and wife; young children were left with their mothers. They could not have visitors from the mainland before their cases had been decided. The immigrants usually spent their time in their dormitories having access to separate small, fenced, outdoor recreation yards (Lai, Lim, & Yung, 1991, p. 15; Lee & Yung, 2010, pp. 95–102).

However, while this material space acted to hold the Chinese, the Chinese in turn used this material to literally and metaphorically write their narratives of resistance into the walls that contained them. Written in Chinese characters, the poems were composed in pencil or ink, and sometimes even carved into the wooden walls. The "delivery" of these poems raises interesting questions, since they existed in public under the watch of the authorities and yet were available only to those who could read the characters, providing a public critique to a specific audience of fellow detainees.

Though the people who wrote these poems were immigrants and arriving in America for the first time, *they* locate themselves in America, perhaps not as Americans, but certainly not as outsiders. Their detainment on Angel Island is a historical moment that creates an exigency for subsequent Asian American rhetorical production, developing *topoi* concerning immigration, the racialized body, social (in)justice, and political engagement. In the following examples from *Island: Poetry and History of Chinese Immigrants on Angel Island, 1910–1940* (Lai et al., 1991), there are explicit references to containment, to the fact that these people are being restricted to the island, to their barracks. There is a spatial awareness in these poems, seeing space both in its material and metaphorical senses, and that this space prevents these Chinese immigrants from attaining their dreams of wealth and success in the Gold Mountain.

> #23
> This place is called an island of immortals,
> When, in fact, this mountain wilderness is a prison.
> Once you see the open net, why throw yourself in?
> It is only because of empty pockets I can do nothing else.

> #24
> I, a seven foot man, am ashamed I cannot extend myself.
> Curled up in an enclosure, my movements are dictated by others.
> Enduring a hundred humiliations, I can only cry in vain.
> This person's tears fall, but what can the blue heavens do?

> #25
> I have infinite feelings that the ocean has changed into a mulberry grove.
> My body is detained in this building.

I cannot fly from this grassy hill,
And green waters block the hero.
Impetuously, I threw away my writing brush.
My efforts have all been in vain.
It is up to me to answer carefully.
I have no words to murmur against the east wind.

The narrative of these poems, but of many in the collection as well, position the writers not as outsiders coming to America with lofty dreams, nor as grateful newcomers unwilling to critique America. Rather, the narratives position the writers *in relation* to America: they comment, criticize, even challenge America as active participants in America, even if limited by the boundaries of Angel Island. But I would also like to make the point that these writers are also participating in a type of cultural transformation as they write about America in their own Chinese dialect and poetic forms. Such an act is subtle, and even subversive, as the poems were written on the walls for other detainees to see. The meta-awareness of these poems and of the function of these poems illustrates the power of this particular rhetorical space:

#31
There are tens of thousands of poems composed on these walls.
They are all cries of complaint and sadness.
The day I am rid of this prison and attain success,
I must remember that this chapter once existed.
In my daily needs, I must be frugal.
Needless extravagance leads youth to ruin.
All my compatriots should please be mindful.
Once you have some small gains, return home early.

In the situation of Angel Island we see how place, history, and experience create the conditions for and shape the rhetorical acts of the immigrants who found themselves detained there. We also see in these poems examples of hybridity and, perhaps, nascent creolization, the development of a new discourse to respond to a particular exigency in Angel Island, but also an exigency that crosses time and space as we take the broader view of history and understand the experience of Asians and Asian Americans in the United States The immigrants described here are neither Asian nor American but caught in a liminal space, manifested by Angel Island, where they must reimagine and reposition themselves in order to act and to draw on the variety of symbolic resources, newly acquired or already available, to respond rhetorically.

Hole Hole Bushi as Asian American Rhetoric

As a site of Asian American and Pacific Islander rhetoric, Hawai'i has had to deal with the ongoing representation and negotiation of many traditions that, through historical, social, and cultural forces, have had profound material effects on that place. Thus, while Hawai'i has often been invoked as a metaphorical Paradise—for its pure natives and unspoiled natural landscape in the 19th century, or for its multicultural harmony in the 20th century,—it more often functions as a hybrid or creole space in what Wilson (2000) has described as the "dirty, magical Pacific" (p. 283), where cultures from across the Pacific and Asia have conflicted and collaborated under the U.S. metropole and have not fulfilled the American master tropes of the "melting pot" or James Michener's "Golden Man" (*sic*).

The rise of the sugar plantation in Hawai'i in the mid-19th century dramatically changed the makeup of Hawai'i's population. By 1920 over 300,000 Asians (from China, Korea, Okinawa, the Philippines, and, above all, Japan) came to Hawai'i to work on the plantations, transforming a population that had been 97 percent Native Hawaiian/part-Hawaiian and 2 percent white in 1853 to a population that was 62 percent Asian, 16.3 percent Native Hawaiian/part-Hawaiian, and 7.7 percent white in 1920 (Takaki, 1998, p. 132). In 2010, the population of Hawai'i continued to reflect the impact of the plantation era with a make-up that is 38.6 percent Asian, 10 percent Native Hawaiian/Pacific Islander, and 24.7 percent white (United States Census Bureau, 2010).

While many of these contract laborers imagined that their time in Hawai'i would be limited as they earned their fortunes and returned home rich, this did not turn out to be the case. In fact the economics of the plantation often kept these laborers not only in Hawai'i unable to return their homelands, but literally on the plantation, as workers lived in plantation camps, were forced to buy all of their necessities at the plantation store, and could never earn enough in a reasonable amount of time to improve their conditions and move off the plantation.

As Okihiro (1991) points out in his historical study, *Cane Fires*, the plantations exerted their will over their workers through legislation (Masters and Servants Act), labor contracts, the courts and police, plantation rules, a system of punishment and fines, physical abuse, and fear (p. 35). In short, the plantations were able to utilize not only their own systems of ordering and discipline, but also to employ and manipulate the systems of government and larger culture in the exploitation of workers who were openly discriminated against because of race.

As one form of response to plantation culture, Japanese and Japanese American field workers composed and performed *hole hole bushi*, cane-stripping songs. The production and form of these songs can be considered typically "local," with the name itself made up of the Hawaiian *hole hole* meaning "stripping cane" and the Japanese *bushi* for "song." The tunes were often based on Japanese folk melodies, while the lyrics incorporated the "new" subject matter of Hawai'i. We find, then, in these songs perhaps not only some of the first Japanese *American* verse and literature produced in Hawai'i, but also an important Japanese American cultural and rhetorical practice that functions to critique American society. As Okihiro (1991) argues:

> *Hole hole bushi*, nonetheless, like the "blues" for African Americans, were both looking glass and mirror, clarifying and baring a minority group's

experiences in America and, in reflection, American society as a whole. Further, the beginnings of *hole hole bushi* locate the germination of a people, neither Japanese nor European American, but uniquely indigenous and American, deeply rooted and "with green leaves."

(p. 33)

While these songs serve to critique and to create "new" relations between an emergent culture and the dominant culture, even if only on the surface, these songs are also rhetorical, the persuasive act of workers who locate themselves and create a space for negotiation and refutation with dominant cultural practices within the specific occasion and space of the plantation and in the larger creole space of Hawai'i.

More than merely laments or complaints by workers about their lives, these songs are sharp in their criticism, often referring to specific events or people, but they are also witty and ironic, commenting on the routine of everyday life, the grand dreams they had expected to fulfill in Hawai'i, and the material conditions of their existence. For example:[1]

> Wonderful Hawai'i, or so I heard
> One look and it seems like Hell
> The manager's the Devil and
> His *lunas* are demons.

> Shall I go to America
> Or shall I go home to Japan?
> I'm lost in thoughts
> Here in Hawai'i.

> Starting out so early
> Lunches on our shoulders
> Off to our *hole hole* work
> Never seems to be enough.

> My husband cuts the cane,
> I do the *hole hole*.
> By sweat and tears
> We get by.

> Worse than the birds crying
> Or the temple bells tolling
> Is the plantation bell
> Calling us to another day.

> Today's hoe *hana* work
> Doesn't seem so hard

> Because last night I received
> A letter from home.

In each of these songs the *topoi* of the plantation serves to generate specific critiques of plantation culture and practices. There is a clear tension as we hear the workers oppose the plantation or its agents and oppose the system that they are working under, but are tied (or even compelled) to the plantation. The workers sing about their poor treatment and about a hard life made harder by an oppressive plantation. They sing about their personal lives, the impossibility of separating those lives from the plantation, and the ties between their labor and their bodies. However, while the plantation may treat workers simply as bodies, these workers embody their rhetoric as they create and perform their songs in the fields, giving meaning to their labor beyond what is required by the plantation. As Reynolds (2004) has argued:

> Only bodies can make places meaningful, and the bodies that occupy a place give it meaning. Bodies that are beautiful, bodies that are big, bodies that are slow, bodies that are pregnant, bodies that are tattooed (or corseted): all of these bodies make their way through social space, being imprinted by place as they also leave their trace upon places.
>
> *(pp. 144–145)*

The plantation "calls" and the workers answer. And yet their answers are quietly subversive (and counter-hegemonic, as opposed to simply resistant) because of the nature of the songs. Sung in the field under the watch of the *luna* (overseer), the songs made their criticisms of the plantation literally right in front of plantation officials. Or when the plantation employed *hippari-men* to work in the fields, songs were sung in conjunction with the plantation as a "call and response" took place between these special workers hired to work faster and the regular workers who had to keep up.[2]

An ethos is generated from the *hole hole bushi* that is similar to the "ethos of the blues" described by Neal (1993). The blues, in Neal's view, are not about resignation, not a lament about a past history, nor a bleak assessment of the future. Rather, the blues are about survival and the creation of "lyric responses to the facts of life" (p. 56). But, while the blues is often seen as a personal response, both the blues and the *hole hole bushi* in fact become important community responses, and, as Neal suggests, stand for a "collective sensibility of a people at particular stages of cultural, social, and political development" (p. 59). Thus the themes of labor and oppression that characterize the *hole hole bushi* (as well as the blues) are very necessary in the impulse by the workers to respond creatively to their circumstances. In short, these songs are about workers and their bodies: how they are driven, how they are disciplined, how they are "owned." The following *hole hole bushi* makes the point simply: their bodies exist to produce profits:

Why settle for 35 cents
Doing *hole hole* all day
When I can make a dollar
Sleeping with that *pake*?

Thus, like the African American *blues*, the *hole hole bushi* are about a human condition, a condition of racialized bodies, a condition of oppression. And the plantation operates not only to produce profits, but also to reduce persons to bodies. Foucault's (1979) study of the body in 18th-century France, *Discipline & Punish*, provides an important description of the function of the body in oppressive conditions:

> The body now serves as an instrument or intermediary: if one intervenes upon it to imprison it, or to make it work, it is in order to deprive the individual of liberty that is regarded both as a right and as property. The body, according to this penalty, is caught up in a system of constraints and privations, obligations and prohibitions. Physical pain, the pain of the body itself, is no longer the constituent element of the penalty. From being an art of unbearable sensations punishment has become an economy of suspended rights.
>
> *(p. 11)*

The plantation economy of Hawai'i served to deprive the workers of their liberties, especially those of the Japanese who found themselves (along with other imported labor from Asia) among the lowest paid and often the target of overt racism. It was no longer the physical pain alone from grueling work that marked the condition of the Japanese laborers, but the systematic suspension of basic rights as they were subjected to harsh penalties under both plantation rules and territorial laws. And even as the pipeline of cheap labor closed and plantation owners were forced to negotiate with a growing collective labor body, the residual paternalism still maintained control of workers' bodies and how they were used.

Thus, despite the oppressive conditions of the plantation, these Japanese and Japanese American field workers (among the many diverse field workers who labored hard) found themselves in a productive rhetorical space that allowed them to address the hardships they experienced. And part of this rhetorical space is shaped by the creole nature of the community that brought together different discourses and created new forms and expressions to address specific conditions. While improvement in material, political, and social conditions were slow and still affect social relations in Hawai'i today, we also see the emergence of an Asian American rhetoric that functioned to critique and argue against the plantation.

What I hope to have illustrated in this chapter is how both Angel Island and the plantation in Hawai'i have functioned as a specific rhetorical space that, as Mountford (2001) has described, is "a physical representation of relationships and ideas." In this sense Angel Island and Hawai'i's plantations are both *topoi* and trope, sites where the topics for inquiry and consideration are generated, and metaphors for the experiences and means of persuasion employed by Asians and Asian Americans. However, each is a particular manifestation of the Asian American experience as a creole rhetorical space, as a place that carries "the residue of history." Thus, as the Angel Island poems and the *hole hole bushi* illustrate, the rhetorical work generated in these creole rhetorical spaces reflects and negotiates a history and legacy of Asians in America, its transformation of the community, and the ongoing give and take that continues for those whose lives are informed by the Asian American experience.

Finally, this examination of two instances of Asian American rhetoric also provides historical context for the study of Asian American rhetorical and literacy practices that have begun to emerge in the field of rhetoric and composition. For example, Monberg (2008) has extended Ratcliffe's concept of "rhetorical listening" to uncover the spatial metaphors and other pedagogical theories in the work of Filipino American activist, Dorothy Laigo Cordova, to challenge the binary between rhetorical theory and practice, and to "recover" the rhetorical legacy of Cordova as an important site of community memory. Shimabukuro's (2008) work has focused on one World War II internment camp in Heart Mountain, Wyoming, to examine how a group of Japanese American internees in this community collaboratively wrote, published, and distributed bulletins that explicitly refused the military draft as long as the community was still "interned" against their will. Finally, in her work Hoang (2008) examines the racialization of language and literacy as applied to the Asian American subject, in particular focusing on the development of ethos and the use of memory by Asian American students to create rhetorical situations that challenge racism. What is exciting about the work of these three scholars and the emerging scholarship in cultural rhetorics is that it crosses historical boundaries, moving from the not too distant past to the contemporary, examines the use of rhetoric and writing across genres and purposes, and seeks to understand specifically the relationship between Asian Americans and their use of rhetoric. In these sites of rhetorical activity, we see rhetoric that creates, challenges, and makes space for Asian Americans and helps us to reimagine rhetoric and composition as a field.

Notes

1   The *hole hole bushi* cited are from Okihiro (1991). Some of them also appear in Odo and Urata (1990), and in slightly different translation in Takaki (1983) and Uyehara (1980). For a fuller treatment of *hole hole bushi*, see *Voices from the Canefield* by Franklin Odo (Oxford University Press, forthcoming).
2   See Uyehara (1980). The *hippari-men* were paid 10 cents more a day than the regular workers. The term is derived from the Japanese word *hipparu*, meaning "to drag, to pull, to draw" (pp. 115–116, 119, n.11).

References

Foucault, M. (1979). *Discipline & punish: The birth of the prison* (A. Sheridan, Trans.). New York, NY: Vintage Books.

Hoang, H. (2008). Asian American rhetorical memory and a "Memory that is only sometimes our own." In L. Mao & M. Young (Eds.), *Representations: Doing Asian American
rhetoric* (pp. 62–82). Logan, UT: Utah State University Press.

Lai, H. M., Lim, G., & Yung, J. (Eds.) (1991). *Island: Poetry and history of Chinese immigrants
on Angel Island, 1910–1940*. Seattle, WA: University of Washington Press.

Lee, E., & Yung, J. (2010). *Angel island: Immigrant gateway to America*. New York, NY:
Oxford University Press.

Mao, L. (2005). Rhetorical borderlands: Chinese American rhetoric in the making. *College
Composition and Communication, 56*(3), 426–469.

Mao, L., & Young, M. (2008a). Introduction: Performing Asian American rhetoric in
the American imaginary. In L. Mao, & M. Young (Eds.), *Representations: Doing Asian
American rhetoric* (pp. 1–22). Logan, UT: Utah State University Press.

Mao, L., & Young, M. (Eds.). (2008b). *Representations: Doing Asian American rhetoric*.
Logan, UT: Utah State University Press.

Monberg, T. G. (2008). Listening for legacies; or, how I began to hear Dorothy Laigo
Cordova, the Pinay behind the podium known as FANHS. In L. Mao & M. Young
(Eds.), *Representations: Doing Asian American rhetoric* (pp. 83–105). Logan, UT: Utah
State University Press.

Mountford, R. (2001). On gender and rhetorical space. *Rhetoric Society Quarterly, 30*(1),
41–71. doi:10.1080/02773940109391194.

Neal, L. (1993). The ethos of blues. In G. Early (Ed.), *Speech and power: The African American essay and its cultural content, from polemics to pulpit* (Vol. 2, pp. 55–62). Hopewell, NJ:
Ecco Press.

Odo, F. (forthcoming). *Songs from the canefield*. Oxford, UK: Oxford University Press.

Odo, F., & Urata, H. M. (1990, May 18). Hole hole bushi. *The Hawaii Herald, 11*(10),
20–22.

Okihiro, G. (1991). *Cane fires: The anti-Japanese movement in Hawaii, 1865–1945*. Philadelphia, PA: Temple University Press.

Reynolds, N. (2004). *Geographies of writing: Inhabiting places and encountering difference*.
Carbondale, IL: Southern Illinois University Press.

Shimabukuro, M. (2008). Relocating authority: coauthor(iz)ing a Japanese American ethos
of resistance under mass incarceration. In L. Mao & M. Young (Eds.), *Representations:
Doing Asian American rhetoric* (pp. 127–149). Logan, UT: Utah State University Press.

Takaki, R. (1983). *Pau Hana: Plantation life and labor in Hawaii, 1835–1920*. Honolulu, HI:
University of Hawaii Press.

Takaki, R. (1998). *Strangers from a different shore: A history of Asian Americans*. Boston, MA:
Bay Books/Little, Brown & Co.

United States Census Bureau (2010). *United States census 2010*. Retrieved from http://2010.
census.gov/2010census (accessed Nov. 15, 2012).

Uyehara, Y. (1980). The *Horehore Bushi*: A type of Japanese folksong developed and sung
among the early immigrants in Hawaii. *Social Process in Hawaii, 28,* 110–120.

Wilson, R. (2000). *Reimagining the American Pacific: From South Pacific to Bamboo Ridge and
beyond*. Durham, NC: Duke University Press.

Young, M. (2011). Foreign and domestic: Gender and the place(s) of Asian American
rhetoric. In D. Journet, B. A. Boehm, & C. E. Britt (Eds.), *Narrative acts: Rhetoric, race,
and identity, knowledge* (pp. 67–82). New York, NY: Hampton Press.

7

CONFRONTING THE WOUNDS OF COLONIALISM THROUGH WORDS

Jon Reyhner

This chapter examines current efforts by indigenous peoples to revitalize their languages and cultures as a part of a process of healing wounds caused by the history of colonialism they have endured. In schools in much of the colonized world, indigenous cultures were devalued and children were punished for practicing them in order to replace them with the cultures of the colonizers. Labeled barbaric and uncivilized based on cursory examinations, indigenous languages and cultures went largely unstudied and unappreciated except by a few linguists and anthropologists who presented nuanced views of indigenous peoples in their writings. Too often, indigenous cultures were, and are, at best romanticized and at worse described as backward or savage.

Today, we can describe colonization to include "cultural genocide" that has had disastrous effects on the wellbeing of the colonized. As teacher, school administrator, and Indian agent Kneale (1950) noted, the U.S. government's Indian Bureau "went on the assumption that any Indian custom was, *per se*, objectionable, whereas the customs of whites were the ways of civilization" (p. 4). This systematic attack on indigenous identity along with the expropriation of their lands often destroyed cohesive, functioning tribal societies without an adequate replacement structures, leading to all kinds of social ills today.

Too often today the colonized continue to colonize themselves as they copy the thinking they learned in schools controlled by colonial governments, as Alexie (2007) can be accused of doing in his 2007 National Book Award-winning young adult semi-autobiographical novel *The Absolutely True Diary of a Part-Time Indian*. In the novel Alexie paints an especially bleak picture of life on the Spokane Indian Reservation in the United States, and the main character, Arnold, escapes by enrolling in the "white" school located off the reservation. A non-Indian teacher tells Arnold, "That's how we were taught to teach you. We were supposed to kill the Indian to save the child … We were supposed to make you give up being Indian. Your songs and stories and language and dancing. Everything. We weren't trying to kill Indian people. We were trying to kill Indian culture" (p. 35). Because Arnold chooses to go to a white school to get a better education, he is labeled an "apple" (red on the outside and white culturally on the inside) by those he leaves behind. School success is viewed as only obtainable by assimilating into the dominant colonizing culture. Similarly, anthropologist Stocker's (2005) *I Won't Stay Indian, I'll Keep Studying*, set in Costa Rica, examines a problem shared by indigenous peoples worldwide that "the label Indian had connotations of backwardness and even inferior intellect … Being Indian automatically set students up for being treated as inferior" and that "for most students from the [Indian] reservation, projecting an Indian identity seemed incompatible with school success" (p. 2).

Alexie's writing is a continuation of an upsurge of indigenous authorship that can be traced back in the United States to at least the Civil Rights Movement. Leading American Indian authors include Pulitzer Prize winner N. Scott Momaday, Vine Deloria, Jr., and, most recently, Alexie. Today, most indigenous authors write in their national rather than tribal languages, because these are the languages they know, and their use opens up their work to a wide readership. Through their writings indigenous authors seek to understand and explain the indigenous colonial experience, and in doing so they cross the various boundaries real and imagined existing between indigenous peoples and the immigrant settler populations they are in contact with. These boundaries reflect the differences in the languages and cultures of the people involved, but they are not hard and fast. Rather the boundaries are porous, with words and cultural practices seeping back and forth across them.

Religious Boundaries

The writing systems for many indigenous languages were developed centuries ago by Christian missionaries in order to make religious writings accessible to both potential and actual converts. Missionaries, producing dictionaries and translated bibles, took indigenous words and concepts and shaded them with Christian theological meanings. These translation efforts crossed boundaries between traditional cultures and the Christianity of colonial societies. In contrast, government-run boarding schools for indigenous youth in Australia, Canada, New Zealand, and the United States suppressed indigenous languages and taught Christianity and the colonizing culture with an English-only curriculum (Reyhner & Eder, 2004).

For indigenous peoples there is often not a simple dichotomy between the missionary-labeled devil's indigenous paganism and Christianity. Eastman (1980), who attended a mission school in 19th-century South Dakota that taught reading and writing first in his Dakota language, became convinced after observing the materialism of late 19th-century America that "Christianity and modern civilization are opposed and irreconcilable, and that the spirit of Christianity and of our ancient [Sioux] religion is essentially the same" (p. 24). While Eastman and many other indigenous people accepted Christianity, sometimes after identifying it with their indigenous heritage, others did not. Hopi artist Kabotie (1977) recalled, "I've found the more outside education I receive, the more I appreciate the true Hopi way. When the missionaries would come into the village and try to convert us, I used to wonder why anyone would want to be a Christian if it meant becoming like those people" (p. 12).

Christianity and colonial languages usually went hand in hand, but missionaries who preached and wrote in indigenous languages as well in the colonizing language, as was the case in the school Eastman attended, could be quite effective. Bender (2009) notes that speaking the Cherokee language today in North Carolina is associated with older devout Christians. In contrast, some other indigenous Christian converts and their descendents today fear indigenous language revitalization efforts may promote the revival of indigenous religious beliefs (Parsons-Yazzie, 2003). Then there are those indigenous people with a syncretic approach to religion who see no boundaries. The anthropologist Farella (1993) recalls a dialogue with a Navajo:

> There is one community with a lot of medicine men, one that is always referred to as traditional by those who know about such things, where I had the following conversation over and over again: Are you a medicine man? Yes. Do you believe in the traditional religion? Yes. Are you a Catholic? Yes. Native American Church? Sometimes. Well, which is it, traditional, Catholic or peyote? Yes.
>
> *(p. 12)*

Christianity and cultural assimilation especially appealed to indigenous peoples whose lives were turned upside down by virgin-ground epidemics, loss of land, and other traumatic experiences that severely disrupted their way of life. It also appealed to the poor in less egalitarian indigenous societies.

Socio-Economic Boundaries

Maslow's (1954) "hierarchy of needs" seems to be operant where indigenous people learn English and other "world" languages in order to get jobs so they can buy food and keep a roof over their head. Economic survival tends to take precedence over efforts to maintain heritage languages and cultures. However, if one has met the lower level needs in Maslow's hierarchy, then one can have the time and energy to work on something like indigenous language revitalization that probably has no immediate economic payback.

Canagarajah (2011) examined how Tamils from different social classes who immigrated to the United States and Canada from Sri Lanka have either held onto or jettisoned their heritage language. The upper classes that learned English before emigrating as "professionals" and speak a Tamil dialect of English are more interested in passing on Tamil to their children than the lower socio-economic status Tamils who emigrated as "victims" of the Sri Lankan Civil War or who are women. The latter group sees learning standard English as a way to enter the middle class in the United States and Canada. For them, Tamil currently lacks utility and has little attraction, in contrast to during the Sri Lankan Civil War when families sent "their children to die as suicide bombers for language rights" (p. 95). Among the Navajo in the United States, those able to accumulate large herds of sheep and occupy better grazing land are more likely to have political power within the Navajo tribal government where speaking Navajo is still important (though minutes of meetings are written in English) and practice traditional Navajo religion and speak Navajo, whereas "*Poorer people in Navajo terms have more incentive to adopt white ways than those who are wealthier*," including Christianity and speaking English (Levy & Kunitz, 1974, p. 186, italics in original).

Colonial languages were often promoted using the argument that learning them was a way for indigenous people to advance economically as well as the way to become more "civilized." However, that promised success often does not materialize with the switch to speaking only English. Within most poverty stricken American Indian nations in the United States today, English is the first language of almost all the residents. The same is true for the Maori of New Zealand, Aborigines in Australia, and many other indigenous peoples who have not shared equally in the wealth of their countries, and naturally they can be very envious of that wealth and shamed by their own lack of it.

Prestige Boundaries

Gilmore (2011) notes how studies of indigenous language loss "voice complex narratives of shame, stigma, humiliation, and a deficit discourse surrounding languages and identities" as well as "counter-themes of pride in identity, use of the home language, and respect for community values, rituals, and knowledge" to assimilation (pp. 123–124). The languages of those in power in national governments are usually seen as superior to the languages of ethnic minorities, which are associated with being, rural, backward, poor, and generally inferior. English and other international languages are seen as languages of prosperity, modernity, civilization, and progress. Anthropologists tend to see the notion of colonial superiority emanating from ethnocentrism, where people see the characteristics of the group they are born into, including language, to be the norm against which other cultures are measured, and those that are most different are seen as the most barbaric.

The tendency of those in power is either to subordinate and/or seek to assimilate people who are different. In the United States with its ideology of equality, assimilation is seen as the way to make subordinate ethnic and racial minorities gain equality with the "white" majority in a big "melting pot." However, as indicated previously, giving up one's minority ethnic identity and language and speaking English have often not led to more economic success.

Indigenous languages were once all oral languages, but written languages have a prestige and a utility that unwritten languages lack. To survive in this modern world, it helps to have a written format, which requires some standardization. The Basque are one example of a group that worked to increase the prestige of their language by developing a writing system. Basque dialects in the south (northwestern Spain) and north (southwestern France) of the Basque Country varied enough to cause difficulty with mutual intelligibility. For the purposes of writing and teaching in schools, central dialects were used to create a standardized Basque that would be understandable to all sections of the Basque Country (Irujo Ametzaga, 2009). The creation of a Basque written corpus helps counter the rural backwater stereotype that speakers of indigenous languages can suffer under. To further increase the prestige and prove that it was "capable of expressing anything written in any human language," classics of world literature were translated into Basque (Irujo Ametzaga, 2009, p. 52). Ironically, however, for Basque authors to achieve a wider readership they need to write in a "world language" or have their works translated. As Basque author Zaldua (2009) notes, English is "the only language that allows any literature to be known worldwide: it is the passport to The World Republic (that is to say market) of Letters" (p. 100).

"Purism" and "Golden Age" Boundaries

All languages change over time, and elders of all cultures can be dismayed by the "slang" dialect that youth often speak. Linguist Field (2009) notes that Navajo elders who voice their criticism of the way young people speak an indigenous language "may trigger linguistic insecurity on the part of younger imperfect speakers, which may lead to younger speakers' refusal to speak the language and intensify language shift" to English (p. 47). She notes how young Navajo adults and adolescents can "enthusiastically embrace code-mixing, and perhaps less consciously, changes to Navajo grammar" (p. 43). Another contentious idea is that indigenous languages are only for esoteric—not for public consumption—traditional/ceremonial practices.

In the 1990s while teaching and taking classes at Navajo Community College (NCC, now called Diné College), House (2002) found that approaches used to valorize and revitalize Navajo language and culture did so by oppositioning it to and devaluing "white" culture. This is a sort of revenge for the history of non-Indians systematically devaluing Navajo and other indigenous cultures. However, a nostalgic, but unrealistic, turning back to "sheepherding and growing a small garden, living in a hogan, and driving a team of horses" does nothing to help Navajos face the complex issues facing their future (p. 87). House notes how the Navajo, as is the case with other indigenous peoples, "are faced with the dilemma of how to create an authentic yet viable Navajo identity in an irreversibly modern world" (p. xxvii).

There are also romanticized notions of indigenous languages being linked to "a more harmonious or spiritual worldview" and English as a "cold" noun-based language that is "'dead' in both a spiritual and expressive sense" (Gómez de García, Axelrod, & Lachler, 2009, pp. 100, 109 and 121). In contrast, native languages are seen as verb-based and more expressive and spiritual, which is associated with the fact that, sometimes, the spiritual and ceremonial domains are the only ones left for the native language. One can speculate whether this perception results from many people not learning English beyond a conversational proficiency and never accessing its vast literature. House (2002) also found in some classrooms at NCC the "white man's shadow" phenomenon, where "white" culture is portrayed as monolithically greedy, materialistic, etc. and natives are the opposite—generous, spiritual, etc. (Simard, 1990). This dichotimization goes against many, if not most, of the traditional values of most indigenous peoples. For example, Hopi scholar Nicholas (2011) notes, "The fundamental principles of the Hopi way of life are those of reciprocity and humility" (p. 60).

Another barrier that can be thrown up to language revitalization is illustrated in Jaffe's (2011) examination of how Corsican is taught in schools. Language purists look for some untainted form of their language before it was impacted by French, Spanish, English, Portuguese, or some other more "powerful" language, but there is no such "golden age." Such efforts can lead to teaching a form of a language, in this case Corsican, that is only taught and used in classrooms. Such efforts produce a school-based "monoglot standard" that has little likelihood of catching on more widely. This same language artificiality is noted by King and Haboud (2011) in Ecuador. There, in the last two decades, Quichua has left the home and become mainly a school subject.

On the colonizers side, the inaccurate belief in a "linguistic form of social Darwinism" that a "superior," more fit language, like English, will naturally replace an "inferior," more "savage" language can damage outside support for indigenous language revitalization efforts (Loether, 2009, p. 245). Boas (1940), known as the father of American anthropology, put forward the concept of "cultural relativism," where cultures cannot be ranked as more or less inferior or superior; they are just different. Linguists take the same view of languages.

Generational Boundaries

Elders see their language as a way of passing down important cultural values and the wisdom of the ages, not teaching math, science, and other school subjects. Of course those subjects can be taught in any language, and teaching them in an immersion school in the indigenous language, as is done in Hawaiian and Māori language immersion schools, does not preclude teaching traditional values as well.

Nicholas (2011) notes that Hopi elders see the current decline in speaking Hopi as associated with youth's "unHopi" behavior, leading to gang activity and disrespect for elders, whereas the Hopi language, as previously mentioned, is associated with traditional values of hard work and, as previously mentioned, reciprocity and humility. La Farge's (1929) Pulitzer-prize winning 1929 novel *Laughing Boy* attempts to give a flavor of what Navajo language and culture are like as written in English, and shows the impact of colonization. He links the decline in his heroine's moral values and behavior to her English-only assimilationist education in government boarding schools and living closer to the reservation boundary and interacting with non-Navajos.

At Rock Point, located in the interior of the Navajo Nation in the 1970s, the all-Navajo school board concluded "that it was the breakdown of a working knowledge of Navajo kinship that caused much of what they perceived as inappropriate, un-Navajo, behavior; the way back, they felt was to teach students that system" (Holm & Holm, 1990, p. 178). Navajo and other indigenous grandparents can sometimes not even talk to their grandchildren who only know English. To counteract this collapse, the Rock Point School Board established a successful Navajo–English bilingual program in their school that emphasized Navajo social studies and the Navajo beliefs about kinship. For the Navajo and other tribes, kinship through extended family and clans establishes rules for interacting respectfully, and this interaction is reflected in the language itself.

Navajo and many other indigenous languages subordinate nouns to verbs. Linguists describe it as a polysynthetic language. According to linguist Midgette (1997), sentences in these languages "often consist of single, very complex words, with roots, prefixes and suffices occurring in a fixed order, as opposed to English, which is an analytic language, which accumulates a number of relatively short and simple words" (p. 33). She also gives a Navajo example of how translation from one language to another can be difficult, using the Navajo word *hózhó*, which lies at the "heart of their world view," writing "This word can only be translated by three separate English words: 'peace,' 'harmony,' and 'beauty'" (p. 40).

In her doctoral research, Parsons-Yazzie (1995) found, "Elder Navajos want to pass on their knowledge and wisdom to the younger generation. … Today the younger generation does not know the language and is unable to accept the words of wisdom" (p. 1). She concludes, "The use of the native tongue is like therapy, specific native words express love and caring. Knowing the language presents one with a strong self-identity, a culture with which to identify, and a sense of wellness" (p. 3).

Ethnocentric National Boundaries

In the United States and Europe, demographics are changing, resulting in ethnic minorities becoming a larger percentage of many nations' populations. A reaction to this change, which can be seen as endangering the hegemony of English, is the current effort by some conservatives to pass a constitutional amendment making English the official language of the United States. Combs, González, and Moll (2011) note how in the American southwest there has been a long-term and still ongoing "concerted effort of assimilation and subordination of the Mexican population, especially through coercive Americanization programs in the schools and the imposition of the English language at all costs" (p. 185). Historian Blanton (2004) documents how, through most of history, English-only education for Mexican Americans has disadvantaged them. An attempt was made in the United States, starting in 1968 with the passage of the Bilingual Education Act, to provide more culturally appropriate education, but the fear initiated by the rising tide of Spanish-speaking immigrants from Latin America that can be seen as drowning the descendents of the old immigrant population from Europe helped lead to the passage of the No Child Left Behind Act of 2001, which focused on English-language acquisition without native language support.

There is an ideology, especially espoused in the United States by conservative politicians, that the national language, in their case English, is the "glue" that holds the nation together (see, e.g., Reyhner, 2001). This ignores multiple civil wars across the globe, including the United States' bloodiest war, in which both sides spoke the same language. This ideology of "one nation, one language" ignores stable multilingual countries, of which Switzerland is an exemplar, and presupposes a standard version of a language despite the fact that languages vary from place to place. Gillmore (2011) notes, "equating language and nation is an historical and ideological construct" (p. 125). What has the potential of holding nations and the world together is a commitment to liberty and justice for all and a respect for everyone's human rights. With the formation of the United Nations after World War II there has been a steady development of human rights declarations and conventions, culminating in the adoption of the UN's Declaration on the Rights of Indigenous Peoples in 2007 (Reyhner & Singh, 2010).

With globalization and the "flattening" of the world, the suppression of minority languages that was practiced by many nation states is easing and there is a growing respect for cultural pluralism. For example, with the development of the European Union, it was necessary to protect the languages of the various member states, and that in turn is a wedge used to protect all languages spoken in Europe. According to the European Union's European Commission on Multilingualism (2012), "The EU's language policy promotes multilingualism and aims for a situation in which every EU citizen can speak at least two foreign languages in addition to their mother tongue" (n.p.). Article 22 of the Charter of Fundamental Rights of the European Union states, "The Union shall respect cultural, religious and linguistic diversity."

In addition, the Council of Europe (1995), which includes even more member states than the European Union, has a Framework Convention for the Protection of National Minorities. Section II, Article 5 of the convention declares, "The Parties undertake to promote the conditions necessary for persons belonging to national minorities to maintain and develop their culture, and to preserve the essential elements of their identity, namely their religion, language, traditions and cultural heritage" (n.p.). As Korkeakivi (2008), Head of the Council of Europe's Secretariat on the Framework Convention for the Protection of National Minorities, notes, what is unique about the convention is that it includes a monitoring provision to gain compliance by signatory states and Article 15 that "guarantees effective participation of minorities in decision-making" (p. 149).

Conclusion

Many of the perceived boundaries among cultures and nations are based on superficial observations of different cultures, as well as some very real differences, compounded by the inability to understand each other's languages. As explorer and first director of the U.S. Bureau of Ethnology, Powell (1896) noted, over a century ago:

> so few Americans yet realize that of all the people on this continent, including even ourselves, the most profoundly religious, if by religion is meant fidelity to teachings and observations that are regarded as sacred, are the American Indians, especially wherever still unchanged from their early condition, and this deeply religious feeling of theirs might, if properly appreciated, be made use of, not weakened or destroyed by premature opposition.
>
> *(pp. 112–113)*

Close observation of even widely different cultures tends to show a common humanity that is masked by language, dress, and other differences.

The wounds indigenous peoples have suffered from ethnocentric assimilationist colonial policies are still being inflicted, but the various international human rights initiatives today are promising a better future. The unfulfilled promises of assimilation, including learning English, and a concomitant decline in traditional values, leading to dysfunctional behavior, especially among the young, is one cause for the current interest in indigenous language revitalization. In addition, even though more and more American Indian and other indigenous children speak only English, Spanish or some other colonial language, the economic and educational gap between them and "white" non-indigenous peoples remains.

Alexie's successful escape from the poverty and problems of his Spokane Indian Reservation by attending a "white" school off the reservation fictionalized in his *The Absolutely True Diary of a Part-Time Indian* is an option available to a gifted few (Alexie, 2007). One can argue that language-immersion schools that promote a strong sense of indigenous identity while supporting academic achievement are an alternative that show great promise, even though they are only available to a few in the United States. Hill and May (2011) note that learning Māori in

New Zealand immersion schools helps children know who they are and, as they were told by one interviewee, "if they know who they are, they are able to stand strong in the world," and they see the goal of Māori-medium education is for students to "*become citizens of the world*" (pp. 172–173, emphasis in original). Their research finds that seven years of Māori-medium education starting in preschool gives children a solid foundation that can withstand the onslaught of learning and becoming very competent in world languages such as English. This is the approach being taken by the European Union and Council of Europe towards languages, and other countries need to see indigenous language revitalization as a basic human right. In our new globalized and "flat" world we need citizens who are multilingual and who can cross boundaries and overcome ethnocentrism to understand and appreciate better other cultures that often appear, on the surface, to be so very different from their own.

Alexie's advice is to leave the reservation with its poor schools located in a dysfunctional, poverty-stricken environment, but that is not really an option for many indigenous people. Inner-city urban schools that serve the urban poor are as noted for their lack of educational success as are reservation schools (Berliner, 2009). Alexie (2007) especially confronts the necessity to become educated and deal with life today. However, indigenous people can find strength to confront the modern world in their traditional languages and cultures. Towards the end of Alexie's book, Arnold, recovering from the death of his sister, discusses his many identities:

> Reservations were meant to be prisons, you know? Indians were supposed to move onto reservations and die. We were supposed to disappear.
>
> But somehow or another, Indians have forgotten that reservations were meant to be death camps …
>
> I realized that, sure, I was a Spokane Indian. I belonged to that tribe. But I also belonged to the tribe of American immigrants. And to the tribe of basketball players. And to the tribe of bookworms.
>
> *(pp. 216–217)*

While in some places language and culture are viewed as inseparable, in other places native identity is linked to cultural activities that can be practiced in an English-speaking environment, as Alexie describes on the Spokane Reservation in Washington State. However, as a language becomes more endangered it can become "a badge of identity" (Field & Kroskrity, 2009, p. 20). "What many Native groups say they really want to teach is identity, and language serves as part of that identity" (Gómez de García et al., 2009, p. 118). A strong positive identity can be seen as the key to success in life.

Speaking at the U.S. Office of Indian Education's Language and Culture Preservation Conference in Albuquerque, New Mexico in 2004, former Menominee Nation chairperson Apesanahkwat recalled that, in Catholic school, the nuns, in effect, told their students "to throw stones at the Elders." He opined that Indians today "have tasted cherry pie [the good things of modern America] and we like it." However, Indians today are "like fish lying on the beach ... we need to be in that water" of our culture (Apesanahkwat, personal communication, March 8, 2004).

References

Alexie, S. (2007). *The absolutely true diary of a part-time Indian.* New York, NY: Little Brown and Company.

Bender, M. (2009). Visibility, authenticity, and insiderness in Cherokee language ideologies. In P. V. Kroskrity & M. C. Field (Eds.), *Native American language ideologies: Beliefs, practices and struggles in Indian country* (pp. 123–147). Tucson, AZ: University of Arizona Press.

Berliner, D. (2009). *Poverty and potential: Out-of-school factors and school success.* Boulder, CO: Education and the Public Interest Center & Education Policy Research Unit. Retrieved from http://epicpolicy.org/files/PB-Berliner-NON-SCHOOL.pdf (accessed Nov. 15, 2012).

Blanton, C. (2004). *The strange career of bilingual education in Texas 1836–1981.* College Station, TX: Texas A&M University Press.

Boas, F. (1940). *Race, language and culture.* Chicago, IL: University of Chicago Press.

Canagarajah, A. S. (2011). Diaspora communities, language maintenance, and policy dilemmas. In T. L. McCarty (Ed.), *Ethnography and language policy* (pp. 77–97). New York, NY: Routledge.

Combs, M. C., González, N., & Moll, L. (2011). US Latinos and the learning of English: The metonymy of language policy. In T. L. McCarty (Ed.), *Ethnography and language policy* (pp. 185–203). New York, NY: Routledge.

Council of Europe. (1995). *Framework convention for the protection of national minorities.* Retrieved from http://conventions.coe.int/Treaty/en/Treaties/html/157.htm (accessed Nov. 15, 2012).

Eastman, C. A. (Ohiyesa). (1980). *The soul of the Indian: An interpretation.* Lincoln, NE: University of Nebraska Press.

European Commission on Multilingualism. (2012). *EU language policy.* Retrieved from http://p21208.typo3server.info/89.0.html (accessed Nov. 15, 2012).

Farella, J. (1993). *The wind in a jar.* Albuquerque, NM: University of New Mexico Press.

Field, M. C. (2009). Changing Navajo language ideologies and changing language use. In P. V. Kroskrity & M. C. Field (Eds.), *Native American language ideologies: Beliefs, practices and struggles in Indian country* (pp. 31–47). Tucson, AZ: University of Arizona Press.

Field, M. C., & Kroskrity, P. V. (2009). Introduction: Revealing Native American language identities. In P. V. Kroskrity & M. C. Field (Eds.), *Native American language ideologies: Beliefs, practices and struggles in Indian country* (pp. 3–28). Tucson, AZ: University of Arizona Press.

Gilmore, P. (2011). Language ideologies, ethnography, and ethnology: New directions in anthropological approaches to language policy. In T. L. McCarty (Ed.), *Ethnography and language policy* (pp. 121–127). New York, NY: Routledge.

Gómez de García, J., Axelrod, M., & Lachler, J. (2009). English is the dead language: Native perspectives on bilingualism. In P. V. Kroskrity & M. C. Field (Eds.), *Native American language ideologies: Beliefs, practices and struggles in Indian country* (pp. 99–122). Tucson, AZ: University of Arizona Press.

Hill, R., & May, S. (2011). Exploring biliteracy in Māori-medium education. In T. L. McCarty (Ed.), *Ethnography and language policy* (pp. 161–183). New York, NY: Routledge.

Holm, A., & Holm, W. (1990). Rock Point, a Navajo way to go to school: A valediction. *The Annals of the American Academy of Political and Social Science, 508*, 170–184. doi:10.1177/0002716290508001014.

House, D. (2002). *Language shift among the Navajos: Identity politics and cultural continuity.* Tucson, AZ: University of Arizona Press.

Irujo Ametzaga, X. I. (2009). Introduction to a political history of the Basque language and literature. *Tinta, 9*, 31–69.

Jaffe, A. (2011). Critical perspectives on language-in-education policy: The Corsican example. In T. L. McCarty (Ed.), *Ethnography and language policy* (pp. 205–229). New York, NY: Routledge.

Kabotie, F. (1977). *Fred Kabotie, Hopi Indian artist: An autobiography told with Bill Belknap.* Flagstaff, AZ: Museum of Northern Arizona.

King, K. A., & Haboud, M. (2011). International migration and Quichua language shift in the Ecuadorian Andes. In T. L. McCarty (Ed.), *Ethnography and language policy* (pp. 139–159). New York, NY: Routledge.

Kneale, A. (1950). *Indian agent.* Caldwell, ID: Caxton.

Korkeakivi, A. (2008). In defense of speaking out: The European human rights regime and the protection of minority languages. *Intercultural Human Rights Law Review, 3*, 137–149.

La Farge, O. (1929). *Laughing boy.* Boston, MA: Houghton Mifflin.

Levy, J., & Kunitz, S. (1974). *Indian drinking: Navajo practices and Anglo-American theories.* New York, NY: John Wiley and Sons.

Loether, C. (2009). Language revitalization and the manipulation of language ideologies A Shoshoni case study. In P. V. Kroskrity & M. C. Field (Eds.), *Native American language ideologies: Beliefs, practices and struggles in Indian country* (pp. 239–254). Tucson, AZ: University of Arizona Press.

Maslow, A. (1954). *Motivation and personality.* New York, NY: Harper

Midgette, S. (1997). The native languages of North America: Structure and survival. In D. Morrison (Ed.), *American Indian studies* (pp. 27–45). New York, NY: Peter Lang.

Nicholas, S. E. (2011). "How are you Hopi if you can't speak it?": An ethnographic study of language as cultural practice among contemporary Hopi youth. In T. L. McCarty (Ed.), *Ethnography and language policy* (pp. 53–75). New York, NY: Routledge.

Parsons-Yazzie, E. (1995). A Study of Reasons for Navajo Language Attrition as Perceived by Navajo Speaking Parents. EdD dissertation, Northern Arizona University.

Parsons-Yazzie, E. (2003). Missionaries and American Indian languages. In J. Reyhner, O. Trujillo, R. L. Carrasco, & L. Lockard (Eds.), *Nurturing native languages* (pp. 165–178). Flagstaff, AZ: Northern Arizona University. Retrieved from http://jan.ucc.nau.edu/~jar/NNL/NNL_14.pdf (accessed Nov. 15, 2012).

Powell, J. W. (1896). The need of studying the Indian in order to teach him. In *Annual report of the Board of Indian Commissioners* (pp. 109–15). Washington, DC: U.S. Government Printing Office.

Reyhner, J. (2001). Cultural survival vs. forced assimilation: The renewed war on diversity. *Cultural Survival Quarterly, 25*(2), 22–25.

Reyhner, J., & Eder, J. (2004). *American Indian education: A history.* Norman, OK: University of Oklahoma Press.

Reyhner, J., & Singh, N. K. (2010). Cultural genocide in Australia, Canada, New Zealand, and the United States: The destruction and transformation of indigenous cultures. *Indigenous Policy Journal, 21*(4).

Simard, J. J. (1990). White ghosts, red shadows: The reduction of North American Indians. In J. A. Clifton (Ed.), *The invented Indian: Cultural fictions and government policies* (pp. 333–369). New Brunswick, NJ: Transaction Publishers.

Stocker, K. (2005). *I won't stay Indian, I'll keep studying.* Boulder, CO: University Press of Colorado.

Zaldua, I. (2009). Eight crucial decisions (a Basque writer is obliged to face). In M. J. Olaziregi (Ed.), *Writers in between languages: Minority literatures in the global scene* (pp. 89–112). Reno, NV: Center for Basque Studies, University of Nevada.

8

THE CHEROKEE SYLLABARY: THE EVOLUTION OF WRITING IN SEQUOYAN

Ellen Cushman

In 1821, a Cherokee man named Sequoyah presented his invention of a non-alphabetic writing system to the Cherokee Tribal Council in Echota. This system relies upon 86 characters that were originally designed in longhand before being reduced to print and are now seen in Unicode-based fonts on the Internet and in text messaging. In this chapter, I overview the evolution of this writing system from script, to print, to digital forms to demonstrate how Cherokees weave Sequoyan alongside the alphabet today to maintain a unique written legacy that is directly related to language preservation efforts. This indigenous writing system—developed outside of an alphabetic influence, though alongside this predominant script—challenges what counts as literacy (it's not just about the letter) and demands a larger understanding of meaning-making with writing systems that are othered by the ubiquity of the alphabet.

Drawing on evidence gathered over six years of ethnohistorical research, this chapter expands on the work of Mignolo (2003), Baca (2008), and Baca and Villanueva (2010), who help us move past the alphabetic bias and situate texts that accommodate hybrid codes and conventions. In the ongoing effort to free literacy scholars from the Western bias of American literacy history, Mignolo's (1992) seminal work on literacy and programs of colonization in the Americas explored how literacy became part and parcel of the colonization of American Indians. This colonization included writing grammars of indigenous languages through "an ideological program that impinged on the jurisdiction and implementation of spreading Western literacy in the New World" (p. 50). Viewing all meaning-making through an alphabetic screen, this program worked simultaneously at the instrumental and ideological levels of influence (p. 48). Building on Mignolo's (1992, 2003) path-breaking work, Baca's (2008) book exploring Mestiz@ scripts corrects "the rigid evolutionary proposition that all writing systems profess toward the letter, that alphabetic literacy is the pinnacle of all other systems of recorded knowledge" (p. 7). Drawing scholarly attention to hybrid scripts, Baca examines the material reality of meaning-making to correct the Western bias in literacy studies as he illuminates the importance of reading and writing for colonized groups. These corrective studies do double duty: on the one hand, they afford a theoretical lens through which writing systems can be understood from an indigenous perspective; and on the other, they add to the growing body of research that demonstrates the meaning-making potentials of othered writing systems.

When a writing system succeeds in resisting an alphabetic bias to become a permanent instructional resource for native peoples, it satisfies several instrumental and cultural needs of the people using it. Anthropologist Walker (1969) finds, "The history of the nineteenth century suggests that native literacy is accepted to the extent that it is based on a syllabic writing system, it is available to adults, it is adapted to both sacred and secular contexts, and perhaps most importantly, that it is disseminated independently of White educational institutions" (p. 166). Certainly the Cherokee syllabary met all of these demands in its script and print forms.

The Cherokee writing system was first learned in manuscript form and was disseminated quickly throughout the tribe within three years of its introduction, without print or mass education. With the advent of Cherokee in print in 1827, a literary legacy became public and broadly disseminated through newspapers, hymnals, the New Testament, primers, and the Cherokee almanac. It was used up until the early 1900s throughout the tribe's educational institutions, even as English was fast becoming the official language of the nation and Cherokee schools. After allotment ended in 1906, the tribal government was dissolved and with it went a tremendous amount of publication of Sequoyan, though the writing remained in use in communities through manuscript form in the Baptist churches, stomp grounds, and in texts used by medicine people. With the Indian Self Determination Act in 1972, the Cherokee Nation was reestablished and developed bilingual education materials in print along with online language-learning materials for the language classes and immersion school. Most recently, Sequoyan can be seen online in Facebook pages, in text messaging, on iPod applications, and in Wikipedia. This evolutionary story of the Cherokee syllabary from script to print begs the question: What aspects of its instrumentality might have lent to its adaptability and longstanding use?

A Writing System in Its Own Right

To answer the above question, scholars need to understand this writing system in its own right (Cushman, 2011c), viewing it apart from an alphabetic bias that tends to see it using the Roman alphabet as a baseline for analysis. Though the Cherokee syllabary is not an alphabet, it is often approached as though it was. In her exploration of the materiality of the letter, Drucker (1997) incorrectly insists that Sequoyah, who was never a chief, borrowed heavily from the designs of the alphabet when he invented the Cherokee syllabary (p. 38). Anthropologist Mooney (1892) claims the syllabary has "several defects," and uses the words "syllabary" and "alphabet" interchangeably to describe Sequoyah's invention (p. 64). And Holmes and Smith (1976), authors of the go-to book for Cherokee-language learners, incorrectly classify the syllabary "as a variety of alphabet" (p. 8). All judge the design and utility of the Cherokee writing system using an alphabetic baseline for comparison. All analyze the Cherokee writing system from an alphabetic perspective. And all rely on the syllabary chart shown here in Figure 8.1 as their primary source of evidence for their claims. In so doing, the potential visual and linguistic powers of the original syllabary are lost on literacy scholars and language learners who rely on this chart.

Sequoyah eschewed English (Cushman 2011a), originally wrote the syllabary in longhand characters that bore no resemblance to alphabetic letters (Cushman 2011b, 2011c; Walker & Sarbaugh 1993), and arranged it in an order that drew upon a visual mnemonic (Cushman, 2010). The Cherokee quickly became fluent in Sequoyan within just a few years of its introduction in longhand. A reduction of the longhand characters to print forms was in use in 1825, two years before Samuel Worcester even arrived at Brainerd Mission to work with the Cherokees. Cherokees alone developed the script and printed designs for these characters from a shorthand that had been in use for six years before print. A visual analysis of each script and print form revealed that 67 of 85 of characters (78.8 percent) took their visual cues from the original longhand versions. Roman glyphs were borrowed when they retained some element of the original characters. In other words, any connection the Cherokee syllabary may have to the Roman alphabet has been imagined more than real. When it moved to print, the manuscript form retained some elements of the longhand, which helps to explain why no decrease in reading and writing rates were noticed during this time. While much of the visual information was retained, important linguistic information was obscured when it moved to print, thanks to Worcester (Cushman 2010).

In 1827, the original arrangement (longhand) and shorthand of the writing system had been standardized into print using this arrangement made popular by Moravian missionary, Samuel Worcester. Worcester had reordered the original characters of the Cherokee syllabary following the orthographic rules of the Latin alphabet (Figure 8.1). Just under "The Cherokee Alphabet," two complete sets of characters are included: "Characters as Arranged by the Inventor" and "Characters Systematically Arranged with the Sounds" (Figure 8.2), assuming, of course, that Sequoyah's arrangement had no system. The vowels were then listed in alphabetic order and the combinations were roughly arranged alphabetically, save for the d/t combinations of sounds, which in Cherokee can sound similar. Each character was assigned a transliteration to roughly equivalent sounds in English. By 1846 the new arrangement of the "Cherokee Alphabet" had become standardized, in part, through these two publications (Cushman, 2010, 2011c).

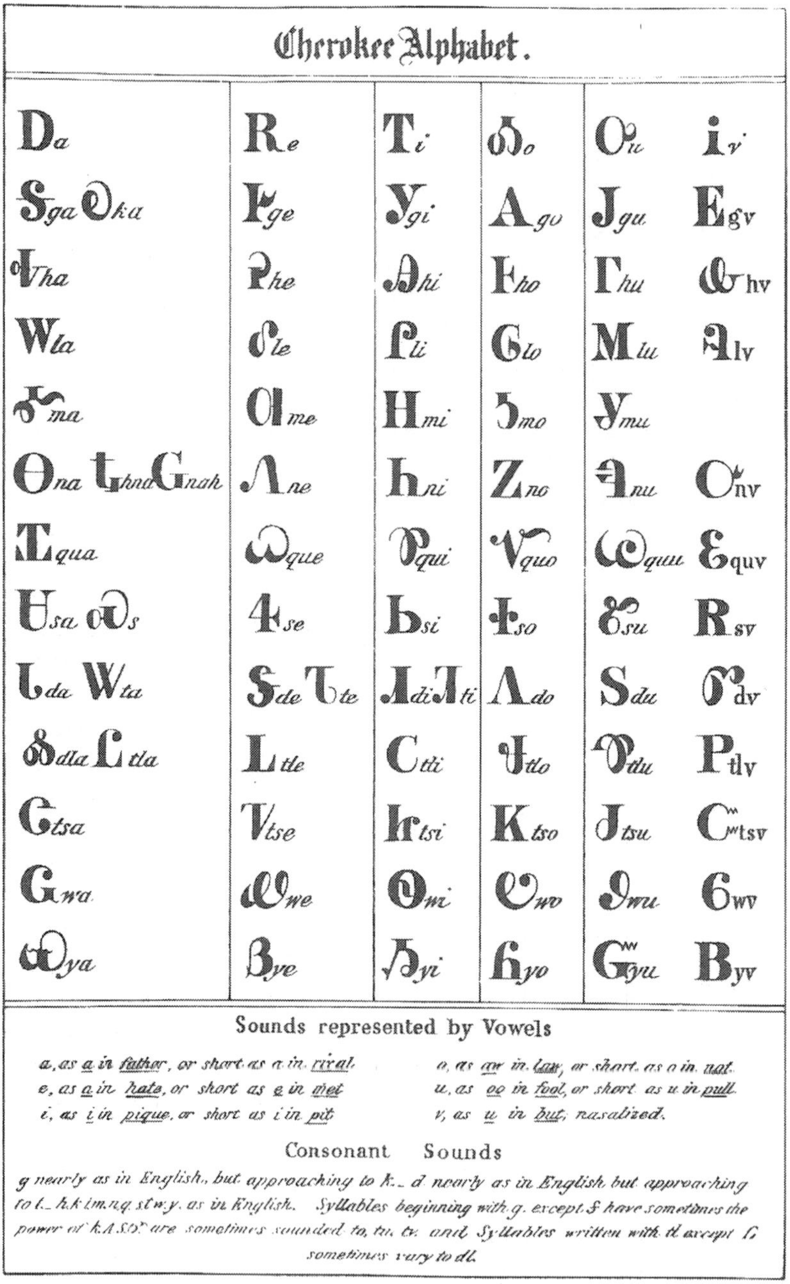

Cherokee Alphabet.

D a	R e	T i	Ꮼ o	O u	i v
S ga Ꮼ ka	Ᏸ ge	Ᏻ gi	A go	J gu	E gv
Ꮣ ha	Ꭾ he	Ꭿ hi	Ᏽ ho	Ꭱ hu	Ꮕ hv
W la	� le	Ꮈ li	Ꮆ lo	M lu	Ꭰ lv
Ꮉ ma	Ꮝ me	H mi	Ꮼ mo	Ꮽ mu	
Ꮟ na Ꮏ hna Ꮐ nah	Ꭽ ne	Ꮒ ni	Z no	Ꮴ nu	Ꮕ nv
Ꮖ qua	Ꮗ que	Ꮙ qui	Ꮚ quo	Ꮜ quu	Ꮝ quv
Ꮞ sa Ꮤ s	Ꮢ se	Ꮘ si	Ꮼ so	Ꮖ su	R sv
Ꮣ da Ꮤ ta	Ꮥ de Ꮦ te	Ꮧ di Ꮨ ti	Ꭿ do	S du	Ꮩ dv
Ꮪ dla Ꮣ tla	Ꮫ tle	C tti	Ꮬ tlo	Ꮭ tlu	P tlv
Ꮳ tsa	Ꮴ tse	Ꮵ tsi	K tso	Ꮶ tsu	Ꮷ tsv
Ꮹ wa	Ꮺ we	Ꮻ wi	Ꮼ wo	Ꮽ wu	Ꮾ wv
Ꮿ ya	Ᏸ ye	Ᏹ yi	Ᏺ yo	Ᏻ yu	Ᏼ yv

Sounds represented by Vowels

a, as a in father, or short as a in rival.
e, as a in hate, or short as e in met.
i, as i in pique, or short as i in pit

o, as aw in law, or short as o in not.
u, as oo in fool, or short as u in pull.
v, as u in but, nasalized.

Consonant Sounds

g nearly as in English, but approaching to k. d nearly as in English but approaching to t. h k l m n q s t w y, as in English. Syllables beginning with g except Ꭶ have sometimes the power of k. A S Ꮷ are sometimes sounded to, tu, tv, and Syllables written with tl except Ꮭ sometimes vary to dl.

FIGURE 8.1 Samuel Worcester's arrangement of the Cherokee syllabary, misnamed as a "Cherokee Alphabet"

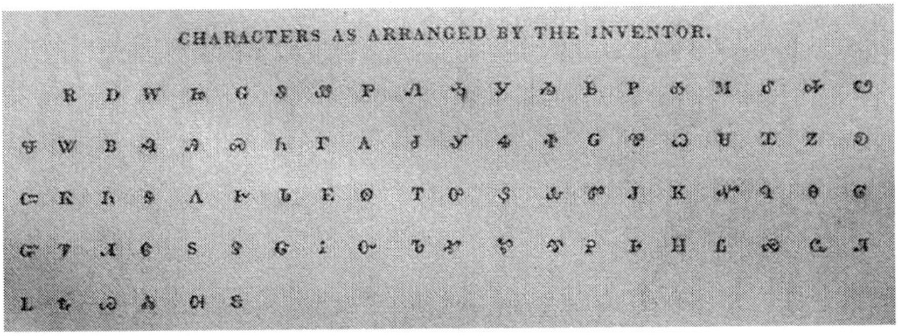

FIGURE 8.2 The "Cherokee Alphabet," initially published in issue 1 of the *Cherokee Phoenix* (February 21, 1828) by Samuel Worcester, with its "characters systematically arranged with the sounds," and republished in the inaugural issue of the *Cherokee Messenger* in 1844

The characters were "systematically arranged" in a way that mimics the way English alphabetic writing is ordered and taught (Figure 8.2). Though it is not an alphabet, calling the syllabary a "Cherokee Alphabet" had a rhetorical effect for settlers, political leaders, and reformers, who perceived Cherokees as more civilized because of this "alphabet."[1] The rearrangement of characters rests on conventions similar to those used in alphabetic literacy primers that organized spelling and vocabulary lessons around consonant–vowel combinations. The arrangement in print versions of the syllabary should have had little impact on people's abilities to learn it. In fact, given the ways in which this standardized version is keyed to the alphabet, it should have made learning Cherokee much easier for those whose first language was English. But that was not the case.

For English speakers, this standardized arrangement of the syllabary may have drawn too much attention to the sounds of characters, diverting attention from the ways in which the syllabary actually represents much more than sound. Mooney (1892) describes how difficult it was for English speakers to learn the Cherokee syllabary through the standardized syllabary chart: "A number of the characters are so nearly alike that they can scarcely be distinguished even in the most carefully written manuscript. There is no logical connection of characters denoting related sounds—as *tsa*, *tse*, *tsi*, etc.—and finally each character commonly requires several strokes in the making" (p. 63).

The Cherokee syllabary is difficult to learn for those raised with English as their first language. As Mooney noted, characters resemble each other and require several strokes, sometimes seeming to show no "logical" connection between the characters and related sounds. Though the Cherokee writing system is difficult to learn for people whose first language is English, it carries its own cultural logics, meanings, and values that abide today, if we view it outside of the alphabetic lens.

Relying on this standardized chart, scholars, well-meaning missionaries, and the general public alike have misunderstood the history and instrumentality of the Cherokee writing system, approaching it as though it was more akin to the Latin alphabet than it actually is. When seen through an alphabetic lens, though, the instrumentality of the Cherokee syllabary is reduced to its simplest function: it seems to merely encode sound with each character. To say that the instrumental workings of the Cherokee syllabary rest at the level of character–sound correspondence, however, underestimates the potential representational power of each character in a word. Not every character has the same depth of representational power. For example, the character Ꭿ /hi/ can be both a pronoun prefix as well as suffix in the same verb phrase—the meaning potential is activated by its location in the verb phrase. If only understood as working at the phonetic level, though, the potential heuristic power of the syllabary is lost on Cherokee-language learners and scholars.

To free the Cherokee syllabary from the alphabetic bias, then, involves a shift in the terms that one might typically use to describe reading and writing: letters, literacy, literate, and the alphabet. These words, so taken for granted in discussions of reading and writing, are no longer useful for describing the Cherokee writing system, if indeed they ever were. The etymologies of these words link them to one writing system alone: *letters* are only of alphabets; *literacy* in its denotative sense is to work fluently with letter–sound correspondences; to be *literate* is to be fluent with the letter or to be lettered, from the Latin, *literatus*; and the word *alphabet* represents the first two Greek letters alpha and beta taken to mean the whole set of letters. This constellation of terms always links reading and writing to the letter, indeed links seemingly all domains of knowledge and knowledge-making to literacy (Wysocki & Johnson-Eiola, 1999). This chapter changes the terms on which and through which reading and writing in Cherokee is understood.

The term *character* describes each individual mark in the Cherokee syllabary, because it reflects more closely the ways in which these were created, designed, and redesigned for print, and the ways these work instrumentally. Some of the Cherokee people with whom I work are fluent readers and writers of *Sequoyan*, and they may also be *literate* in the Roman alphabet. And the Cherokee writing system as a whole is described as a *syllabary* that shows *morphographic* qualities; while each character in the writing system represents sound units, it also can potentially represent additional linguistic information depending on the order of the syllables. Let me illustrate this last rather remarkable claim.

Not Just a Syllabary

In the first evolutionary phase of the Cherokee writing system, Sequoyah invented a system wherein each character can potentially represent not just sound, but semantic, morphological, and syntactical information as well. For example, the verb phrase ᏦᎯᏧ /tohitsu/ is a common greeting used with a familiar person, loosely translating to "how are you?" But its exact translation reveals more:

ᏦᎯ   /dohi/ is a root meaning "at peace, well, harmony, balanced"
Ꮶ   /tsu/ is a 2nd person singular pronoun meaning "you"
ᏦᎯ   /dohi/ can also be used as an adjective meaning well (health).
      In response to this phrase a Cherokee speaking formally would reply:
      ᏦᎯᏇ ᎠᏇ, ᏂᎯᏁ? /tohiquu aya, nihina/, loosely translated to "I am well, and you?" Again, the exact translations of each character reveals more meaning.
ᏦᎯ   /dohi/ is a root meaning "at peace, well, harmony, balanced"
Ꮻ   /quu/ first person singular pronoun meaning I
ᎠᏇ   /aya/ myself, my person
ᏂᎯ   /nihi/ second person pronoun you
Ꮎ   /na/ pronoun suffix meaning, "and what about?"

Cherokee is what linguists call a "polysynthetic language," in which words can consist of a high number of morphemes, those smallest meaningful units in the grammar of a language. Said another way, one multisyllabic word in Cherokee can be an entire sentence in which each syllable uttered carries with it meaning (e.g. the Cherokee word for goodbye is a sentence that reads: ᏦᎰᏝᎪᏫᎢ /don-adagohvi/, "you and I saw each other again"). In Cherokee, a verb phrase like this is a complete sentence that has morphological rules governing which syllables can be used as prefixes, roots, and suffixes. These verb phrases paint pictures of the action unfolding, can be up to 14 syllables, and can potentially indicate where, who, with what, to whom, doing what, how, and when, in one word.

This polysynthetic structure of Cherokee lends itself well to a writing system in which each grapheme represents more than just sound, but also the potential underlying morphological elements of the language. Over the decade or so it took Sequoyah to invent this system, he reported to interviewers that he had tried two other forms of representation, pictographs and logographs (Cushman, 2011a, 2011b). He created a system that blends the economy of a syllabary with the meaningfulness of morphographic systems and, in so doing, Sequoyan closely represents this polysynthetic language.[2] Unfortunately, this instrumentality is lost upon English-language speakers using Worcester's alphabetical orthography. With Worcester's arrangement as a key to the language, scholars and Cherokee-language learners are misled to assume that they only need to look for a simple decoding of phonetic information. Character represents sound, just like an alphabet, end of story.

When Cherokee moved into print, its instrumentality, largely obscured to English-speaking audiences, remained present for Cherokees, who printed millions of pages of documents in Sequoyan and continued to use it in manuscript form as well from 1827 to the 1900s. "In addition to numerous Bible translations, hymn books, and other religious works," writes Mooney (1900), "there have been printed in the Cherokee language and syllabary the *Cherokee Phoenix* (journal), Cherokee Advocate (journal), *Cherokee Messenger* (periodical), *Cherokee Almanac* (annual), Cherokee spelling books, arithmetic's, and other schoolbooks for those unable to read English, several editions of the laws of the Nation, and a large body of tracts and minor publications" (p. 112). Public uses of the syllabary were equally diverse and widespread: handwritten Cherokee was found in "letter writing, council records, personal memoranda, etc.," as well as extensive recording and documentation of medicines and prayers "for the purpose of preserving to their successors the—ancient rituals and secret knowledge of the tribe" (p. 112). Three presses contributed to the flourishing of literature published for Cherokees during this time: the Park Hill Press, Cherokee Nation Press, and Baptist Mission Press. Between 1835 and 1860 the Park Hill Press run by Samuel Worcester took partial responsibility for the proliferation of printed materials available in Cherokee and English. "This press printed 13,980,000 pages of books, tracts, pamphlets, and passages from the Bible in both the Cherokee writing system and alphabet" (White, 1962, p. 511). The ubiquity of manuscript and print coupled with the ease of use of the syllabary made it a powerful tool in persevering in the Cherokee language for everyday life as well as documenting and codifying traditional ways and histories. Numerous manuscript items also remain as part of a legacy of social documents that Cherokees wrote in their everyday lives.

The manuscript forms of writing, along with the printed *New Testament* and *Hymns*, became a literary legacy that allowed Cherokees to continue writing and reading the language throughout some of the darkest years after the Dawes General Allotment Act disbanded tribal governments and divided all commonly held lands into individual parcels of private property (Cushman, 2006). Cherokees who spoke and wrote the language during this time did so in what Wahrhaftig (1998) called a "calculated inconspicuousness" (p. 96). Cherokees in small towns in Oklahoma, organized around traditional stomp and Cherokee Baptist churches, continued practicing the language, reading and writing in Cherokee. They opted out of white mainstream institutions that failed to support, indeed often violently repressed, the Cherokee language. When external validation of the Cherokee language became more apparent, a slow, but steady groundswell of Cherokee-language use emerged in print, type, and script, even appearing in comics, newspapers, and gift store items.

In the 1990s the Cherokee Nation recognized the need to protect the language and did so with the 1991 Language Revitalization Act. The Cherokee Nation recognized the growing problem of language erosion and passed legislation in 1991 to address the problem. Under the Act Relating to the Tribal Policy for the Promotion and Preservation of Cherokee Language, History and Culture (Cherokee Nation, 1991), Cherokee and English were finally recognized as the official language of the tribe, providing even more validity and impetus for the use of Cherokee. Cherokees from rural communities might again begin to see the nation's valuing of the language through its use in official functions. The Cherokee Nation would try to use both Cherokee and English when providing services, resources, and information and communicating concerns to members of the tribal council.

In 2000, the Nation conducted a survey of Cherokee-language speakers that "showed nearly 64 percent of Cherokee citizens do not speak or understand the language. About 5 percent understand the language but cannot speak it, 17 percent understand and have some speaking ability, 3 percent are conversational, 10 percent are highly fluent, and only 1 percent have mastery of the language" (Chavez, 2009, p. 1). It is even more disturbing that so few children raised in homes where Cherokee is the primary language spoken are retaining their language once they enter English-speaking schools. Importantly, though, 95 percent of the respondents surveyed agreed that ensuring the vitality of the language was important to Cherokee identity and heritage (Chavez, 2009). This suggests that the language is valued as part of identity and heritage, that language loss is an important issue to address in order to maintain Cherokee peoplehood, and that those Cherokees who still speak, read, and write the language are valued assets. With these alarming statistics, the Cherokee Nation developed a Cherokee immersion school, privileged the Cherokee language in their public communications, and developed several K-12 programs through their co-partner Johnson O'Malley Program.

These policies and programs, along with the proliferation of new media, have again made Sequoyan and Cherokee-langauge use possible across more contexts and for more purposes, though the language might still be characterized as endangered at the stage 6 level (Fishman, as cited in Reyhner 2007, pp. 88–109) where there is some intergenerational use of the language. Digital media have also afforded a closer linking of the sounds, uses, practices, and values of the langauge with the writing system that so closely represents it. Syllabary charts that still use the one standardized by Worcester link an audio file with the sound of the glyph that plays when users click on each character. Digital videos can be found on the Cherokee Nation website where childrens' books in Cherokee are read aloud and where Cherokee songs and prayers are coupled with images. To be certain, these digital remediations do not replace the need for more contexts in which Cherokee can be used meaningfully. Cherokee-langauge learners learn best in "*context*[s] that [are] real or at least realistic" and in "processing *content* of high interest" to them (Reyhner & Tennant, 1995, pp. 294–295). Nevertheless, digital remediations do help reinforce the ways in which the Cherokee syllabary itself might be helpful in seeing and hearing the relationship of syllables to meaning, if learners are made aware of the instrumentality of Sequoyan.

Two key heuristics can be drawn from tracing the evolution of the Cherokee syllabary: (1) knowledge of the English writing system interferes with learning Sequoyan (e.g., the habit of seeing R as looking like the letter "R," as in /Robert/, which hinders Cherokee learners from reading its Cherokee sound /sv/); and (2) the original learners of this system were all fluent Cherokee speakers who were learning to read and write in their first language—suggesting they would have understood the semantic potential of each character when used in relation to others. Writing-systems scholar Daniels (2009) and anthropologist Bender (2002) suggested the morphographical nature of the Cherokee syllabary. This research confirms their hyphotheses through linguistic analysis of the writing system, qualitative data, and historical evidence (Cushman, 2010, 2011b, 2011c).

Implications

My goal with this brief history of the Cherokee writing system has been to tell the story of a writing system developed in resistance to alphabetic scripts, in an effort to remove the alphabetic lens that for so long has obscured the instrumental workings and cultural logics of Sequoyan. The instrumentality of the Cherokee syllabary is remarkable for its economy, depth, and flexibility: it represents, with fewer exceptions than alphabetic writing in English, the sound system in the language in just 85 characters; it can potentially codify three levels of linguistic information; and it reproduces well no matter what the medium. As opposed to understanding the Cherokee writing system through an alphabet centric perspective (Harris, 2009), an alphabetic lens (Baca, 2008), or a value system that maintains a hierarchy of signs (Cushman, 2011d), this research changes the terms of the discussion. This work asks us to understand writing as including more than the letter, alphabet, and literacy. It asks us to consider the evolution of indigenous writing technologies happening in spite of and alongside a predominant script that has naturalized our monolinguistic assumptions about knowledge, meaning, and rhetoric. It asks us to re-examine the limited and limiting meaning-making potential of alphabetic orthographies in order to better understand and accommodate graphisms, World Englishes, and hybrid codes.

Equally important to correcting the scholarly record about the Cherokee syllabary, this evolutionary history of the Cherokee syllabary has potential heuristic value for language-preservation efforts for the Cherokee language. The extent to which a writing system, especially one based on an alphabetic orthography, might aid in language-preservation efforts geared toward stabilizing an indigenous language has been a matter of some debate. Morgan's (2009) *The Bearer of this Letter* traces the Fort Belknap Indian Community resistance to the introduction of any alphabetically based orthographies to codify their language. Burnaby (2007) has written at length on the status of indigenous-language preservation efforts across Canada and the U.S., finding that writing in orthographies that are alphabetically based has produced mixed and unpromising results in indigenous communities. Bauman suggests "many such academic writing systems are not practical for community use" (as cited in Burnaby, 2007, p. 29) In the introduction to *Stabilizing Indigenous Languages*, Cantoni (2007) presents a list of misperceptions that plague current practices in stabilizing indigenous languages, among them being the idea that "writing a language is what keeps it alive" (p. vi). Rather than seeing the development of a writing system as a central facet of indigenous-language preservation and revitalization, writing needs to be viewed along many other community-based language practices. "Stabilizing an endangered language," Reyhner (2007) finds, "touches all aspects of a community from child-rearing practices and intergenerational communication to economic and political development" (p. 4). Writing in indigenous languages needs to be practiced in all aspects of community life within contexts, genres, and purposes that are meaningful and, often times, in exclusion of English. Because writing pedagogy works best when it is nested in talk, endangered languages have a stronger chance of survival when talk and writing with indigenous systems happen together and often. If Cherokee-language learners and scholars can view the Cherokee syllabary outside of an alphabetic bias and can continue to develop more practices and purposes for writing, hope remains for the Cherokee language.

Finally, the evolution of the Cherokee syllabary fuels the productive line of research called for in the translingual approach to writing research and pedagogy. The "translingual approach argues for (1) honoring the power of all language users to shape language to specific ends; (2) recognizing the linguistic heterogeneity of all users of language both within the United States and globally; and (3) directly confronting English monolingualist expectations by researching and teaching how writers can work with and against, not simply within, those expectations" (Horner, Lu, Royster, & Trimbur, 2011, p. 305). Sequoyan shaped the Cherokee language and national identity in and on Cherokee terms, which, to date, have not been well documented in histories of American literacy. The Cherokee developed this writing system to write the Cherokee language alongside, and in spite of, the predominance of the English language and literacy. Sequoyah's invention allowed Cherokees to confront head on the imperialist agendas that privileged the development of alphabetic orthographies to encode native languages. With a translingual approach, this research helps shift the paradigm of literacy studies, enabling researchers to think more completely through the modes and scripts through which meaning is encoded, adding to the several strands of research developed on multilingual writers (Canagarajah, 2006a, 2006b; Matsuda, 2006) and code-meshing (Michael-Luna & Canagarajah, 2007). In the global world and in the multicultural United States, literacy, that is fluency with the letter, cannot be the only object of study for scholars of reading and writing. As this example of the evolution of Sequoyan demonstrates, scripts have historical, cultural, linguistic, and ideological import for the people who use them. Research on scripts and multilingualism provide useful correctives to scholarship based on monolingual assumptions, which presume alphabetic literacy and instrumentality as a baseline against which all other scripts and meaning-making activities are judged.

Notes

1   The American Board of Commissions of Foreign Missionaries remarks upon the civilizing force of the Cherokee writing system at the moment it moves from script to print: "Among the Cherokees, also, we see established the first regularly elected government … the Christian religion recognized and protected by the government; regular and exemplary Christian churches, and flourishing schools extensively established, and in many instances taught by native Cherokees" (p. 382). See also Samuel Worcester's account of the Cherokee Alphabet in the *Missionary Herald*, May, 1828.

2   So strong was the Cherokee insistence upon seeing Sequoyan in print that the tribal council rejected the alphabetic orthography proposed by John Pickering and favored by the American Board of Foreign Missionaries (ABCFM) with whom Worcester worked for printing all their religious materials. To his credit, Worcester disabused the ABCFM from their favor of Pickering's orthography over Sequoyan and convinced them to print religious materials in Sequoyan (Cushman, 2011a, 2011b).

References

Baca, D. (2008). *Mestiz@ scripts, digital migrations and the territories of writing*. New York, NY: Palgrave Macmillan.

Baca, D., & Villanueva, V. (Eds.) (2010). *Rhetorics of the Americas*. New York, NY: Palgrave.

Bender, M. (2002). *Signs of Cherokee culture: Sequoyah's syllabary in Eastern Cherokee life*. Chapel Hill, NC: University of North Carolina Press.

Burnaby, B. (2007). Aboriginal language maintenance, development, and enhancement. *Stabilizing Indigenous Languages* (pp. 21–38). Flagstaff, AZ: Center for Excellence in Education.

Canagarajah, A. S. (2006a). The place of World Englishes in composition: Pluralization continued. *College Composition and Communication, 57*(4), 586–619.

Canagarajah, A. S. (2006b). Toward a writing pedagogy of shuttling between languages: Learning from multilingual writers. *College English, 68*(6), 589–604. doi:10.2307/25472177.

Cantoni, G (Ed.). (2007). *Stabilizing indigenous languages*. Flagstaff, AZ: Northern Arizona University Press.

Chavez, W. (2009). Long-range language preservation plan in progress. *Cherokee Phoenix*. Retrieved from http://www.cherokeephoenix.org/6/Article.aspx (accessed Nov. 15, 2012).

Cherokee Nation. (1991). *Act relating to the establishment of the tribal policy for the promotion and preservation of Cherokee language, history and culture*. Retrieved from http://cherokee.legi-star.com/LegislationDetail.aspx?ID=266941&GUID=C8EC5F0A-E523-49A0-92BD-42041FCE32EA&Options =ID|Text|&Search=10 91 (accessed Nov. 15, 2012).

Cushman, E. (2006). Toward a praxis of new media: The allotment period in Cherokee history. *Reflections on Community-Based Writing Instruction, 4*(3), 124–143.

Cushman, E. (2010). The Cherokee syllabary from script to print. *Ethnohistory, 57*(4), 625–650.

Cushman, E. (2011a). "We're taking the genius of Sequoyah into this century:" The Cherokee syllabary, peoplehood, and perseverance. *Wicazo Sa Review Journal, 25*(4), 67–83. doi:10.1353/wic.2011.0002.

Cushman, E. (2011b). The Cherokee syllabary: A writing system in its own right. *Written Communication, 28*(3), 255–281. doi:10.1177/0741088311410172.

Cushman, E. (2011c). *The Cherokee syllabary: Writing the people's perseverance.* Norman, OK: University of Oklahoma Press.

Cushman, E. (2011d). New media scholarship and teaching: Challenging the hierarchy of signs. *Pedagogy, 11*(1), 63–80. doi:10.1215/15314200-2010-017.

Daniels, P. (2009). Grammatology. In D. Olson, & N. Torrance (Eds.), *The Cambridge handbook of literacy* (pp. 25–45). Cambridge: Cambridge University Press.

Drucker, J. (1997). *The visible word: Experimental typography and modern art, 1909–1923* (2nd ed.). Chicago, IL: University Of Chicago Press.

Harris, R. (2009). *Rationality and the literate mind.* New York, NY: Taylor and Francis, Routledge.

Holmes, R. B., & Smith, B. S. (1976). *Beginning Cherokee.* Norman, OK: University of Oklahoma Press.

Horner, B., Lu, M. Z., Royster, J. J., & Trimbur, J. (2011). Language difference in writing: Toward a translingual approach. *College English, 73*(3), 303–321.

Matsuda, P. K. (2006). The myth of linguistic homogeneity in U.S. college composition. *College English, 68*(6), 637–651. doi:10.2307/25472180.

Michael-Luna, S., & Canagarajah, A. S. (2007). Multilingual academic literacies: Pedagogical foundations for code meshing in primary and higher education. *Journal of Applied Linguistics, 4*(1), 55–77.

Mignolo, W. D. (1992) "On the colonization of Amerindian languages and memories: Renaissance theories of writing and the discontinuity of the classical tradition. *Comparative Studies in Society and History, 34*(2), 301–330. doi:10.1017/S0010417500017709.

Mignolo, W. D. (2003). *The darker side of the Renaissance: Literacy, territoriality, and colonization* (2nd ed.). Ann Arbor, MI: University of Michigan Press.

Mooney, J. (1892). Improved Cherokee alphabets. *American Anthropologist, 5*(1), 63–64. doi:10.1525/aa.1892.5.1.02a00080.

Mooney, J. (1900). *Myths of the Cherokees.* Washington, DC: Bureau of American Ethnology.

Morgan, M. (2009). *The bearer of this letter: Language ideologies, literacy practices, and the Fort Belknap Indian community.* Lincoln, NE: University of Nebraska Press.

Reyhner, J. (2007). Rationale and needs for stabilizing indigenous languages. In G. Cantoni (Ed.), *Stabilizing indigenous languages* (pp. 3–14). Flagstaff, AZ: Northern Arizona University Press.

Reyhner, J., & Tennant, E. (1995). Maintaining and renewing native languages. *The Bilingual Research Journal, 19*(2), 279–304.

Wahrhaftig, A. (1998). Looking back to Tahlequah: Robert K. Thomas' role among the Oklahoma Cherokee, 1963–1967. In S. Pavlik (Ed.), *A good Cherokee, a good anthropologist* (pp. 93–105). Los Angeles, CA: UCLA University Press.

Walker, W. (1969). Notes on native writing systems and the design of native literacy programs. *Anthropological Linguistics, 11*(5), 148–66.

Walker, W., & Sarbaugh, J. (1993). The early history of the Cherokee syllabary. *Ethnohistory, 40*(1), 70–94. doi:10.2307/482159.

White, J. (1962). On the revival of printing in the Cherokee language. *Current Anthropology, 3*(5), 511–514. doi:10.1086/200321.

Wysocki, A. F., & Johnson-Eilola, J. (1999). Blinded by the letter: Why are we using literacy as a metaphor for everything else? In G. E. Hawisher & C. L. Selfe (Eds.), *Passions pedagogies and 21st century technologies* (pp. 349–368). Logan, UT: Utah State University Press.

9

HI-*EIN*, HI يين OR يين HI? TRANSLINGUAL PRACTICES FROM LEBANON AND MAINSTREAM LITERACY EDUCATION

Nancy Bou Ayash

The code-meshed title is illustrative of the challenge of representing translingual relations that most fully capture the complexity of language interactions as Lebanese language users negotiate tensions between different communication. The unconventional addition of يين next to *Hi* opens up various possibilities tied to the movement of meanings in this translingual design in light of locally constructed social relations, meanings that I will explore in a later section in this chapter.

A "translingual" approach to language difference in writing, as advanced by Horner, Lu, Royster, and Trimbur (2011) embraces the "variety, fluidity, intermingling, and changeability of languages" and language practices (p. 301). The current chapter answers the calls of Horner et al.'s (2011) position statement for advancing a translingual approach in U.S. writing programs. With perspectives from the specific location of Lebanon, I adopt a translingual approach to linguistic practices in that site, both on the street and in educational settings, in order to tease out the strategies both language users and literacy laborers adopt in the face of residual monolingual ideologies in various domains of life. Local language practices in Lebanon, as I will demonstrate, do indeed prove the validity of seeing English as "a language always in translation," as Pennycook (2008) puts it, and as emerging in response to linguistic, cultural, historical, geopolitical, and economic relations of difference. Through a description of translingual language relations in Lebanese sociolinguistic landscapes and how these get (or do not get) translated into curricular design, I demonstrate that the productivity of efforts towards institutionalizing translingualism in mainstream literacy pedagogy largely depends on laboring over the close alignment of writing curricula with the specificity of sociolinguistic landscaping.

Language Relations: Sociolinguistic Landscapes and Curricular Design

English and Other Languages on the Ground

Lebanon is a multilingual nation with a dynamic use of Arabic, French, and English that serves basic communicative, vocational, and educational purposes.[1] An oral Lebanese Arabic variety, used for conducting daily affairs, and a written Modern Standard Arabic version, used only in formal domains, co-exist among its discourse communities. While traveling in various Lebanese social circles, it is not uncommon to hear the conversation in public spaces easily mesh Lebanese Arabic with English and French. Sections on basic Lebanese–Arabic phrases that interactive online travel guides provide are particularly illustrative of such local language practices. In its Lebanese Arabic phrasebook, for instance, Wikitravel helpfully advises tourists to use an English–Lebanese Arabic–French mixture of *Sorry, wein il toilette?* for "Excuse me, where is the bathroom?" should they need to find a bathroom. It also instructs hungry foreigners and tourists to inquire whether a Lebanese bar provides snacks using *3endkoon Bar Snacks?* for "Do you have bar snacks?"[2]

In citing these examples and the ones that follow, my purpose is not to use them simply to conduct an "enumeration of languages," but rather to illustrate, using a spatio-temporal lens, the complexity of translingual language practices on the ground (Pennycook, 2010, pp. 10, 97). I argue, following Pennycook's (2010) calls for the exigence for a "qualitative understanding of the traffic of meaning" instead of a "quantitative strategy" towards linguistic diversity (p. 68), that such local language practices resemble glosso-diversity or the "diversity of languages" as well as semio-diversity or the "diversity within language," i.e. the diversity of meanings (p. 100). A close look at language relations in the cosmo-politan capital city Beirut transports you into the spatiality of language in the way language users from all areas of life put their cultural and linguistic resources into action as day-to-day affairs on the street are being conducted, and into the temporality of language through the process of sedimentation emerging from pre-colonial, colonial, and post-colonial history. This sense of "flow" in language use, as described by Pennycook, characterizes ongoing language sedimented through creative, thoughtful repetitions over time and across space.

A representative demonstration of the process of relocalization and creation of semio-diversity in the contemporary Lebanese society is the local language prac-tice of attaching the Arabic dual number suffix -ein (ﻳﲔ) in response to French or English greetings, such as in Bonjourein (two bonjour's to you), Bonsoirein (two bonsoir's), Hi-ein (two hi's), or Hello-ein (two hello's). This widespread trans-lingual practice was mainly started by taxi drivers in the city as a sign of Lebanese hospitality and generosity to tourists or even courtesy to national citizens (Laser Films, 2010). Aligned with a Lebanese tradition of giving with profusion and with a famous Lebanese saying that "more of everything never hurt anyone," this numerical representation in the greeting where the person at the receiving end is not merely greeted with one salutation but two is conveyed through a high rising intonation with a distinctive elongated final syllable signifying a welcoming gesture. These idiosyncratic linguistic designs are distinguished from their more monolingual counterparts such as bonjour, bonsoir, hi, and hello not only in form but also in their unique meaning as a representation of a different kind of inter-personal relations between language users. Western, colonial languages of English and French in this relocalized language practice are deterritorialized into the micro space of the cab driver as a "meso-political action" mediating between broader social, cultural, and linguistic structures on one hand and more local activity on another (Pennycook, 2010, p. 29). Actively intervening with the dominant trade model, the driver's language creation reverses the power relations between lab-orer and buyer of labor through establishing the identity of its user, not only as a driver but also as a host in relation to riders. In this way, a Lebanese driver doesn't need to ask his "guests" relaxing in the back of his cab "Do you mind if I talk to you?" anymore, and is rather empowered by his relocalized greeting to impart his own world views, lived experiences, and acquired wisdom on them.

In a culture that adopts an iconic greeting of *Hi!* كيفك؟ *Ça va?* (pronounced as *Hi! Kifak? Ça va?*, the equivalent for "Hi, how are you doing? Are you fine?"), what I'll refer to as "mix-and-match" language practices, with all three languages meshed together, in daily communication are widely accepted and even expected in Lebanese society. This translingual greeting became initially popular among the young population as a distinctive marker of high social class and education through replacing the monolingual Lebanese Arabic greeting *marhaba*, the French *salut*, or the English *hi* that are inadequate for the intended type of meaning-ful social relations. Resorting to mixed-and-matched options of *Hi! Kifak? Ça va?* not only helps Lebanese youth mark generational and class differences but also perform a modern, hybrid identity more aligned with the transcultural and translingual flows in the cosmopolitan Beiruti culture, thereby resisting the more singular, fixed, and compartmentalized identities that the monolingual greetings impart. Repetitions of this linguistic construction over time have generated new meanings of subversion to elitism as it is currently used among different social groups to symbolize national identity and authenticity. The relocalization of this language practice in space and time is a reflection of newness, renewal, and differ-ence, or what Pennycook labels as "fertile mimesis" (2010, p. 37). In the vicinity of *Kifak* and *Ça va*, the English *Hi* generates new social and cultural relations between its language users that mark them as "different" and "Lebanese," with full ownership of their daily language use, meaningful relations not captured by an English-only construction. To appreciate more fully the dynamic use of language resources by ordinary language users, I consider in the next section one aspect of the macro context of local language practices, which is the educational and the ideological landscape informing and informed by such practices.

Writing Instruction and Translation[3]

The past couple of years have witnessed new efforts among a number of professional writing teachers to redesign writing assignments in ways that further
promote cross-language relations in their writing classrooms. Several instructors of international business writing and technical communication courses have
acknowledged the importance of translating the linguistic realities and challenges
of cross-border exchanges in local and global relations in the business world into
their own classrooms through encouraging the process of composing business and
technical documents in Arabic and French alongside English. On an instructional
level, my personal experience working with such translingual writing assignments
in my technical writing courses, which are a requirement for students majoring
in engineering, architecture, and graphic design, proved to be a great opportunity
for students to examine the use of their native language in the world of marketing and business in a fast, capitalist world amid the hegemony of English. Such
discussions led to unsolicited explorations of stylistic structures that incorporate
the unwritten vernacular using the Standard Arabic calligraphy or Latin encod-
ing (what is commonly known as "transliteration"), with special symbols used
to replace the missing phonemes as in the motto of a popular Lebanese industry
campaign *Bit7eb Lebnen 7eb Sina3to* for "If you love Lebanon, love its local products."[4] Conversations about such relocalized language practices that were carried
over from instant messaging and social networking into the advertisement domain
encouraged a critical examination of the wide range of literate practices available
to multilingual Lebanese students both inside and outside the writing classroom,
such as decisions about when, how, and why they resort to translingual options
like *Hi!* كيفك؟ *Ça va?* or *Hi-ein*.

Though the diverse language situation in Lebanon has found its way into
professional writing classrooms, academic writing teachers are still very hesitant
to encourage cross-language relations in their own writing pedagogies. Strong
justifications from the push of the job market in Lebanon have empowered only
professional writing teachers for pursuing translingual work, but the dominance
of monolingual ideologies in the academic knowledge market in Lebanon as
well as internationally has kept those in the academic realm clinging to conformity to standardized rules and prescribed writing conventions. Educators
and academics are constantly pressured by the allegedly universal demands of
educational and job opportunities over the reproduction of language standards
when the professional world is, in reality, much less stringent than they like
to acknowledge, and they in turn transport dominant conceptions about such
ostensibly necessary prerequisites for social and personal development to their
students. A key point of interest here is the precedence of the professional realm
over the academic, particularly in revising and adapting curriculum design and
pedagogy for closer alignment with prevailing translingualism in sociolinguistic
and business landscapes.

Similar ideological differences can be observed even in applied translation courses that are designed to capture the politics of translingual meaning-making.[5] One introductory translation course is offered by the Department of Arabic and Near Eastern Languages and mostly involves English–Arabic translation. As stated in the syllabus, work in this course is conducive to "a better understanding of both languages, and of the ways they interact, in the translation context" and to a critical engagement with the "static lexical and otherwise dynamic meanings" in various compositions (course syllabus, Arabic 225: Translation, March 1, 2011). With translation viewed as "the first step towards cultural cross-pollination," the course is described as an opportunity to explore the "intricacies of both languages together, or the fundamentals of one through the understanding of the intricacies of the other." However, such translingual work remains hindered by dominant expectations for a finished, monolingual product and insistence on standardized versions. With emphasis on the significance of the "mastery of the fundamentals," the course syllabus portrays appeals to traditional language standards aesthetic through warning against translated products that "corrupt language, talent, and taste":

> We, the citizens of universities, are the guards of proper understanding and correct communication. We cannot trade in incomprehensible texts that corrupt language, talent, and taste. We shall therefore approach translation as an academic enterprise governed by criteria of correctness and precision.
>
> *(Course syllabus, Arabic 225: Translation, American University of Beirut)*

Another translation course, on the other hand, offered by the English department and recently approved as a humanities general education course, allows for a more critical engagement with language standards. This course, as indicated in its syllabus, mainly involves Arabic–English translation activities and is designed to help university students "reflect on what they do, how they do it, and why they do it in a particular way when other options are available" (course syllabus, English 233: Introduction to Translation). The theoretical component deemed most relevant to students in this course is that of "language in use rather than … language as an abstract system of phonemes, morphemes, lexemes, etc." and of the lack of "one-to-one correspondence between words and meaning constituents within or across languages," with focus on the multiplicity and ramification of meanings instead. This course encourages students to negotiate their way through literary, nonliterary, multimodal, and multimedia texts with constant negotiations of tensions between the multiplicity of discourses, genres, languages, and language practices. Such differences in the commitment level to translingualism in various translation courses speak directly to the residual force of monolingual ideologies seeping even into heavily based translingual work.

Implications for Mainstream Literacy Pedagogy

What exactly does an actively translingual site like Lebanon in its daily lived experiences and business transactions and some pockets of educational institutions have to offer mainstream literacy pedagogy? In light of perspectives from a statistically and culturally sustained translingual space, local sociolinguistic and business landscaping, which are fertile grounds for translingual language practices, are generally neglected sites of language use in many academic contexts that need to be addressed more aggressively in curriculum planning and design. Involving a high frequency of trafficking across meanings, genres, disciplines, languages, and language practices, the local specificity of sociolinguistic and business landscaping is situated in stark opposition with the stringency of the academic world (also see Tupas, 2006), thereby challenging the intrinsic value of monolingual practices primarily accorded by academia. The nature of language relations characterizing the business landscaping and day-to-day experiences is in itself an asset that calls for compositionists' close attention, particularly in pursuing more translingual work in writing programs and writing classrooms. Texts from various areas of life, including digital composing spaces, can be used as interactive course materials for highlighting processes of relocalization in every act of reading and writing and for engaging students of business and technical writing courses or even first-year composition courses in prolific translingual work.

Laboring with, on, and across, not just within, English and other languages and critically engaging with the politics and problematics of translation is the dream of many literacy specialists and composition teachers. Pennycook (2010) argues that the language teaching enterprise, and I would add writing instruction, is "indelibly tied to translation and the diversity of meanings" (p. 141; see also Kramsch, 2006). Among the globally exploding influences of the hegemony of English are its unnatural promotion of monolingual ideologies amid actively multilingual societies and its eschewal of the productivity of imagining literacy instruction as a "project of translation" (Pennycook, 2008, p. 43). There is a growing need to continue vigilantly fighting monolingualist ideologies (see Canagarajah, 2006; Horner & Lu, 2009; Horner & Trimbur, 2002, Horner et al., 2011), particularly in course design, through institutionalizing courses in translation theory and practice similar to those offered in Lebanon, in addition to weaving in work of translation across languages, language practices, disciplines, and genres into existing professional and academic writing curricula. Designing translation assignments with attention to the politics of meaning-making for writing students who are constantly composing, thinking, and living their daily lives in translation lies at the heart of translingualism and is a necessary start for any writing classroom. As writing teachers, we can start by bringing translation to the forefront in writing pedagogy, through integrating translation activity into existing writing courses for an enhanced awareness among our students of the dynamic interaction between English, other languages, and the language practices inevitably occurring in their daily encounters. A translingual writing classroom then foregrounds the creation of semio-diversity or the multiplicity of meanings on top of glosso-diversity.

Acknowledgments

I would like to thank Dr Min-Zhan Lu for her helpful suggestions on various versions of this paper in her seminar on revision theory and practice, and for her continuous support and encouragement to this day.

Notes

1   French and English in Lebanon were first introduced through the arrival of missionaries in the first half of the 19th century, the most prominent of which were the French Jesuits and the American Evangelical Protestants. The French language in Lebanon gained its high status after the colonial French rule in the middle of the 20th century, which chiefly promoted its use. Today, alongside the native Arabic language, the Lebanese speak French as a second foreign language after English, or as the first foreign language and English as the second, with English increasingly becoming the more widely used language.
2   The number 3 is used for voiced pharyngeal fricatives.
3   Perspectives here are drawn from one particular American-style university, the American University of Beirut, based on my past teaching experiences and personal communication and emails with local practitioners.
4   The number 7 is used for voiceless pharyngeal fricatives.
5   Textual analysis here is based on information from course descriptions in the university catalogue, course syllabi, and assignment prompts from undergraduate level translation courses (i.e. Arabic 225: Translation; and English 233: Introduction to Translation), all of which were obtained either through department websites or personal communication with translation instructors and students enrolled in these courses.

References

American University of Beirut. (n.d.). *Arabic 225: Translation. Syllabus and policies.* Retrieved from Faculty of Arts and Sciences website: http://www.aub.edu.lb/fas/fas_home/faculty_resources/Documents/arab225.pdf (accessed Nov. 15, 2012).

Canagarajah, S. (2006). The place of World Englishes in composition: Pluralization continued. *College Composition and Communication,* 57 (4), 586–619.

Horner, B., & Lu, M. (2009). Resisting monolingualism in "English": Reading and writing the politics of language. In V. Ellis, C. Fox & B. Street (Eds.), *Rethinking English in schools: A new and constructive stage* (pp. 141–57). London, UK: Continuum.

Horner, B., Lu, M., Royster, J., & Trimbur, J. (2011). Language difference: Toward a translingual approach. *College English,* 73(3), 299–317.

Horner, B., & Trimbur, J. (2002). English only and U.S. college composition. *College Composition and Communication,* 53, 594–630.

Kramsch, C. (2006). The traffic in meaning. *Asia Pacific Journal of Education,* 26(1), 99–104.

Laser Films (producer). (2010). *La France au Liban* "*TAXI*" [video file]. Retrieved from http://www.youtube.com/watch?v=UzoDp6JciM4&feature=related (accessed Nov. 15, 2012).

Pennycook, A. (2008). English as a language always in translation. *European Journal of English Studies, 12*(1), 33–47.

Pennycook, A. (2010). *Language as a local practice.* Abingdon: Routledge.

Tupas, T. R. F. (2006). Standard Englishes, pedagogical paradigms, and their conditions of (im)possibility. In R. Rubdy & M. Saraceni (Eds.), *English in the world: Global rules, global roles* (pp. 169–185). London: Continuum.

Wikitravel. (n.d.). *Lebanese Arabic phrasebook.* Retrieved from http://wikitravel.org/en/Lebanese_Arabic_phrasebook (accessed Nov. 15, 2012).

10

TRANSLINGUAL PRACTICES IN KENYAN HIPHOP: PEDAGOGICAL IMPLICATIONS

Esther Milu

Introduction

In the essay "Towards a Mestiza Rhetoric: Gloria Anzaldúa on Composition and Postcoloniality," Lunsford (2009) laments that the field of composition studies has not done enough to help writing instructors promote language diversity and multiculturalism in their classrooms. In her essay, which is based on an interview with Gloria Anzaldúa, both scholars concur that the field's lack of concerted effort to promote language and cultural diversity has worked to disadvantage monolingual American students. This is because the students not only fail to recognize the language and cultural diversity of others, but their very own diversity. Anzaldúa proposes one way of helping monolingual students recognize their diversity is by "jerking them out into another country where they don't speak the language, they don't know the food. It's like taking a fish out of water" (as cited in Lunsford, 2009, p. 1413). An exposure to difference, she argues, will enable students to recognize the multiple voices, linguistic, cultural, and rhetorical identities they embody.

In this chapter I heed Anzaldúa's proposal. I argue that writing teachers need to explore diverse cultures to theorize pedagogies to teach language diversity. I propose global hiphop, or cipha, as one of the cultural sites that can offer students the kind of stimulation Anzaldúa conceptualizes. While my definition of global hiphop, or cipha, also includes U.S.-based hiphop, here, I encourage teachers to consider more than ever before teaching with and about hiphop from other parts of the world, in addition to U.S. hiphop. I make this recommendation based on the assumption that, in the past, many hiphop pedagogies applied in U.S. writing classrooms have been theorized and exclusively relied on U.S.-based hiphop, particularly African American hiphop. Like Ibrahim (2009), I argue that hiphop from other parts of the world is rich and unique in the sense that it is characterized by musical, cultural, and linguistic creolization or *métissage*. "*Métissage*" he explains, "assumes two or more cultural entities that are equally valorized; hence it is egalitarian hybridity, where ambiguity, multiplicity, fragmentation, and plurality become the new landscape" (p. 233).

Kenyan hiphop, which is used in this chapter to theorize a translingual pedagogy, is characterized by hybridization of hiphop, dance hall, reggae, and traditional African music forms. At the language level, the artists cross Kenyan language boundaries to include many non-indigenous languages. Other common languages used include African American language (AAL) and Caribbean-based languages such as Jamaican Patois and Dread Talk. The interaction of multiple and diverse cultures, music genres, and languages is, according to Ibrahim (2009), an indicator of how hiphop outside the United States emphasizes and engages in a "dialectic relation between the global and the local (a point that some U.S.-based hiphop is yet to fully understand)" (p. 236).

The Linguistic Situation of Kenyan Hiphop

Kenya is a very linguistically diverse nation. There are three major indigenous speaking groups in the country: the Cushites, the Bantu, and the Nilotes. Under these three broad categories are over 40 indigenous languages. Kiswahili and English are recognized as the country's official and national languages. English, introduced in Kenya through the British colonization, is privileged as the official language of instruction and business. Kiswahili, also called Swahili, is a mandatory and examinable subject in elementary and secondary schools. In addition, Kiswahili serves as the main language of inter-ethnic communication, and is also spoken regionally in several countries in East and sub-Saharan Africa.

Because of the popularity of Kiswahili and English, the two are now becoming the preferred languages for many, especially in Kenya's urban cities. Consequently, this has influenced and shaped the language of Kenyan hiphop, in that English and Kiswahili are the main, or base, languages of composition, arguably aimed at reaching a wider national, regional, and international audience. Some artists incorporate Kenya's indigenous languages in their compositions. However, one should note that, even though the composing is mainly done in Kiswahili and English, the artists are by no means adhering to the "standard" grammar rules of either language. Defying the languages' rules has been made possible through a translanguaging practice referred to as "Sheng," which I briefly discuss below.

Sheng as a Translingual Discourse

To appreciate translingual practices in Kenyan hiphop, one has to understand the languaging practices of Sheng because they significantly shape the identity of Kenyan hiphop. Sheng has been defined and described by linguists as the mixing of several languages in spoken and, to some extent, written communication. In his extensive study on Sheng, Githinji (2006) established that Sheng means different things to different people in Kenya. Perhaps the varied interpretations and meanings arise from one notable finding of his study, that is, Sheng defies all the established rules that govern the definitions of a language, a dialect, pidgin, Creole, jargon, and slang. Because of this fluidity, his study concluded, "a critical look at Sheng shows that while it does display aspects of all these linguistic categories, it cannot conclusively be classified into any of them without raising problems of definition" (p. 43).

A common Kenyan understanding of Sheng is that it is a strategy of switching and mixing of languages, and also a language in its own right, that is, a hybrid linguistic code for Kenyan urban youth (Abdulaziz & Osinde, 1997; Githiora, 2002; Ogechi, 2005; Spyropoulos, 1987). From a historical viewpoint, these studies posit that Sheng emerged from the densely populated multilingual Kenyan urban centers as result of mixing of English and Swahili. Sheng thus became the second facilitator of interethnic communication among the youth, allowing them to switch and borrow from either language if they felt limited in terms of proficiency in using either Swahili or English. Momanyi (2009) notes that, while this was initially the case, today Sheng crosses language boundaries to include other languages in its construction.

A number of authors have argued that Sheng adopts Swahili language structure. With Kiswahili being a Bantu language, Ogechi (2005) coined the term "Bantuization" to refer to a process where words whose syllables do not follow the "primitive" Bantu syllable structure of consonant–vowel (CV), are manipulated or adjusted to fit the structure. According to Ogechi (2005), words borrowed from a non-Bantu language have to be first "Bantuized" to become Sheng. To demonstrate this process, a word like *mababi* in the song *Bamba* by Esir, K-Rupt, and Big Pin (2001, Track 3) is borrowed from the word "Babylon." The word is truncated to *babi* and a prefix *ma-* is added to it to create a new word *mababi*, singular *mbabi* or *babi*. The newly formed word, *mababi*, means oppressors or people in power in Kenyan context, especially the police or political elite. *Mababi* has also been used to refer to the west or imperialists. The word Babylon, which is the name of the ancient city of Mesopotamia, and historically associated with corruption and the persecution of Jews, has, over the years entered the lexicon of the Rastafarian movement and culture to refer to corrupt government personalities, institutions, or systems. Babylon is now part of Jamaican dance hall and reggae lexicon, two music forms that have greatly influenced Kenyan hiphop. Richardson (2006) observes that these two music forms are influenced by Rasta ideology and symbology. Thus, Kenyan hiphop artists borrowed and reinvented the word Babylon by linguistically repurposing it through Sheng to fit a Kenyan localized reality and worldview. This example demonstrates not only Sheng's languaging practices but also how diverse linguistic, cultural, and music creolization shapes the language practices of Kenyan hiphop artists.

However, because of Sheng's fluidity, Kenyan hiphop artists continue to challenge fixed rules like Bantuization, as they come up with new languaging practices every day. In this chapter, I argue that Sheng as a translingual practice allows artists to manipulate a variety of languages for their diverse purposes, and in ways that push the linguistic boundaries of the languages involved.

Translingualism at the Lexical Level

Sheng's translingual practices in Kenyan hiphop occur at different levels. At the lexical level, artists mix two or more languages to form a word, for example, through the Bantuization process described above. Another way is through linguistic inventiveness. An example of this is the word *unbwogable* in the hiphop song *Who can Bwogo Me?* by Gidi Gidi Maji Maji (2002, Track 2). The prefix *un-* and the Luo word *bwogo*, which means to scare or defeat, and the suffix *-able* are combined to form the word *unbwogable*. Luo is one of the indigenous languages spoken in Kenya under the Nilotic speaking group. To say "I am unbwogable" means I am unbeatable or I am not scared. Because of the song's mass appeal, it became a campaign anthem and slogan for the then major opposition party, the National Rainbow Coalition (NARC), during Kenya's 2002 general elections. As a campaign tool, the word and its accompanying message had a dramatic influence on Kenya's national politics, contributing significantly to persuading the electorate to end President Moi's totalitarian leadership of 25 years, and the Kenya African National Union (KANU) party's autonomous rule of 40 years.

Linguistic inventiveness as a translanguaging practice reveals the artists' high level of metalinguistic awareness and linguistic creativity, which is conscious of historical, cultural, economic, and socio-political factors. In their critical and rhetorical analysis of the song, Nyairo and Ogunde (2005) observe that, "it is due to [the] common cultural context rooted in shared experiences that a song like *Unbwogable* acquires its social agency because it resonates with the political impulses and anxieties of the moment" (p. 239). This is one example among many that hiphop artists come up with every day in their composing and performing practices.

Translingualism at Morpho-Syntactical Level

The realization of Sheng as translingual form at this level is comparable to what is referred to in linguistic terms as "code-mixing." Bokamba (1998) defines code-mixing as the "the embedding or mixing of various linguistic units, i.e., affixes, words, phrases, and clauses from two distinct grammatical systems or subsystems within the same sentence and same speech situation" (p. 24). The following excerpt from *Hiphop Halisi* by Ukoo Flani and Nazizi (2008, Track 1) is an example of a code-mixing of Swahili and English morphemes and clauses in a hiphop lyrical composition. The excerpt represents a common or the typical case of translingual composing in Kenyan hiphop. I have highlighted the phrases below to demonstrate the process. A hyphen indicates the point of mixing.

Tafadhali expect First Lady *kwa* beat
kama hii **iki-pump** kwa **ma-streets** za Nai
robbery town **tuki-represent** *washe*
na wadhii wanaojiunga nami
juu hii sound *ya* Ukoo Flani *na mi* N̲azizi
toka Mau Mau *wapate uhuru sa* **tuko-free**
ku-rock ma-crowds so *wanacheza nasi*
hawawezi kataa instead **wana-agree**
that we the *illest*★ *kwa hii* crowd *ya wasanii*
that's why *tunachaguliwa na* **ma-teen-ie**

Transcription code: *italics*—Swahili; **bold**—code-mixed Swahili and English morphemes; Roman—English, ★AAL lexicon

The morpheme ★illest in the excerpt above is lexicon borrowed from AAL. AAL, which is a distinct linguistic system with its own lexicon, grammar, and phonological patterns of usage, has been crossing into Kenyan hiphop. This can be attributed to the influence of African American hiphop on Kenyan hiphop, and to the globalization of hiphop and hiphop nation language.

In addition, AAL syntactical features are prevalent in Kenyan hiphop. In the song *Bamba* by Esir, K-rupt, and Big Pin (2001, Track 3), the artists use the habitual "be" when they rap "we be partying." Similarly, Ukoo Flani Mau Mau's lyrics are strewn with zero copula syntactical forms. For example, in *All Over the World* (2004, Track 6), they rap, "we rolling," while in *Burn Dem* (2008, Track 2), they rap, "we still livin this ghetto life." The reduction of the final consonant sound to a single sound so that a word like "living" becomes "livin" is also prevalent in Kenyan hiphop, and is consistent with AAL grammar.

The harmonious incorporation of AAL syntactical forms within English, Kiswahili, and Kenyan indigenous languages grammar(s) is a translanguaging practice. Ludi (2003) explains this process where "rules and norms are activated that overlap single languages and govern the harmonic, i.e. the 'grammatical' mixing of elements from different languages" (as cited in Garcia 2008, p. 46). Such a practice allows the artists to mesh more than two languages with distinct syntactic systems in their lyrics; a testament of how two or more languages can be accommodated within the bounds of a single text (Canagarajah, 2006).

In conclusion, the use of multiple languages in Kenyan hiphop shows the artists' freedom and agency to use all the languages in their repertoire to compose their music. Such a practice is consistent with Kellman's (2000) argument that " translinguals move beyond their native languages … theirs is an aspiration to transcend language in general, to be pandictic, to utter everything"(p. 16). On another level, translanguaging is also a way for the artists to index their postcolonial identities. Omoniyi (2009) identifies a number of identities that African rappers have to negotiate through their choice of language in composing their music: nationality, religion, ethnicity, home versus diasporic and global relations and connections, and collaborations with "global" or U.S. rappers. Omoniyi sees one function of switching between languages by the rappers is to "produce appropriate alignments, stances or positionings in relation to any of these identities" (p. 130). Translanguaging thus allows the artists to index their membership in different discourse communities: local, regional, diasporic, global, and hiphop nation.

Towards a Translingual Hiphop Pedagogy

A pedagogy inspired by hiphop would be guided but not limited to the following objectives: (1) To expose students to other cultures, languages and Englishes; (2) to explore the affordances of multilingual composing; and (3) to develop in students a metalinguistic awareness through critical and a rhetorical analysis of multilingual hiphop texts. Teachers would need to provide their students with a brief overview of the historical, social, and cultural context of all the languages used. Like in any other class, the learning goals should be designed to equip students with the right values, attitudes, knowledge, and skills about the importance of language in their writing.

To facilitate a better understanding of the message in the music, a combination of print, audio, and visual elements of the lyrics is necessary. As Canagarajah (2011) observes, a translingual text has an expanded spatial dimension, which invites readers and participants to be sensitive to its visual and aesthetic elements. It is also multimodal and "performative" in the way it is read and understood. As such, it has an orientation different from a text produced in the autonomous literacy model (p. 19). Playing hiphop music videos, along with print texts of the lyrics gives the students an opportunity to interact and engage creatively with the text.

Next, the teacher can have students undertake small group discussions, which can be guided by a number of activities where students:

- Identify English lexemes and syntactical forms that are mixed with other languages or that may seem idiosyncratic. Have them discuss how the mixing affects the "grammar" of languages involved or how it contradicts conventional orthography and pronunciation.
- Discuss possible reasons why artists may be using several languages in writing their lyrics. Think about purpose and audience and how these may influence an artist's choice of a particular language(s).
- Do a rhetorical and critical analysis of the hiphop lyrics to identify the different linguistic strategies employed, such as code-mixing, code-switching, linguistic borrowing/crossing, and inventiveness. Discuss the opportunities it offers the artists.
- Discuss and share the possible genres or contexts in which the students do multilingual composing, either consciously or unconsciously.

In this pedagogy, the teacher's roles are the following:

- to facilitate a dialogue where the entire class shares and reflects on activities arising from the small group discussions
- to have students attempt a multilingual composition or write in a language other than their primary one.

Implications

A rhetorical or critical analysis of why, when, and how hiphop artists use multiple languages in their compositions helps students develop a metalinguistic awareness through an understanding that language is not a "static thing" but is a process and a system with the potential to be manipulated to achieve rhetorical ends. In addition, having students interrogate what is "(un)grammatical" about some words or having them make sense of the idiosyncratic syntactical forms in the lyrics helps tease out their awareness of other Englishes.

A focus on examining what may seem to be grammar and usage errors allows students to critically analyze the creative, critical, and ideological role of grammar. The teacher should facilitate a discussion to help students critically explore whether "errors" are indeed grammar errors, or whether they are related to another language or hiphop genre. This is an opportunity to begin questioning the notions of what constitutes Standard English and whom it serves. Students' recognition of the artists' agency to manipulate language helps them realize they too have agency to use language creatively and purposefully and for a range of reasons and in a variety of contexts.

Hiphop exposes students not only to languages and cultures in local communities, but also to a number of world Englishes, such as AAL and Sheng/Kenyan English. Students get an opportunity to discuss issues related to the evolution, variation, and fluidity of the English language. This is also an opportunity to learn the historical and social–cultural context of the languages. A study of the Englishes used in Kenyan hiphop, for example, gives the teacher an opportunity to help students explore the historical, racial and cultural relationship between Africans (Kenyans), Jamaicans, and African Americans. Students and teachers get an opportunity to learn something about the communities/cultures where these languages spring up.

In addition, examining the discrepancy or contradiction in orthography (what is written in the text), and how it is pronounced in the video is intended to shatter the assumption made by teachers and students alike that English is a phonetically regular language (Delpit, 1996, p. 61). Teachers and students become sensitive to varied pronunciations of particular English forms. Such sensitivity works in reversing the negative attitudes that students and teachers harbor about other people's languages and Englishes.

It is my hope that one big take away from this discussion would be that instructors can begin to view global cipha as a site where they can explore and theorize more pedagogies for teaching language diversity. A translingual hiphop pedagogy, as shown in this discussion, resists linguistic imperialism and calls for a pluralism in all composing. It also allows multiple languages and stylistic types of both "standard" and "non-standard" to mesh in a creative, critical, and productive way.

References

Abdulaziz, M., & Osinde, K. (1997). Sheng and Engsh: Development of mixed codes among the urban youth in Kenya. *International Journal of the Sociology of Language, 125*, 43–64.

Bokamba, E. G. (1998). Codemixing, language variation, and linguistic theory: Evidence from Bantu languages. *Lingua, 76*(1), 21–62.

Canagarajah, A. S. (2006). The place of world Englishes: Pluralization continued. *College Composition and Communication, 57*(4), 586–619.

Canagarajah, A. S. (2011). Translanguaging in the classroom: Emerging issues for research and pedagogy. *Applied Linguistics Review, 2*, 1–27. doi:10.1515/9783110239331.1.

Delpit, L. (1995). *Other people's children: Cultural conflict in the classroom.* New York, NY: New Press.

Esir, K-rupt, & Big Pin. (2001). Bamba. *Nimefika.* Nairobi, Kenya: Ogopa DJs.

García, O. (2008). *Bilingual education in the 21st century: A global perspective.* Malden, MA: Wiley-Blackwell.

Gidi Gidi Maji Maji. (2002). Who can bwogo me? *Unbwogable.* Nairobi, Kenya: Blue Zebra Records.

Githinji, P. (2006). Sheng and variation: The construction and negotiation of multiple identities. (Unpublished doctoral dissertation). Michigan State University, East Lansing, MI.

Githiora, C. (2002). Sheng: Peer language, Swahili dialect or emerging Creole. *Journal of African Cultural Studies, 15*(2), 159–181. doi:10.1080/1369681022000042637.

Ibrahim, A. (2009). Takin hip hop to a whole nother level. In S. Alim, A, Ibrahim, & A. Pennycook (Eds.), *Global linguistics flows: Hip hop cultures, youth identities, and the politics of language* (pp. 239–348). New York, NY: Routledge.

Kellman, S. G. (2000). *The translingual imagination.* Lincoln, NE: University of Nebraska Press.

Lunsford, A. (2009). Towards a mestiza rhetoric: Gloria Anzaldúa on composition and postcoloniality. In S. Miller (Ed.), *The Norton book of composition studies* (pp. 1401–1428). New York, NY: Norton.

Momanyi, C. (2009). The effects of "Sheng" in the teaching of Kiswahili in Kenyan schools. *The Journal of Pan African Studies, 2*(8), 127–138.

Nyairo, J. & Ogunde, J. (2005). Popular music, popular politics: *Unbwogable* and the idioms of freedom in Kenyan popular music. *African Affairs, 104*, 225–245. doi:10.1093/afraf/adi012.

Ogechi, N. (2005). On lexicalization in Sheng. *Nordic Journal of African Studies, 14*(3), 334–355.

Omoniyi, T. (2009). So I choose to do am Naija style: Hiphop, language, and postcolonial identities. In S. Alim, A. Ibrahim, & A. Pennycook (Eds.), *Global linguistic flows: Hiphop culture, youth identities and the politics of language* (pp. 113–135). New York, NY: Routledge.

Richardson, E. B. (2006). *Hiphop literacies.* New York, NY: Routledge.

Spyropoulos, M. (1987). Sheng: Some preliminary investigations into a recently emerged Nairobi street language. *Journal of the Anthropological Society of Oxford, 18*(1), 125–136.

Ukoo Flani & Nazizi. (2008). Hiphop halisi. *Kaya hiphop.* Mombasa, Kenya: Basetown Records and Headbangaz Entertainment.

Ukoo Flani Mau Mau. (2004). All over the world. *Kilio cha haki.* Nairobi, Kenya: UpToYouToo.

Ukoo Flani Mau Mau. (2008). Burn dem. *Kaya hiphop.* Mombasa, Kenya: Basetown Records and Headbangaz Entertainment.

PART III
Code-Meshing Orientations

valorizing vs legitimizing

Nelson-Whyte + Young

Issues when

= People use terms imprecisely + don't really
immerse themselves in the scholarship
they claim to be relying on

- Students are viewed as passive
recipients of these philosophies &
approaches. Need to collaborate w/
students

11

PEDAGOGICAL AND SOCIO-POLITICAL IMPLICATIONS OF CODE-MESHING IN CLASSROOMS: SOME CONSIDERATIONS FOR A TRANSLINGUAL ORIENTATION TO WRITING

Vivette Milson-Whyte

The current focus on language by some U.S. rhetoric and composition scholars is a refreshing turn for educator-researchers for whom proposals such as code-meshing and translingualism represent a lived reality. As a Jamaican educator-researcher who has lived and studied in the United States of America, I consider code-meshing as one instantiation of a translingual approach to writing—even though proposals for code-meshing preceded an elaboration of translingualism. In this chapter, I raise three concerns about these proposals: problems regarding valorizing, yet not legitimizing, minoritized languages; problems arising from language users' inability to code-switch effectively; and the potential for ignoring sameness and difference while attempting to address difference in language use, with *naturalized* double consciousness and *transferred* mainstreamers being among categories/groupings that are ignored/erased. I begin by presenting an aspect of the background to linguistic behavior in postcolonial societies (especially in the Americas), and then I outline the proposals for code-meshing and translingualism and list their potential benefits to lead into an elaboration of their implications for Jamaican (and other American) students in U.S. classrooms. I examine a code-meshed artifact from Jamaica to illustrate the concerns, most of which relate to code-meshing but which present important considerations for a translingual orientation to writing in any multilingual context.

Languaging in Postcolonial Societies

Postcolonial societies have been marked by linguistic chauvinism—the belief in the superiority of one's language, especially in the case of a standard language such as English—and linguistic imperialism—the imposition of one language (such as

English) as dominant over another or others (see Skutnabb-Kangas, 2002), often with the selected official dialect, the standard, being considered as linguistic capital (see Bourdieu, 1991), and being promoted/treated as *Language* rather than as *a language*. Given this erroneous association of the standard with *Language* and not just *a language*, other dialects (and other standards) are simultaneously rendered peripheral or minoritized—as are their users. Arising from these divisions and treatments of language varieties have been considerations of languages in contact as systems that are either discrete or integrated, with these considerations suggesting whether or not the contact languages are compatible.

The more blurred the boundaries between language varieties in a setting, the more compatible the languages are thought to be. This blurriness/fuzziness is perhaps most evident where standard and non-standard languages that share some feature such as lexis co-exist—as in a situation such as the United States with African American Vernacular English and Standard American English (SAE), or Jamaica where Jamaican Creole (JC) and Standard English (SE) share vocabulary. Some policy-makers and educators consider this blurriness a hindrance to standard language and literacy development; however, for others the students' repertoire of languages is on a continuum and the languages operate as resources rather than hindrances to language development in general.

Where a continuum exists or is accepted, and even where the languages are distinct (i.e., not sharing any linguistic feature), speakers' linguistic behavior is marked heavily by code-switching (movement back and forth between codes), code-shifting (movement from one code to another and remaining in the latter during interaction), code-mixing (blending codes in varying degrees), and so on (see Isaacs, 2006, for some definitions). These linguistic moves are sometimes motivated by social dictates; by ignorance; by desires to make one language contest or complement the other, or to signal social or cultural affiliation, or to show dexterity in switching, or to achieve other specific purposes; or for no apparent reason but the fact that more than one code is available to speakers.

Strategy Proposed for Languaging in U.S. Classrooms: Code-Meshing

Considering the fuzziness that can manifest where a continuum is acknowledged, and considering the underachievement in African Americans who are told to code-switch (in the sense of style shifting), Young (2007) proposes that teachers should allow students to write as they speak in everyday situations; that is, to code-mesh. For Young, what he calls Black English Vernacular (BEV) and White English Vernacular (WEV) are not all that different. Eschewing the binaristic logic that often attends discussions about the two varieties, Young opines that the differences between WEV and BEV are exaggerated, resulting in pedagogies that yield limited numbers of African Americans who master the standard language (p. 134). To address this problem, Young proposes that educators allow African American students to use "a thorough, seamless mixture" (p. 106) of their vernacular and the standard—as happens in everyday language use. The benefits, he believes, would "extend beyond producing better papers" and have an affective value because teachers would stop considering students' "linguistic habits as subliterate, fundamentally incompatible with what's considered standard" (p. 106). Young demonstrates that African American students rarely use only one dialect; instead, they operate in fluid ways, mingling and blending BEV and WEV. Young does not consider such comingling to be erroneous. He proposes that should African American students be allowed to engage in a similar blending of codes in classrooms, such students would feel that they and their language habits are validated and would probably engage more with school and realize increased literacy levels.

Canagarajah (2006), drawing on both the complementary and contestable relations among languages in his culture, proposes that students in the United States be allowed to include their non-standard dialects and other Englishes in the standard code. In Canagarajah's (2009) cultural tradition, writers have used languages to contest each other, thereby "elevat[ing] the respectability of the vernacular and democratiz[ing] the elite language]" (p. 27). However, because of the highly multilingual nature of his and other such societies, languages are often complementary. Canagarajah (2006) has also observed the tendency among some of his African American and World Englishes-speaking students to refuse (or be unable) to edit out their dialects and languages from materials in SAE (p. 597). For him, these inclusions are fruitful rather than distracting. Based on his experiences and observations, Canagarajah views code-meshing as a way to acknowledge all of the linguistic resources of multilingual students, and wishes other educators would acknowledge same.

Philosophy Proposed to Guide Languaging in U.S. Classrooms: Translingualism

Proposals for code-meshing preceded the definition of an overarching philosophy for languaging in U.S. classrooms proposed by Horner, Lu, Royster, and Trimbur (2011). Beyond addressing African Americans or speakers of World Englishes, Horner et al. consider all language users for whom a translingual approach would be useful in this age. In this orientation, "approach" is stressed rather than any fixed form. A review of this approach bears representing in the co-authors' words.

"This approach," the authors say, "sees difference in language not as a barrier to overcome or as a problem to manage, but as a resource for producing meaning in writing, speaking, reading, and listening" (Horner et al., 2011, p. 303). It "treats standardized rules as historical codifications of language that inevitably change through dynamic processes of use," and it "proclaims that writers can, do, and must negotiate standardized rules in light of the contexts of specific instances of writing" (p. 305). This approach accepts and emphasizes "the inevitability and necessity of interaction among languages, within languages, and across language practices" (p. 307). Horner et al. (2011) conclude that "translingualism teaches language users to assume and expect that each new instance of language use brings the need and opportunity to develop new ways of using language, and to draw on a range of language resources" (p. 312).

Potential Benefits of Code-Meshing as Strategy and of Translingualism as Philosophy

Given the facts of increasing migration and late globalization, and the attendant contact of languages and cultures, and reshaping of literacy practices to address these developments, as well as the glaring underachievement of significant numbers of students from certain social groups, proposals for code-meshing and translingualism are welcome. Indeed, as a Jamaican educator-researcher with similar concerns to Young (2007) about the underachievement of students from certain socio-economic backgrounds, and considering the ways that languages, cultures, and peoples will continue to intersect thanks to continued migration and technoglobalism, I am fascinated by these proposals. Where code-meshing is concerned, I can envisage the intertwined socio-political, psychological, and pedagogical benefits of helping to valorize minoritized languages, counter linguistic prejudices, and therefore subvert the hegemony of standardized languages. Code-meshing could also help students develop cognitive fluency and increase their engagement with learning (see Milson-Whyte, 2011). A translingual approach, as a philosophy on languaging, could prove useful for both educator and student—foregrounding student writers' agency, allowing for discussion and negotiations of what is written, and increasing learning for both parties.

Concerns Regarding Code-Meshing and Translingualism

However, how these proposals are to be realized amongst specific linguistic and cultural groups could be problematic. Indeed, these proposals evoke some serious concerns with regard to Jamaican (and other *American*) students in U.S. classrooms. (Here, I dare to use the term "American" loosely to include North American, Central American, Caribbean, and South American.) What are these concerns? First, there are problems with valorizing, yet not legitimizing, minoritized languages; second, there are/can be problems arising from a lack of adequate knowledge about "the rhetorical strategies of switching" (Canagarajah, 2006, p. 602); and, third, there is the potential for ignoring sameness and difference while attempting to address difference in language use.

With regard to the first concern, proposals for including other codes/varieties in classrooms where standard English is required usually mention the benefits of valorizing minoritized students' languages simultaneous with developing students' writing in English (see Bean et al., 2003; Elbow, 1999). However, I suspect that educators could help minoritized students address the two-fold goal of making meaning and communicating that meaning not simply by valorizing

Varieties of Latin American Spanish!

How to do this? "legitimacy" in what sense?

language varieties, but also by helping to establish their legitimacy. Indeed, I find
that code-meshing and/or a translingual approach may be problematic with specific regard to Jamaican Creole (JC). (Of course, problems could arise too with
regard to some standards, such as Spanish, when the language is tied to a country
such as Mexico rather than to Spain.) The need to first establish the legitimacy of
this non-standard language (JC) seems critical so that, when students include JC
items in standardized English, students will understand the terms as such and be
able to interrogate the power structures attending such items as well as those in
English. What are the reasons?

with students w/in the class? In the institution? Socially?

One reason is that JC is a contact language that is stigmatized. Formed in the
crucible of the plantation from the contact between European, African, and indigenous Caribbean languages, the Creole language epitomizes transculturation (see
Pratt, 1991). With English providing the lexis for Creole and this shared base rendering both languages similar, JC has been denigrated for centuries (see Milson-
Whyte, 2006). Creole-speaking Jamaicans have internalized the stigma attached
to the Creole, developing a contradictory attitude to SE and to JC—what Kachru
and Nelson (2001) call "attitudinal schizophrenia" (p. 15). In this kind of situation, people consider the languages as distinct, in that speakers associate JC with
their culture and identity and want it kept separate from SE for educational purposes because they feel it could prevent them from learning SE (in much the same
way that some Spanish-speaking parents in the United States react to bilingual
programs when these parents' main concern is for their children to learn English).
At the same time, these JC speakers self-identify as English speakers, feeling that
they know a range of Englishes and produce SE (see Nero, 1997, 2006).

complaint w/ multi-cult. approches generally?

Another reason is that Jamaica's linguistic context defies facile descriptions. There
is lack of agreement among Creole linguists regarding the specific linguistic model
that obtains in the Jamaican language situation because of very complex variability
in the country. For a long time, Jamaica has been described as diglossic, since there
are "two separate language varieties, each with its own specific functions within the
society" (Devonish, 1986, p. 9)—for example, JC for informal situations and SE for
official business. However, linguists also speak of a continuum ranging from basi-
lectal Creole (varieties most removed from English and associated with rural areas),
through mesolectal Creole (spoken in urban areas), to acrolectal English (varieties
closest to the standard and associated with educated speakers). Devonish explains
that "because of the similarity of the vocabulary of Creole and English, there has
been a tendency … to develop a series of language varieties in between the most
Creole varieties of language on the one hand, and the most standard varieties of
English, on the other" (p. 115). The term "Creole continuum" is, therefore, used
to refer to the range of varieties between the Creole base and standard English.

No simple "JC" exists

The use of the term *continuum* is, however, as problematic as the determination
of the boundary between Creole and English. Craig (2006) notes that English
Creole, varieties that constitute the mesolect, and Standard English are "more
distinguishable in theory than in reality" (p. 108). Observing changes in the use of

official and non-standard languages, another Caribbean linguist Robertson (1996) maintains that the Creole and standard languages in the Caribbean are not really in a "complementary or diglossic relationship" (p. 113). Kachru (1992) aptly summarized the complexity in Jamaica when he acknowledged that "countries such as South Africa or Jamaica are difficult to place within the concentric circles. In terms of the English-using populations and the functions of English, their situations are rather complex" (p. 362).

Compounding this complexity is the fact that JC is largely oral and students are not literate in it. In this situation, Jamaicans are taught English as a first language—on the basis that the two languages are (lexically) similar. The result has been widespread problems: The close lexical similarity between JC and SE often poses problems for students whose receptive skills are higher than their productive skills, and these high receptive skills sometimes cause students to leave intact in writing Creole expressions that look/sound like English (see Craig, 1999; Nero, 2006).

Given these reasons, students need to be able to distinguish JC from SE if they are to understand when they are code-meshing—in terms of actually blending two different varieties. However, for this to be done on a large scale, the country and the speakers themselves need to recognize the legitimacy of JC. Although there is increasing valorization of JC, Jamaicans are still a far way from legitimizing it for more than passing/peripheral use in official circumstances—and legitimizing is crucial to linguistic and other forms of development. As Winford (1994) writes, "there is growing consensus among Caribbeanists that recognition of the autonomy of Creole vernaculars as distinct systems from the lexically related official languages is a prerequisite to addressing practical concerns such as reform of educational policy, improvement of literacy, and the instrumentalization of Creole in wider areas of public life" (p. 58).

The second concern speaks to a related problem regarding speakers' inability to switch smoothly from one language to the next. This is the situation for weaker writers who are not able to distinguish between JC and SE. They tend to mix languages but in ways that might not be effective—in terms of readily communicating a message to an English-speaking audience. Rather than code-switch, these students may code-shift to Creole (see Craig, 1999, p. 42). Those Jamaican students who would be classified as weaker writers lack metalinguistic awareness of their languages and tend to produce *knotty* writing in English—of the kind described by Irvine and Elsasser (1988) elsewhere in the Caribbean. Nero (1997) provides various accounts of a lack of metalinguistic awareness among Caribbean students and their resultant written products in U.S. classrooms.

This lack of metalinguistic awareness sometimes leads to mixes such as "Is English we speaking" (Morris, 1999, p. 1) or "a hinglish mi a taak" (Pollard, 1998, p. 10). Code-mixing of this kind is facilitated in Jamaica because of the close lexical relationship between Creole and English. As Jamaican educator Pollard says, "The close lexical relationship serves to camouflage the differences of phonology, grammar and idiom" (p. 10). Code-mixing is often confusing to the English speaker, but the "mixer" (who is often a predominantly Creole speaker) is usually unaware of the "mix" and unaware that the "mix" is not English.

The two examples, in which the interlocutor is declaring that he or she is speaking [in] English, raise questions about the nature/proportion of blends in a classroom situation. Young (2009) recommends that the standard would remain dominant but be inflected by students' natural speech habits. In recommending the inclusion of other codes in SAE, Canagarajah (2006) indicates that code-meshing involves the "qualified use of alternate codes into the dominant discourse" (p. 599). However, I wonder about the extent to which that proportion reflects what happens in everyday situations. If the mesh is "studied" in a hybrid composition, to what extent is it reflecting *lived reality*? And if it is natural, could it be seen to be reflecting ignorance of one of the codes?

Why does this matter? Young (2009) says that standard principles of communication still obtain in code-meshed writing (pp. 64–65). Canagarajah (2009) indicates that code-meshing is *work*. For those unfamiliar with the intricacies of code-meshing, it may seem like *too much work*. Canagarajah writes that "what enables multilinguals to communicate across difference is that they instantaneously construct the norms and conventions that will operate during their conversation" (p. 18). He also explains that multilinguals "don't depend on language as a preconstructed system that comes ready-made with forms and meanings. For them meanings and grammars are always emergent" (p. 18). The ahistorical nature of such language use suggests a need to be constantly constructing the norms of conversation. Indeed, Canagarajah's (2006) conclusions indicate the need for deliberate, focused, skilful languaging. He tells readers, "Code meshing calls for multidialectalism not monodialectalism. … [Multilingual students] have to not only master the dominant varieties of English, but also know how to bring in their preferred varieties in rhetorically strategic ways" (p. 598). These efforts are necessary because "code meshing is a complex discursive act for our students (one that involves a polydialectal competence—i.e., familiarity with standard varieties, expert use of local variants, and the rhetorical strategies of switching)" (p. 602). Horner et al. (2011) summarize the challenges when they say that a translingual approach to writing requires "*more*, not less*," from student writers (and educators) in terms of attention to style, register, syntax, and so on (p. 304). It appears then that the intellectual work and conscious languaging attending these proposals could so strain weaker JC students that what they produce could look like the two unacceptable examples given earlier.

The third concern, and perhaps what bothers me the most about proposals for code-meshing and translingual writing, is the potential for ignoring sameness and difference while attempting to address difference, with *naturalized* double consciousness and *transferred* mainstreamers being among the ignored. What do I mean? Teachers have to be prepared to have students decline invitations to code-mesh or disregard translingualism because these students live/operate in situations where languages are still treated as discrete systems. Jamaicans who are adept at code-switching/shifting may have adopted what Villanueva (1993) calls a posture of "racelessness" (p. 39)—as practiced by some minority groups in the United States in their attempts to take on mainstream language and culture. Alternatively, they may lead what Young (2007), drawing on DuBois, calls a *life* of double consciousness (p. 128) but that I call *naturalized* double consciousness. In the former situation (more aptly *classlessness* in Jamaica), students may neglect Jamaican language and culture (Creole) to adopt the dominant language and culture (English). Young (2007) criticizes the latter phenomenon which, I imagine, he would consider an unfortunate reality for many West Indians who use both standard and Creole languages. For individuals who are fluent in these different codes, their different language varieties serve mutually exclusive functions—the one/some for speaking and private affairs, the other(s) for reading and writing. Indeed, double consciousness is the reality for many Jamaicans who reserve Creole for informal situations and English for formal affairs such as reading and writing. Operating thus, these Jamaicans think only in English if they are to speak or write for formal purposes. It is as if they operate an on/off language switch (pace Lu, 2009). So, Yes! I code-mesh when speaking, but as I prepare to write anything, my thoughts shift to English—as I perceive it.

Young (2007) would probably say these Jamaicans (and other Caribbeaners) are performing a problem. He writes that "because the obligation to perform is required and so pervasive, it has become a part of common sense when it shouldn't be. Even those who are most burdened are inclined to accept it" (pp. 130–131). For Young, then, Jamaicans who unquestioningly lead a life of double consciousness are "performing the problem" (p. 131). However, these *doubly conscious* Jamaicans (who would probably prefer to be considered as having *double vision* in Bhabha's (1994) terms) are high achievers who can use codes with dexterity and who, like Canagarajah (2006), can, and do, edit out non-standard or other standards' features from their English writing.

Current proposals do not adequately address individuals who manifest these postures. On one level, these students are often ignored in discussions in the United States about foreign/international students because of the tendency to promote homogeneity—so all international students are simultaneously *different* from U.S. students and *the same* in being grouped as *all ESL*, and need to be taught separate from L1 (English Only) composition students (see critiques of these categories in Matsuda, 2006). What we forget sometimes, it seems, is that *mainstream* (in terms of *class* and not *race*) transfers from one country to another. So when we address mainstream U.S. students, we ought to consider what I call the *transferred mainstreamers* who are expert standard language users from another country and studying in the United States. Transferred mainstream students often do not wish to change the *status quo* in any way, and, in the case of Jamaica, help to maintain the unequal relationship between Creole and English. When these students are sent into special English as a Second Language (ESL) classes, they may escape necessary discussions about language and power and respect for the legitimacy of all languages. On another level, these transferred mainstream students evoke concern *code-meshing to threatens to & familiar ge" + "normalize" linguistic difference?*

about how a translingual approach harbors the potential for eliminating difference when it helps mainstream U.S. students. I wonder about this danger in light of the ways in which standard languages can seem to gobble up others (see similar concerns expressed by Rogers, 2009). Mainstream students, invited to engage in blending styles and codes, may not value the difference in minoritized varieties: once blended into the dominant code, minoritized varieties—previously considered as different, albeit subordinate—can be virtually forgotten.

The other aspect of sameness and difference that I fear could get overlooked has to do with the specific linguistic and cultural groups the proposals are meant to assist the most. So, I'm wondering—if Alleyne (1980) and other linguists are right that the African American situation is parallel to that of Creole-speaking communities and the "distinctiveness" of the two varieties (BEV and WEV) is "an historical and structural fact" (p. 4)—could African Americans benefit from development of metalinguistic awareness of their vernacular in terms of what it is, what its features are, how it differs from other language varieties? That is, if Young (2009) continues to make the argument that the two language varieties are not all that different, could that hinder rather than promote African American students' development? Could an outsider ask, "If the varieties are not that different, why then can the students not produce the standard dialect?"

Translingualism Through Code-Meshing at Work

As stated, code-meshing and other manifestations of translingualism require intellectual work. If JC-speaking students are allowed to code-mesh, then educators have to be prepared for the serious, deliberate, even painful, negotiation that Horner et al. (2011) propose. I demonstrate this through a property sign that was captured by Jamaican photographer Ray Chen and has been popularized on a Jamaican souvenir key ring (Figure 11.1). The artefact bears words that appear part of standard English but have a different resonance in the specific context.

FIGURE 11.1   Code-meshing in a property sign

This is a typical "no trespassing" sign (with the owner's signature expressed as an abbreviation of "the proprietor"). The details provided explain the nature of the problem: Various animals (which the average English speaker will recognize) have been walking in/on/through the property. This seems to be the reason for the details in "Dont Walk Here," with the sign writer either deliberately or unconsciously omitting the apostrophe in "don't." To (over)emphasize the seriousness of the interdiction, the writer includes the Jamaican expletive "a rasscloth." In a word, this expletive could convey the sense of "absolutely" as in "Absolutely no trespassing." However, that specific expletive as spelt here (to rhyme with say "crass" rather than with say "pass") indexes identity. Spelt thus, it seems to be referring to a Rastafarian, with the implication being that either the property owner or the owner of the animals is of that orientation.

If the spelling of the expletive is a genuine error, the explanation could be that neither property nor animal owner is Rastafarian and the sign writer/property owner is simply livid. This latter explanation would be consistent with the use of the expletive, which often suggests that plain terms have failed the user but here conveys multiple realities. One of these realities is the use of JC merely for cursing—because it is not legitimized to be used for other purposes. The anger would explain why the property owner would seem to have directed a sign to animals that cannot read, but seem to have included humans in "other animals."

The sign also reveals how an expert language user (a mainstreamer) can manipulate language. The sign writer conceals various threats in the word "Notice" and in the artifact. Readers are likely to feel that they know English terms such as "walk" but may not realize that the sign writer is also using it to mean "graze." Rather than detect the seriousness in the warning, readers may experience alienation on encountering the expletive that mentions the term "cloth" (as do the other main Jamaican expletives) but is not self-explanatory. Other terms may puzzle readers. That the words "and" and "will be" are minimized and underlined is probably an indication that shooting has already taken place: animals have been shot in the past and will be shot in the future. "Pound," as used, is highly ambiguous. Nothing indicates if the animals have been or will be sent to the public pound or impounded on the property or pounded (as in struck or crushed by beating). As used, "pound" seems to suggest blows will be inflicted on the animals; however, it could be that the author has simply abbreviated the local "go a pound" (meaning "sent to the pound"), or, worse, the abbreviation could mean stray animals will become the property owner's property. The ambiguity inherent in the warning suggests that the writer/property owner is an expert language user who has found ways to manipulate local language varieties and render unfamiliar the familiar or vice versa.

Readers can imagine that far more can be deduced from this short notice which blends English and Jamaican Creole, even though they may not be able to determine if the language user acknowledges the power of all of the attendant language varieties in the blended text. Readers may even be concerned about untranslatable terms or culture-specific inclusions in writing that require much negotiation for interpretation. As stated, JC students, allowed to code-mesh, may include in writing *English words* that carry *JC meanings*. They may also include untranslatable and/or ambiguous terms requiring much negotiation. In a context in which apparently English words have a different indexicality, attempts to decipher them could cause some readers to feel alienated.

Given the negotiation required, I imagine Muchiri, Mulamba, Myers, and Ndoloi (1995) and their other African colleagues saying, "These colleagues in the United States have a vastly different conception of time than colleagues in the rest of the world. All of this time to deliberate over and negotiate differences in writing? Where do they find that time? Who pays for it?" Even if U.S. colleagues have the time and other resources for that kind of deliberation/negotiation, I imagine individual Jamaican students in U.S. classrooms saying, "This program requires four years for completion. I can spare only two, at most three. As colorful as I may know JC elements could make my academic writing, I really don't have the time and means to try to think in JC for academic purposes and then explain any JC elements in writing to a teacher or peers who may speak only one language." These imagined statements are preoccupations shared by other multilingual students such as those about whom Muchiri et al. write.

To Continue Languaging ...

I hasten to note that Young (2007) hints at limitations in code-meshing by acknowledging that it will not solve all of the problems that attend African Americans' education because the linguistic issues are entangled with various racial problems with a long history (p. 8). And Canagarajah (2009) admits that "though code meshing comes naturally/spontaneously to multilinguals, writing proficiency and rhetorical effectiveness are learnt practices. Code-meshing in writing can certainly be enhanced through sound teaching" (p. 44). He emphasizes the need for multilingual students to "be aware that some of their readers are not going to negotiate to the same extent and in the same manner as their fellow multilinguals do. ... They may also learn to build in more redundancy in their writing so that readers may recover meanings through multiple affordances" (p. 45). However, besides these problems to which Young (2007) and Canagarajah (2009) allude, there are those other concerns that I have raised about code-meshing in classrooms and translingualism as an overriding philosophy—efforts that valorize, yet not legitimize, minoritized languages; problems arising from inability to code-switch effectively; and the potential for ignoring sameness and difference while attempting to address difference in language use.

Readers in some areas in the Americas may ask why they/we should care about the illustrated Jamaican situation. I'd say the experience of Jamaican students is shared by many other communities with pidgins, creoles, or devalued dialects in and beyond the Americas. And, thanks to the airways and electronic highways, we are likely to meet each other in many global contact zones. How will we interact across our language boundaries to negotiate our differences? How will we interact with both the weak writers and expert language users we encounter in classrooms in the Americas and elsewhere? The concerns raised appear to be necessary considerations for recent proposals about languaging in translingual ways not only in U.S. writing classrooms but also in other contexts in which some students/groups are minoritized.

References

Alleyne, M. (1980). *Comparative Afro-American: An historical-comparative study of English-based Afro-American dialects of the new world*. Ann Arbor, MI: Karoma.

Bean, J., Eddy, R., Grego, R., Irvine, P., Kurtz, E., Matsuda, P. K., Cucchiara, M., Elbow, P., Haswell, R., Kennedy, E., & Lehner, A. (2003). Should we invite students to write in home languages? Complicating the yes/no debate. *Composition Studies, 31,* 25–42.

Bhabha, H. K. (1994). *The location of culture*. London: Routledge.

Bourdieu, P. (1991). *Language and symbolic power* (J. B. Thompson, Ed.; G. Raymond & M. Adamson, Trans.) Cambridge, MA: Harvard University Press.

Canagarajah, A. S. (2006). The place of world Englishes in composition: Pluralization continued. *College Composition and Communication, 57,* 586–619.

Canagarajah, A. S. (2009). Multilingual strategies of negotiating English: From conversation to writing. *JAC: A Journal of Composition Theory, 29*(1–2), 17–48.

Craig, D. (1999). *Teaching language and literacy: Policies and procedures for vernacular situations*. Georgetown, Guyana: Education and Development Services.

Craig, D. (2006). The use of the vernacular in West Indian education. In H. Simmons-McDonald & I. Robertson (Eds.), *Exploring the boundaries of Caribbean Creole languages* (pp. 99–117). Kingston, Jamaica: The University of the West Indies Press.

Devonish, H. (1986). *Language and liberation: Creole language politics in the Caribbean*. London, UK: Karia Press.

Elbow, P. (1999). Inviting the mother tongue: Beyond "mistake," "bad English," and "wrong language." *JAC: A Journal of Composition Theory, 19*(3), 359–388.

Horner, B., Lu, M. Z., Royster, J. J., & Trimbur, J. (2011). Opinion: Language difference in writing: Toward a translingual approach. *College English, 73,* 303–321.

Irvine, P., & Elsasser, N. (1988). The ecology of literacy: Negotiating writing standards in a Caribbean setting. In B. A. Rafoth & D. L. Rubin (Eds.), *The social construction of written communication* (pp. 304–320). Norwood, NJ: Ablex.

Isaacs, M. (2006). Asou down-there: Code-mixing in a bilingual community. In H. Simmons-McDonald & I. Robertson (Eds.), *Exploring the boundaries of Caribbean Creole languages* (pp. 211–229). Kingston, Jamaica: The University of the West Indies Press.

Kachru, B. B. (1992). Teaching world Englishes. In B. B. Kachru (Ed.), *The other tongue: English across cultures* (2nd ed.) (pp. 544–565). Urbana, IL: University of Illinois Press.

Kachru, B. B., & Nelson, C. (2001). World Englishes. In A. Burns & C. Coffin (Eds.), *Analysing English in a global context* (pp. 9–25). New York: Routledge.

Lu, M. Z. (2009). Metaphors matter: Transcultural literacy. *JAC: A Journal of Composition Theory, 29*(1–2), 285–293.

Matsuda, P. K. (2006). The myth of linguistic homogeneity in U.S. college composition. *College English, 68,* 637–651. doi:10.2307/25472180.

Milson-Whyte, V. (2006). A comparison of the structural composition of the auxiliary in Standard American English and in Jamaican Creole. *Arizona Working Papers in Second Language Acquisition and Teaching (SLAT)*, *13*, 93–116. Retrieved from http://slat.arizona.edu/sites/slat/files/page/awp13milsonwhyte.pdf (accessed 15 November 2012).

Milson-Whyte, V. (2011). Dialogism in Gina Valdés "English con Salsa": A poetic address on accommodating linguistic diversity through code meshing. In V. A. Young & A. Martinez (Eds.), *Code meshing as world English: Policy, pedagogy, performance* (pp. 143–167). Urbana, IL: NCTE.

Morris, M. (1999). *Is English we speaking and other essays*. Kingston, Jamaica: Ian Randle Publishers.

Muchiri, M., Mulamba, N. G., Myers, G., & Ndoloi, D. B. (1995). Importing composition: Teaching and researching academic writing beyond North America. *College Composition and Communication*, *46*, 175–198. doi:10.2307/358427.

Nero, S. J. (1997). English is my native language … or so I believe. *TESOL Quarterly*, *31*, 585–593. doi:10.2307/3587842.

Nero, S. J. (2006). Language, identity, and education of Caribbean English speakers. *World Englishes*, *25*, 501–511.

Pollard, V. (1998). Code switching and code mixing: Language in the Jamaican classroom. *Caribbean Journal of Education*, *20*(1), 9–20.

Pratt, M. L. (1991). Arts of the contact zone. *Profession*, *91*, 33–40.

Robertson, I. (1996). Language education policy (1): Towards a rational approach for Caribbean states. In P. Christie (Ed.), *Caribbean language issues: Old and new. Papers in honour of Mervyn Alleyne on the occasion of his sixtieth birthday* (pp. 112–119). Kingston, Jamaica: The University of the West Indies Press.

Rogers, S. L. (2009). On politics, praxis and "working" English in the real world. *JAC: A Journal of Composition Theory*, *29*(1–2), 276–280.

Skutnabb-Kangas, T. (2002). *Linguistic genocide in education or worldwide diversity and human rights?* Mahwah, NJ: Lawrence Erlbaum.

Villanueva, V. (1993). *Bootstraps: From an American academic of color*. Urbana, IL: NCTE.

Winford, D. (1994). Sociolinguistic approaches to language use in the Anglophone Caribbean. In M. Morgan (Ed.), *Language and the social construction of identity in Creole situations* (pp. 43–62). Los Angeles, CA: UCLA Center for Afro-American Studies.

Young, V. A. (2007). *Your average nigga: Performing race, literacy, and masculinity*. Detroit, MI: Wayne State University Press.

Young, V. A. (2009). "Nah, we straight": An argument against code switching. *JAC: A Journal of Composition Theory*, *29*(1–2), 49–76.

12

IT'S THE WILD WEST OUT THERE: A NEW LINGUISTIC FRONTIER IN U.S. COLLEGE COMPOSITION

Paul Kei Matsuda

In recent years, language issues have come to receive unprecedented attention in U.S. college composition. Articles on language-related topics appear regularly on the pages of prominent journals in the field, and the number of edited volumes is also on the rise (e.g., Horner, Lu, & Matsuda, 2010; Schroeder, Fox, & Bizzell, 2002; Smitherman & Villanueva, 2003; Young & Martinez, 2011). Many of the prestigious awards have been given to publications related to language issues, including the Richard Braddock Award (Canagarajah, 2006; Horner & Trimbur, 2002; Lu, 2004; Pedersen, 2010), Richard Ohmann Award (Matsuda, 2006; Romano, 2004), and CCCC Outstanding Book Award (Horner et al., 2010). At the annual meetings of the Conference on College Composition and Communication (CCCC), sessions related to language issues have regularly been elevated to the status of featured sessions. Several key independent conferences that do not normally focus on language issues—including the Thomas Watson Conference (2010) and the Penn State Rhetoric and Composition Conference (2011)—have also dedicated their conferences to themes related to language issues. Increasingly, these conferences and sessions on language issues are well attended both by established members of the field as well as by relative newcomers who are eager to learn about the latest developments and new opportunities for research and teaching. It seems as if U.S. college composition has discovered a new frontier.

I do not mean to suggest that language-related topics have not been discussed previously—far from it. In fact, there have been numerous attempts to address language issues throughout the relatively short history of U.S. college composition. Yet, the previous attempts at linguistic turns did not quite turn the field around; many of them have been rejected or ignored by the mainstream discourse of U.S. college composition for various reasons (Matsuda, 2012). How is the current iteration of the linguistic turn different from any other that came before? Addressing this question will be my task in this chapter.

The Struggle Away From Language Issues

The history of U.S. college composition through the 1980s can be characterized as a struggle to dissociate itself from language issues, marked by a series of attempts to integrate language issues immediately followed by strong oppositions. Connors (2000b) explained the decline of sentence pedagogy in terms of anti-formalism and anti-scientism that had become pervasive in the field by the 1980s. In my own work, I have argued that the general apathy toward language issues stems from the myth of linguistic homogeneity—the faulty assumption that students in the composition classrooms are always already proficient users of privileged varieties of English, and therefore they need no further attention to language issues thank you very much (Matsuda, 2006). The decline of interest in language issues is also a function of the disciplinary division of labor, where the sense of disciplinary identity limits the scope of professional activities (Matsuda, 1999). The disciplinary division continues to live strong; as a senior member of the field put it during a discussion session: "I am a compositionist, not a linguist."

Another important consideration is the increasing tendency to compartmentalize, which is one of the long-term consequences of professionalization. U.S. college composition in the early years was issue driven, highly interdisciplinary, and multimodal. The first-generation composition specialists were trained in various other disciplines, such as applied linguistics, communication, creative writing, education, linguistics, literary studies, psychology, and rhetoric. Although they brought different theoretical and methodological orientations, they came together to address a common concern—the teaching of composition—by forming a multimodal discipline (Lauer, 1984). The relationship among these diverse perspectives, however, has never been completely harmonious and, as the field grew, the competition among methodological camps became even keener (North, 1987). Furthermore, as U.S. college composition became highly specialized and began to establish a field of its own with a growing number of doctoral programs (Connors, 2000a), the professional literature grew exponentially, and the scope of the field also expanded well beyond the confines of first-year composition to include basic writing, writing across the curriculum, the writing center, professional and technical communication, writing in the disciplines, public discourses, and community literacy. As a result, it became increasingly difficult for newcomers—and even old timers—to stay abreast of all the developments.

It is under these circumstances that language issues have come to be dismissed as both too mundane and too technical at the same time, taking away time and energy from ostensibly more interesting and exciting questions. There are, of course, some notable exceptions who have carved out a niche market for themselves and continued to pursue language-related research and scholarship. Yet, language research in U.S. college composition, even when it did not encounter strong oppositions, has been largely regarded as a special interest. In the meantime, a generation of senior composition scholars who came into the field with a strong background in language studies either have "cut their losses and gone on" (Connors, 2000b, p. 122) or are retiring—if they have not retired already—from the profession (MacDonald, 2005, p. 619), leaving a huge void in the knowledge of language issues in U.S. college composition. It is in the context of this knowledge desert that the current iteration of linguistic turn is taking place.

The New Linguistic Frontier

Because the movement is so widespread, it is difficult to pinpoint a single exigency or to date the exact beginning of the current linguistic turn. The synergy that powers the current linguistic turn stems from multiple exigencies and multiple lines of research and scholarship. It was in part stimulated by the continued effort to address the issue of language diversity for linguistic minority students in the United States as well as second-language writers, including both resident and international students (e.g., Harklau, Losey, & Siegal, 1999; Matsuda, Cox, Jordan, & Ortmeier-Hooper, 2006; Severino, Guerra, & Butler, 1997; Roberge, Siegal, & Harklau, 2009). The renewed interest in Students' Right to Their Own Language (SRTOL) (Butler, M. A. & Committee on CCCC Language Statement, 1974) has also contributed to the development (e.g., Smitherman & Villanueva, 2003; Wible, 2007). Another impetus was the globalization of U.S. college composition (e.g., Donahue, 2009; Foster & Russell, 2002), which has made it undeniably clear that writing in the global context often entails language issues (Matsuda & Matsuda, 2011). Yet another, and arguably most important, development that contributed to the current interest in language issues was an intellectual movement to see languages not as discrete entities but as situated, dynamic, and negotiated—a movement that has shifted the attention from the simplistic and highly politicized (and racialized) binary between assimilation and segregation to aspects of language that seemed more complex and less mundane.

Circa 2000, Bizzell (1999, 2000) began publishing on the notion of "hybrid" or "mixed" forms of academic writing as a growing phenomenon both in student writing and published writing. Importantly, Bizzell argued that these new forms of academic writing were not lesser forms of writing but a necessity in order to perform intellectual work that would not be possible with traditional forms of academic discourse. The idea intrigued many and stimulated a featured panel on this topic at CCCC as well as the publication in 2002 of an edited collection, *ALT DIS: Alternative Discourses and the Academy* (Schroeder et al., 2002). Granted, the collection was exploratory in nature, and contributions to the book seemed to take the discussion in vastly different directions. Yet, the diverse perspectives represented in the collection proved to be helpful in articulating a wide range of issues surrounding the notion, which I attempted to synthesize in the concluding chapter.

Although *ALT DIS* was inspired at least in part by SRTOL, the discussion focused more on philosophical issues rather than issues of language, which was one of the reasons I was asked to write the final response chapter—from the perspective of someone who is deeply rooted in both writing studies and language studies. Upon reading my response chapter, Horner and Lu approached me about the possibility of collaborating on a series of projects to bring language issues to the forefront of U.S. college composition. The collaboration led to several featured sessions at CCCC, a special issue of *College English*, and an edited volume (Horner et al., 2010).

The current movement to integrate language issues into the mainstream discourse of U.S. college composition is a result of the confluence of these and other new and innovative language scholarship. This movement is distinct from its predecessors in a number of ways. One of the most important differences is that the current movement is not just being advocated by a small group of enthusiastic specialists who have a strong background in language studies. Rather, it seems to be engaging the entire field—both junior and senior members—including those who have primary intellectual interests and training in topics other than language issues. While some members will remain indifferent or even resist integrating language issues into their work, the field as a whole seems to be moving toward a better understanding of how language and writing intersect with various aspects of U.S. college composition.

Another important difference is that it is a proactive, rather than reactive, movement. Unlike many of the linguistic turns of the past, this movement is not a direct response to a single demographic change. This is not to suggest that the demographic changes have stabilized. On the contrary, the linguistic diversity continues to intensify as U.S. institutions of higher education, devastated by economic crises and having depleted local would-be student population, try to make ends meet by recruiting students from other countries—who would pay higher tuition and who would not qualify for student loans or most forms of financial aid. In fact, we are in the middle of another wave of demographic change with the influx of international students from China. While these changes are no doubt contributing factors, they could not be the main impetus because the current rise of interest in language issues seems to have started long before anyone had anticipated the drastic changes in the linguistic profile of college students we have been experiencing in the last few years.

What is probably the most significant difference, however, is that the current linguistic turn is motivated by a new research agenda situated in the intellectual context of U.S. college composition. That is, the issue of language differences is no longer seen as mundane drudgery that took time away from other useful pedagogical concerns or interesting intellectual pursuits; rather, it has joined the ranks of new intellectual undertakings worthy of attention from all U.S. college composition scholars. And since the topic opened up a new frontier in the knowledge desert, there are plenty of opportunities to stake a claim—even for those who have had little experience with language. The word is out: Go west and strike it rich.

Future Challenges: It's the Wild West Out There

One of the major problems of any popular movement is the tendency to despise the old and valorize the new—as was the case with the writing process movement and, more recently, the rise of post-process (Matsuda, 2003). Within the current language movement, it has become fashionable to critique the traditional diglossia between privileged varieties of English and other language varieties; the diglossia in the academy has become the villain to be replaced with the new hero: a translingual approach to writing, which is associated with various terms, including hybrid discourses, alternative discourses, world Englishes, code-meshing, translingual writing, and the like. These concepts are exciting to many because they suggest new possibilities for reimagining issues of language differences in U.S. college composition. At the same time, the exclusive focus on a single aspect of language issues can undermine the real need for some language learners to learn a new language (Matsuda, 2006) or the need for non-dominant languages to be validated or left alone (Lyons, 2010). A broader, more balanced framework for conceptualizing language is therefore needed.

While the enthusiasm for the new approach to language issues is necessary in order for the movement to take off and make an impact on the field as a whole, it also needs to be balanced with critical reflections in order for the movement to become sustainable. What concerns me about the current state of affairs is that the terms and concepts associated with the new linguistic turn have become so valorized that scholars are inhibited from critiquing these ideas lest they appear old fashioned or ideologically suspect. Furthermore, many members of the field seem eager to promote these valorized ideas in their scholarship and teaching that they often ask how these concepts can be used in their work without also considering whether, when, and why they should be used (Bean et al., 2003).

The tendency to valorize language differences is problematic also because it can end up feeding the naïve, feel-good liberalism—you are OK as long as you join everyone in valorizing these terms. Even worse, the hunt for novel examples of language differences can turn the whole discussion into a linguistic freak show. Language differences—or lack thereof—are not inherently good or bad; they just happen. While it is important to destigmatize language differences, valorizing those differences without substantive arguments makes the whole movement vulnerable to criticisms and could lead to its eventual dismissal. It seems that more reflexivity is called for as we continue to pursue these issues.

Another problem is related to the knowledge desert that resulted from the stigmatization of earlier discussions of language issues. As Connors (2000b) and MacDonald (2005) have pointed out, the historical struggle to integrate language issues has left a huge void in U.S. college composition, and the field has not developed a well-informed and socially shared theoretical framework for discussing language issues. In order to fill the knowledge gap, composition theorists have attempted to borrow key terms and concepts from other disciplinary contexts, and, in the process, sometimes create an incongruent representation of those terms and concepts (Matsuda & Jablonski, 2000). Delving into a new intellectual territory as we develop new ways of understanding and discussing language issues can, at least initially, create confusion because the availability of "knowledgeable" peers is limited, and the disciplinary dialectic—the process of peer evaluation that provides checks and balances—may not function properly.

Code-Switching or Code-Meshing? A Terminological Mishmash

A prime example of lawlessness in the linguistic frontier of U.S. college composition—and the wider community of English education—is the debate surrounding the terms *code-switching* and *code-meshing*. In addressing the issue of language diversity in U.S. K-6 schools, Wheeler and Swords (2004) used the term "codeswitching" (spelled as one word). With it, they made the age-old point that the language spoken by many African American students is not an imperfect attempt at using the dominant variety of English but a different "code," and that the students can "codeswitch" between the two varieties of English based on the situational context of communication—i.e., using the privileged variety of English in the classroom and using their own variety of English at home. To describe the co-existence of two separate codes, a more appropriate term would have been "diglossia" (Ferguson, 1959, p. 336). Ostensibly, they borrowed "a cluster of notions," including code-switching, from "applied linguistics" (p. 473); however, they did not specify which applied linguists they were borrowing from, nor did they acknowledge that most applied linguistics would not use the term as they did. (For an insightful review of the history of the term code-switching and its variations, see Nilep, 2006.)

It is unfortunate that neither the manuscript reviewers nor the journal editor caught the incongruity in Wheeler and Swords' use of the term "codeswitching." This incongruous definition was further promulgated through their 2006 book, *Code-switching: Teaching Standard English in Urban Classrooms* (this time with a hyphen), published by the National Council of Teachers of English (NCTE). Wheeler also conducts workshops on this notion, which is promoted by NCTE. The incongruous definition became quite popular, also gaining currency among U.S. college composition specialists. Yet, Wheeler's idea quickly became a target of criticism, bringing down the term "code-switching" along with it.

In his 2007 book, Young critiqued the notion of code-switching as defined by Wheeler and Swords, which stipulated that home and school languages should be completely separated. Rather than citing Wheeler and Swords, however, he characterized the term as "a popular concept and approach to language instruction" and attributed it to "many well-meaning literacy educators who do not wish to impose the burden of racial performance when teaching literacy to black students" (p. 7). Then, as his preferred alternative, he proposed the term "code meshing," which he explained was "based on what linguists have called code mix-ing, to combine dialects, styles and registers" (p. 7). It is important to point out, however, that many applied linguists use the term "code-mixing" interchange-ably with code-switching, which is more or less the same idea as code-meshing.

To his credit, Young later identified Wheeler and Swords' book as a source of the term "code switching" (Young, 2009, p. 50) at the 2009 Watson Conference; however, few of the conference participants, including Young, were aware of the idiosyncrasy of Wheeler and Swords' definition. The incongruity remained virtu-ally unnoticed until it was pointed out during the discussion session at the end of the conference. Canagarajah (2006) also has used the term "code switching" in referring to the separation of codes, although he attributes the same idiosyncratic definition to Peter Elbow. As someone who straddles between the disciplinary worlds of U.S. college composition and applied linguistics, however, Canagarajah was aware of the idiosyncrasy, as he wrote: "Note also that some radical scholars have used the term code switching broadly to signify the same practice that I call code meshing here" (p. 598). Yet, he went on to reify the incongruous defini-tion of code-switching by upholding the distinction between code-switching and code-meshing. Unfortunately, it appears that this incongruent usage is also begin-ning to make its way back to applied linguistics (e.g., Higgins, Nettell, Furukawa & Sakoda, 2012).

During the discussion at the end of the 2009 Watson conference, many par-ticipants seemed eager to embrace the term code-meshing and to apply it to their teaching. Yet, few of the participants were able to define the term or explain what it meant to bring code-meshing to the classroom. There was much con-fusion about what code-meshing was, what it looked like in practice, how it was similar to or different than other similar terms, such as code-switching and code-mixing. The conversation went on without a consistent, shared understand-ing of these key concepts. The only sentiment that many seemed to share was this: Code-meshing, good; code-switching, bad. This kind of empty valorization can undermine the efforts of even those who are defining these terms carefully in their own work. The situation seems to be improving somewhat as a result of a series of conversations at various conferences over the last few years; by 2011, Young, Canagarajah, and others had come to explicitly acknowledge these ter-minological problems.

In this discussion, I have focused on the use of the terms code-switching and code-meshing in U.S. college composition scholarship as a way of illustrating one of the major problems of the current language movement—the lack of a community of knowledgeable peers who can ensure intellectual accountability. Yet, I do not mean to suggest the term "code-meshing" should be banned (although I do believe that the incongruous use of the term "code-switching" ought to be stopped). As I mentioned in response to Young's "code-meshing" performance at the 2011 Penn State Conference on Rhetoric and Composition, code-meshing can be consid-ered as "code-switching with attitude" (code-switching in applied linguists' sense, not Wheeler and Swords'), and it is valuable insofar as it highlights the active and agentive use of language mixing. As long as the users of the term are careful about defining the term clearly and in a nuanced way—reflecting the awareness that it is more or less synonymous with code-switching and code-mixing—the term might continue to serve a useful purpose at least for the time being.

Bringing Order to the Wild West

The debate over the term code-mixing is only one example out of many terminological and conceptual confusions and valorizations that are happening in the discussion of language issues in U.S. college composition. There is still a lot of work to be done. How, then, do we bring order to the Wild West of language scholarship in U.S. college composition? I am not, of course, arguing that we should impose rigid rules from the old world to govern the dynamics of a new field of knowledge. Definitions of terms do shift even within the same field—in fact, there are some variations in the definition of code-switching even among applied linguists—but that does not mean it is a free-for-all. In interdisciplinary scholarly activities, where prospectors from various disciplinary backgrounds come together to explore what a new territory has to offer, it is important to define terms carefully, reflecting an awareness of the origin and history of the term as well as its variations. In coining new terms or proposing a new concept, it is important to survey the new territory to make sure that the land has not been previously inhabited by other peoples. (In fact, much of what passes as new ideas about language in U.S. college composition have already been discussed in applied linguistics.) We also need to take care not to overgeneralize or misrepresent ideas and practices in other fields.

As an attempt to represent the perspectives of other disciplines, many conference organizers have chosen to invite researchers from language-related fields and from other countries to attend U.S.-based composition conferences as featured speakers and invited panel members. While this is a good start, it is often not sufficient in addressing the knowledge gap. When U.S. college composition specialists present incongruent views of language-related concepts at these conferences, language specialists in the audience tend not to challenge those questionable practices directly. Instead, they often look down uncomfortably out of politeness or make eye contact with each other to make sure that they are not the only ones who are puzzled. After one of the language-focused conferences organized by a U.S. college composition specialist, an applied linguist who had been invited to the event told me that she felt awkward speaking up to "correct" people because language specialists were disciplinary outsiders who were invited to someone else's party. On another occasion, one of the international participants mentioned to me that he was not able to relate to the conversation—he and others did not understand why U.S. participants were so excited about what seemed like business as usual to international participants while not showing any interests in what they thought were important issues. While efforts to increase cross-disciplinary collaborations need to continue, we need to keep in mind that bringing experts from outside does not automatically make the conversation richer or more informed. The change also needs to happen from within.

Specifically, there needs to be a much more concerted effort to develop a more robust understanding of language scholarship, both within and outside U.S. college composition. It goes without saying that attempts to borrow—or critique—insights from another disciplinary context should be preceded by efforts to become thoroughly familiar with the discussion of key concepts and issues as they are being discussed in other disciplinary contexts. It would also be a good idea to develop a broad understanding of language-related disciplines, their assumptions and their *modi operandi*. Graduate students might consider taking courses in applied linguistics, such as discourse analysis, first and second language acquisition, pedagogical grammar, second language writing, sociolinguistics, and world Englishes. Another way to learn about recent ideas and developments in language-related fields is to attend conferences populated by language specialists—such as the American Association for Applied Linguistics, International Association for World Englishes, Symposium on Second Language Writing, Second Language Research Forum, and Teachers of English to Speakers of Other Languages. Collaborating with colleagues—or at least starting a conversation with them—is also a useful way of understanding ideas and perspectives from other fields.

Finally, I would like to conclude by encouraging U.S. college composition specialists to start learning additional languages. I am not just talking about developing a "reading knowledge"—just enough knowledge to translate literary passages into English—which is a hopelessly outdated notion of language learning from the early part of the 20th century. Instead, I hope more U.S. college composition scholars will try to develop advanced proficiency in multiple languages—both spoken and written—to understand firsthand what it is like to live the multilingual reality.

Acknowledgments

I am grateful to Christine Tardy, Aya Matsuda, and Vershawn Ashanti Young for their helpful comments.

References

Bean, J., Eddy, R., Grego, R., Irvine, P., Kurtz, E., Matsuda, P. K., Cucchiara, M., Elbow, P., Haswel, R., Kennedy, E., & Lehner, A. (2003). Should we invite students to write in home languages? Complicating the yes/no debate. *Composition Studies, 31*, 25–42.

Bizzell, P. (1999). Hybrid academic discourses: What, why, how. *Composition Studies, 27*, 7–21.

Bizzell, P. (2000). Basic writing and the issue of correctness, or what to do with 'mixed' forms of academic discourse. *Journal of Basic Writing, 19*, 4–12.

Butler, M. A., & Committee on CCCC Language Statement (1974). Students' right to their own language (Special Issue). *College Composition and Communication, 25*, 1–32.

Canagarajah, A. S. (2006). The place of World Englishes in composition: Pluralization continued. *College Composition and Communication, 57*(4), 586–619.

Connors, R. J. (2000a). Composition history and disciplinarity. In M. Rosner, B. Boehm, & D. Journet (Eds.), *History, reflection, and narrative: The professionalization of composition, 1963–1983* (pp. 3–22). Stamford, CT: Ablex.

Connors, R. J. (2000b). The erasure of the sentence. *College Composition and Communication, 52*, 96–128. doi:10.2307/358546.

Donahue, C. (2009). "Internationalization" and composition studies: Reorienting the discourse. *College Composition and Communication, 61*(2), 212–243.

Ferguson, C. (1959). Diglossia. *Word, 15*, 325–340.

Foster, D., & Russell, D. (Eds.). (2002). *Writing and learning in cross-national perspective: Transitions from secondary to higher education.* New York, NY: Routledge.

Harklau, L., Losey, K. M., & Siegal, M. (Eds.). (1999). *Generation 1.5 meets college composition: Issues in the teaching of writing to U.S.-educated learners of ESL.* Mahwah, NJ: Lawrence Erlbaum Associates.

Higgins, C., Nettell, R., Furukawa, G., & Sakod, K. (2012) Beyond contrastive analysis and codeswitching: Student documentary filmmaking as a challenge to linguicism in Hawai'i. *Linguistics and Education, 23*, 49–61.

Horner, B., Lu, M., & Matsuda, P. K. (Eds.). (2010). *Cross-language relations in composition.* Carbondale, IL: Southern Illinois University Press

Horner, B., & Trimbur, J. (2002). English only and U.S. college composition. *College Composition and Communication, 53*(4), 594–630. doi:10.2307/1512118.

Lauer, J. M. (1984). Composition studies: Dappled discipline. *Rhetoric Review, 3*(1), 20–29. doi:10.1080/07350198409359074.

Lu, M. (2004). An essay on the work of composition: Composing English against the order of fast capitalism. *College Composition and Communication, 56*(1), 16–50. doi:10.2307/4140679.

Lyons, S. R. (2010). There's no translation for it: The rhetorical sovereignty of indigenous languages. In B. Horner, M. Lu, & P. K. Matsuda (Eds.), *Cross-language relations in composition* (pp. 127–141). Carbondale, IL: Southern Illinois University Press.

MacDonald, S. P. (2005). The erasure of language. *College Composition and Communication, 58*(4), 585–625.

Matsuda, A., & Matsuda, P. K. (2011). Globalizing writing studies: The case of U.S. technical communication textbooks. *Written Communication, 28*(2), 172–192. doi:10.1177/0741088311399708.

Matsuda, P. K. (1999). Composition studies and ESL writing: A disciplinary division of labor. *College Composition and Communication, 50*(4), 699–721. doi:10.2307/358488.

Matsuda, P. K. (2003). Process and post-process: A discursive history. *Journal of Second Language Writing, 12*(1), 65–83. doi:10.1016/S1060-3743(02)00127-3.

Matsuda, P. K. (2006). The myth of linguistic homogeneity in U.S. college composition. *College English, 68*(6), 637–651. doi:10.2307/25472180.

Matsuda, P. K. (2012). Let's Face It: Language Issues and the Writing Program Administrator. *WPA: Writing Program Administration, 36*(1), 141–163.

Matsuda, P. K., Cox, M., Jordan, J., & Ortmeier-Hooper, C. (Eds.). (2006). *Second-language writing in the composition classroom: A critical sourcebook*. Boston, MA: Bedford/St. Martin's Press.

Matsuda, P. K., & Jablonski, J. (2000). Beyond the L2 metaphor: Towards a mutually transformative model of ESL/WAC collaboration. *Academic Writing, 1*. Retrieved from http://wac.colostate.edu/aw/articles/matsuda_jablonski2000.htm (accessed 15 November 2012).

Nilep, C. (2006). "Code switching" in sociocultural linguistics. *Colorado Research in Linguistics, 19*, 1–22.

North, S. M. (1987). *The making of knowledge in composition*. Portsmouth, NH: Boynton Cook.

Pedersen, A. M. (2010). Negotiating cultural identities through language: Academic English in Jordan. *College Composition and Communication, 62*(2), 283–310.

Roberge, M., Siegal, M., & Harklau, L. (Eds.). (2009). *Generation 1.5 in college composition: Teaching academic writing to U.S.-educated learners of ESL*. London, UK: Taylor and Francis.

Romano, S. (2004). Tlaltelolco: The grammatical–rhetorical Indios of colonial Mexico. *College English, 66*(3), 257–277. doi:10.2307/4140748.

Schroeder, C., Fox, F., & Bizzell, P. (Eds.). (2002). *ALT DIS: Alternative discourses and the academy*. Portsmouth, NH: Boynton/Cook Heinemann.

Severino, C., Guerra, J. C., & Butler, J. E. (Eds.). (1997). *Writing in multicultural settings*. New York, NY: Modern Language Association of America.

Smitherman, G., & Villanueva, V. (Eds.). (2003). *Language diversity in the classroom: From intention to practice*. Carbondale, IL: Southern Illinois University Press.

Wheeler, R. S., & Swords, R. (2004). Codeswitching: Tools of language and culture transform the dialectally diverse classroom. *Language Arts, 81*(6), 470–480.

Wheeler, R. S., & Swords, R. (2006). *Code-switching: Teaching standard English in urban classrooms*. Urbana, IL: National Council of Teachers of English.

Wible, S. (2007). Pedagogies of the "students' right" era: The language curriculum research group's project for linguistic diversity. *College Composition and Communication, 57*(3), 442–478.

Young, V. A. (2007). *Your average nigga: Performing race, literacy, and masculinity*. Detroit, MI: Wayne State University Press.

Young, V. A. (2009). "Nah, we straight": An argument against code switching. *JAC: A Journal of Composition Theory, 29*(1–2), 49–76.

Young, V. A., & Martinez, A. Y. (Eds.). (2011). *Code-meshing as World English: Pedagogy, policy, performance*. Urbana, IL: National Council of Teachers of English.

13

KEEP CODE-MESHING

Vershawn Ashanti Young

[handwritten: Is Young addressing a very particular population / history when he advocates for code-meshing?]

Since coining the neologism "code-meshing" in my article "Your Average Nigga" (Young, 2004, 713n8; Young, 2007) and offering there a fledgling definition, the term and its applications have been just as astutely enlarged by others as it has been ardently debated. Perhaps linguist Suresh Canagarajah stands among the most notable advocates of code-meshing, since it's his theoretical and practical scholarship on the concept that has propelled it from an explanation I put in a footnote to a subject of primary focus in journal articles, edited volumes, dissertations, and published monographs (see, e.g., Canagarajah, 2006).

A Personal Response

I am heartened by both the disagreements and deliberations that code-meshing has sparked, and I want to offer a word or two in response to some of these discussions as it relates, at least, to what was my only goal in first promoting the term: to provide a sociolinguistic framework that would help reduce, if not eliminate, both the racial prejudice against African American English and the linguistic injustice against African American people. My goal was, and remains, in regards to the focus of my work as a scholar of African American literary, language, and cultural studies, to help code-meshing become an acceptable practice for what I hear and see black people doing every day: blending, adjusting, playing, and dancing with standard English and academic discourse when they are jiving on the playground, wielding linguistic charm in the courtroom (e.g., "If it *[handwritten: yeesh]* doesn't fit, you must acquit."), writing police reports for work, and speaking and writing anywhere and everywhere that communication takes place, whether in informal or formal settings. What these black folks I hear, read, and admire are doing is code-meshing, which I continue to see as the strategic, self-conscious and un-self-conscious blending of one's own accent, dialect, and linguistic patterns as they are influenced by a host of folks, environments, and media, including momma, family, school, community, peer groups, reading material, academic study, whatever.

The reason this view of code-meshing is so very important to me is because too many teachers still on one hand praise African American students for their creative voice and renderings of black rhetoric when they write poetry but then condemn those same students when they both un-self-consciously *and* strategically employ those same features when speaking to non-black people, particularly white people, or to professionals of any race, or when they produce critical, academic, or journalistic writing. And even though many of these teachers are very well meaning, often saying that they are preparing these students for the real world, one that doesn't yet value black English (read: black people), they must demand that the students switch back and forth when appropriate; be black, or as they put it, speak black, when it's safe to do so, but not when your job, your grades, or your relationships with other non-black people (and sometimes other blacks who share the same prejudice) are on the line.

For me, code-meshing is a smack in the face to logic that unevenly and unfairly places a societal and racial burden on the shoulders of students who shouldn't have to bear the sole brunt of so thoroughly changing themselves, their language, just so other people will feel comfortable; just so they won't offend and lose out on opportunities that would be theirs if they weren't black. Code-meshing says to this thinking, in all the black gusto it can muster, "Honey, puh'leeze!"

Yes, I recognize that I am challenging and attempting to change the *status quo*, not only regarding writing and literacy instruction but also the court of public opinion. Yes, this court includes other black people, some who even themselves use black English, yet still hate it. And yes, I know that some teachers and the public might respond to what I argue with objections that seek to reaffirm that prescriptive standard English is all that students need for academic and financial success, even if it excludes other dialects and language influences. I also know, however, that there are sympathetic teachers who believe that authorizing diverse language practices, that using black standard English and black academic discourse is a good idea; but they ultimately and unfortunately would rather waffle in the debate than to rally against the world as it is (still prejudiced against blackness) and engage the world as it should be (egalitarian, truly diverse).

Therefore, I want to respond to one of the foremost arguments against code-meshing—one recently expressed by a very erudite and accomplished colleague: literary critic and writing teacher Stanley Fish. When his opinion against linguistic diversity appeared on his *New York Times* Opinionator blog, it received quite a bit of support. It also received some criticism, making it an appropriate response to engage, as I and others urge that people keep code-meshing.

Responding to Debates

The debate between teachers who wish to honor students' native languages and dialects as they teach the English language and its various arts—listening, speaking, reading, writing, viewing, and visually representing[1]—and those who believe students must be taught standard English only, since other Englishes are still believed to have limited value, if any, in academic and professional sites, is presently just as intense as it was in 1974, when advocates of students' rights to their own language published their resolution, which to me should settle the waffling of the sympathetic speech and writing teachers about valuing code-meshing when it states this:

> Resolved, that NCTE [National Council of Teachers of English] promote classroom practices to expose students to the variety of dialects that comprise our multiregional, multiethnic, and multicultural society, so that they too will understand the nature of American English.
>
> *(NCTE, 1974)*

This excerpt is taken directly from the position statement, which argues that language arts instruction should focus on effective language rather than viewing prescriptions of standard language as the only key to success. What's more, an excerpt from the background statement of the resolution asks teachers to think deeply about the consequences of what we teach as English and how we teach it:

> And many of us have taught as though the function of schools and colleges were to erase differences. Should we, on the one hand, urge creativity and individuality in the arts and the sciences, take pride in the diversity of our historical development, and, on the other hand, try to obliterate all the differences in the way Americans speak and write? Our major emphasis has been on uniformity, in both speech and writing; would we accomplish more, both educationally and ethically, if we shifted that emphasis to precise, effective, and appropriate communication in diverse ways, whatever the dialect?
>
> *(Committee on CCCC Language: Background statement, 1974, p. 2)*

As a contemporary advocate of the best features of "Students' Rights," I promote the instructional shift the document urges, from prescriptive instruction to an emphasis on "precise, effective, and appropriate communication … whatever the dialect" or, as I would add, "whatever the meshing of dialects."

However, as I shall again argue here, I am also critical of the prevailing methods that sympathetic teachers use to implement it (see Young, 2011; Young & Martinez, 2011). On one side they simply refuse to teach any effective language that comes from standard English or academic discourse, because they feel as if such school-based language violates students' home language. Not so! The problem is this: reprimanding students for blending dialects and asking them to give up their language in favor of another one, even for a little while, or to put is as it is often phrased, "in appropriate settings." This commits the violation. Students in this scenario are asked to switch from their English to the standard. They are patronized, summarily told that their language shares equal prestige with standard dialect, even as teachers belie this very claim by labeling standard language as "formal" and the students' Englishes as "informal," thus reinforcing a superior/inferior linguistic dichotomy (for a recent example of those who urge that teachers adopt the informal/formal formulation, see Wheeler & Swords, 2006). Although different approaches, i.e., refusing to teach standard English and teaching code-switching, both accede to the monolithic ideal of standard English, the belief that other varieties of English are inherently deficient, should be confined to informal situations, used with close friends and family, and needing the narrow rules of standard English to communicate effectively in wider contexts.

Stanley Fish offered his perspective on the best way to teach writing in his widely read *New York Times* Opinionator blog. His opinion piece illustrates just how opposed some of the professoriate and even more of the public are to ideas and pedagogies that accommodate Englishes. Parroting one of the most tired biased arguments against "Students' Rights," Fish (2009, Sept. 7) writes:

> It may be true that the standard language is an instrument of power and a device for protecting the status quo, but that very truth is a reason for teaching it to students who are being prepared for entry into the world as it now is rather than the world as it might be in some utopian imagination—all dialects equal, all habit of speech and writing equally rewarded. You're not going to be able to change the world if you are not equipped with the tools that speak to its present condition. You don't strike a blow against a power structure by making yourself vulnerable to its prejudices …

Fish, and others who believe as he does, couldn't be more wrong. First, no speaker's or writer's language, dialect, or style makes them "vulnerable to prejudice." Prejudice resides in the eyes and ears of the beholders, from the attitudes people have about certain groups of people, bigoted attitudes (both unintentional and intentional) which get projected onto certain groups' languages (see Lippi-Green, 1997). Despite his flaccid gestures to multilingualism, Fish asserts that there is an essential problem with acknowledging dialects in writing instruction, and argues that we should teach students out of them. For him, dialect prejudice is not his problem, too big to tackle; so we must acquiesce to its power. And this is where he gets especially double-tongued. He says no one can change prejudice if you can't speak using the prescriptive rules of standard English, suggesting that dialects are incapable of expressing complaint and substantial arguments in the efforts of change. He is muttering the understanding that "in order to dismantle the master's house, you have to use his tools." I respond: "Ever heard of a bull-dozer?" Bulldozers don't build houses, but you can knock a house down with one. In my opinion, code-meshing is the bulldozer to linguistic prejudice.

However, to speak directly to Fish's point that if students learn the standard language then they can speak against its dominance, this statement is dishonest at best. Fish doesn't really mean it, since he begins his article recommending just the opposite:

> What would a [writing] course based on the method I urge look like? …
> First, you must clear your mind [of the following]: "We affirm the students'
> right to their own patterns and varieties of language—the dialects of their
> nurture or whatever dialects in which they find their own identity and
> style."
>
> *(Fish, 2009, Sept. 7)*

In other words, Fish is pushing the very people who have learned the stand-ard and who are now teaching it to abandon their efforts to disrupt its unfair supremacy. If Fish were actually sincere about his advice to learn the standard language first and afterward pursue changing it, then the writers of the "Students' Rights"—indeed the resolution itself—would stand as exemplary examples.

But Fish ain't for real about seeking change. He would keep code-meshing advocates spinning their wheels, teaching the dominant standard, under the false belief that becoming a part of the system is the best way to change it—when really what happens is that we few who do make it are then used as examples by Fish and others to say, "Ain't nothing wrong with the system; the problem is with the language of the most who don't make it." We few successful minorities and immigrants thus become the very cogs used that keep the same 'ole wheel of linguistic oppression turning, the very hands that keep the prejudicial butter mill a'churnin.

In addition, Fish encourages teachers to patronize students when it comes to issues of language difference. He writes:

> If students infected with the facile egalitarianism of soft multiculturalism
> declare, "I have a right to my own language," reply, "Yes, you do, and I
> am not here to take that language from you; I'm here to teach you another
> one." (Who could object to learning a second language?) And then get on
> with it.
>
> *(Fish, 2009, Sept. 7)*

Besides being snide, he's promoting that we be hypocritical. He wants us first to discard policies such as "Students Rights" and then says we should tell students, "You do have a right to your language." Huh? What's more, it appears particularly disingenuous for Fish to ask, "Who could object to learning a second language [or dialect]" when it's only those who want to keep their languages, the "multiculturals," that he feels shouldn't object to learning standard language. If indeed Fish believes that no one should object to learning another dialect, then wouldn't he be a supporter of "Students' Rights" and argue for the full implementation of code-meshing? After all, the resolution itself offers the same advice. It encourages the learning of a second, third, and even fourth dialect by all students, when it says that teachers should "expose students to the variety of dialects that comprise our multiregional, multiethnic, and multicultural society." So when Fish asks "Who could object to learning a second language?" The answer is—him!—he does, since he most certainly objects to students learning and using any variety of English other than the "standard."

And here's where I want to speak directly as a teacher to other teachers of oral and written English, whether you teach literature, literacy, communication, or any of its other arts. Too many of us double-speak, claiming out one cheek that varieties of English are fully compatible with and sometimes more expressive than standard English as we currently narrowly conceive of it. Out the other cheek we say, "But students must master the rules of standard English usage for standardized tests, to show that they can be successful as professionals at work, and at various stages of school." "Our hands are tied," some of us say. We then close our eyes as we tie many of our students' tongues, in hopes that a few will be successful, while knowing from history, past experience, and current statistics that most don't succeed, certainly most people classified as minorities won't, not under the current limited rubric of what counts as linguistic success.

Exhortation to Teachers

Yet, English teachers are not brick and mortar laborers. We are mediators of culture, transmitting beliefs and values about people and language in all that we do. Because of this, it's important to be aware of the ideology we spread through our instruction. Though there are more, below are three interconnected beliefs that English teachers sustain when we disregard code-meshing and teach standard language only:

1. When we operate as if it's a fact that standard English is what all professionals and academics use, we ignore the real fact that not all successful professionals and academics write in standard English. We ignore the many examples of effective formal writing composed in accents, in varieties of English other than what's considered standard (see Campbell, 2005; Smitherman, 1977; Young, 2007). Further, we ignore that standard English has been and continues to be a contested concept (see Lippi-Green, 1997; McWhorter, 1998).
2. When we say that our hands are tied because of standardized tests and public perception, we allow test makers, the commercial world, and the general public to dictate our professional responsibilities, to decide in effect what we teach, and negate our own professional training and credentials. We choose

not to use our individual and collective agency to alter the prevailing linguistic prejudice.

3. When we teach standard English only, despite feeling, knowing, or thinking that it limits students and is not the only effective mode, we are asserting standard English as if it's a decree from Hitler, as if it's the official language of a dictator, of a totalitarian government, and certainly not the language of a democracy, where the voices of all peoples should matter, and where diversity is appreciated, encouraged, and accepted. When we fear backlash or that we'll lose our jobs if we follow the resolutions of our national professional organization, shouldn't that very fear indicate that best practices are not driving English education, that democracy is not in action?

In view of the foregoing, I continue to believe that the time is now to teach and learn code-meshing. It seems only right that we at least try. So, as has become my mantra and urging, keep code-meshing, keep code-meshing …

Note

1 The six language arts, as designated by the National Council of Teachers of English (NCTE) and the International Reading Association (IRA) (Standards for the English Language Arts, 1996), are listening, speaking, reading, writing, viewing, and visually representing.

References

Campbell, K. (2005). *Gettin' our groove on: Rhetoric, language, and literacy for the hip hop generation*. Detroit, MI: Wayne State University Press.

Canagarajah, A. S. (2006). The place of world Englishes in composition. *College Composition and Communication, 57*(4), 586–619.

Committee on CCCC Language Statement. (1974). Students' right to their own language (Special Issue). *College Composition and Communication, 25*(3), 1–18.

Fish, S. (2009, Sept. 7). What should colleges teach? Part 3. *New York Times* Opinionator Blog. Retrieved from http://opinionator.blogs.nytimes.com/2009/09/07/what-should-colleges-teach-part-3 (accessed 15 November 2012).

Lippi-Green, R. (1997). *English with an accent: Language, ideology and discrimination in the United States*. London, UK: Routledge.

McWhorter, J. (1998). Word on the street: Debunking the myth of a "pure" Standard English. Cambridge, UK: Perseus Publishing.

NCTE. (1974). *Students' right to their own language*. Retrieved from http://www.ncte.org/library/NCTEFiles/Groups/CCCC/NewSRTOL.pdf (accessed Nov. 15, 2012).

Smitherman, G. (1977) *Talkin' and testifyin': The language of Black America*. Detroit, MI: Wayne State University Press.

Wheeler, R., & Swords, R. (2006). *Code-switching: Teaching standard English in urban classrooms*. Urbana, IL: National Council of Teachers of English.

Young, V. (2007). *Your average nigga: Performing race, literacy, and masculinity*. Detroit, MI: Wayne State University Press.

PART IV

Research Directions

14

NEGOTIATION, TRANSLINGUALITY, AND CROSS-CULTURAL WRITING RESEARCH IN A NEW COMPOSITION ERA

Christiane Donahue

Comparative cultural work, we know well, sharpens our understanding of our own work here in the United States, denaturalizing assumed positions, purposes, and valued practices. It has, for example, in recent years, helped us to think about "composition" in relation to "writing studies," and to reconsider the degree to which what we thought was "the other" (multilingual students for example) is in fact us. This is an era in which our field is infused by attention to languages (including modern language instruction), theories, and methods that are growing and developing out of interactions among multiple disciplinary and international pathways. The "new era in composition" in my title thus refers to the evolution in U.S. composition theory or composition studies, as these various other realities become part of the fabric of our research and teaching.

This new era also involves a willingness to reframe our ways of thinking about international writing studies and writing instruction. Knowledge of this instruction and research in other countries is vitally important to the United States, but often not accessible, for a variety of linguistic and disciplinary reasons: The multiple languages other than English in which publications are appearing; the range of disciplinary backgrounds of teachers and researchers working with writing (linguistics, psychology, didactics, etc.); the different institutional structures that promote or obstruct interactions; the actual differences in daily practice infused by ideology; the neglect of scholarship from other contexts (see Horner, 2010, p. 1).

I would like to resist the dominant U.S. discourses about writing in the non-U.S. world. The stories about writing internationally that we do locate and report are often the familiar ones we were seeking rather than the complex ones that are at play. Indeed, our interactions with others can result in their reframing of themselves through our lenses. On the one hand, there are advantages to non-U.S.

models. The absence of an industry of first-year composition in some countries, for example, is not necessarily a lack (see Leki, 2006; Prendergast, 2010). On the other hand, sometimes we *do* share values and practices, but their different names lead us astray. New lenses can help us to see, for example, that a French "research methods" course has the same activities, purposes, values, and methods as a U.S. writing course.

I want to share part of a project that draws on research traditions from France and the United States to explore first-year student writing in those two national contexts, with students imagined as French or English "monolinguals" by the institutions in question. Given that population, it may seem at first that this is not the kind of work being taken up in this volume. I do not try in this study to show, for example, that students were not the monolinguals their institutions imagined. I'd like instead to show how what's learned in the study, by drilling down, looking at French writing in France, brings insight to our multilingual and translingual interests from a different direction. These insights involve both study results—surprises about what the students' texts had in common rather than in contrast—and methods, what the mixing of research traditions was able to bring out, in terms of understanding students' negotiating movements and pushing forward dialogue about some small part of other traditions of higher education writing research.

I'll briefly discuss the study, the methods, and a sampling of results, in order to focus on the stages my understanding of the project has gone through. These are stages I will propose as reflective of a possible broader trajectory for international research in the U.S. field of composition studies.

The Ground Already Tilled

The belief that no one else (outside the United States) does the work we (in the United States) do prevailed for a time, resisting evidence to the contrary. It has not been until fairly recently that we have thought we might be able to learn from writing research and instruction in other parts of the world. English as a Second Language (ESL) work has also, until fairly recently, remained outside of the mainstream concerns of most U.S. writing faculty—at least, until the gentle but persistent critiques from scholars like Matsuda (1999), Ortmeier-Hooper (2008), and Tardy (2006) began to bring the field around. Fraiberg and You (2010) point to composing as historically multilingual and transnational. Others have helped us to decenter monolingual practices and to consider who *we* are as *global citizens of higher education writing studies* rather than intellectual tourists out to see what's going on beyond our borders.

Within that broader frame, we have celebrated the bi- or multilingual in literature, and promoted learning languages. Our relationship with the multilingual–cultural has also developed sideways, through for example our troubled relationship to "world literatures" (Leki, 2006; Smith, 2011) with readings offered in our courses, or through the hybrid glance we get via our occasional encounters with colleagues at U.S. institutions overseas. Throughout, our fundamental view of language has been one of discrete languages (see, e.g., Horner, Necamp, & Donahue, 2011b; House, 1999) and our approaches to preparing literate students in the 21st century have also been decidedly monolingual or focused on monolingual understandings of our students and their language(s).

These approaches have been unsettled by, among others, Pennycook's (2008) exploration of English—and I believe he would agree that the same could be said of any one language—as "a language always in translation" (p. 34) rather than a "hermetic language that [is] inherently tied to a national culture" (p. 40). If, as Pennycook argues, "all communication involves translation" (p. 40), then the focus on accommodating diversity in successful communication—with communication understood here as meaning-making (Canagarajah, 2006b)—leads us to recognizing multiliteracies (Canagarajah, 2002) as more pertinent to 21st-century communication, and multilinguality as a resource (Kramsch, 2006; Canagarajah, 2003).

As questions about the recently developed fuzzy catchall notions of "globalization" and "internationalization" of writing (research or teaching) have intersected with concrete, specifically focused questions about multilingual learners in U.S. writing classes that had been studied for decades, the U.S. field of composition and rhetoric has felt itself challenged and stretched. Horner, Lu, Royster, and Trimbur (2011a) recently articulated specifically what a paradigm shift away from the mono/multilingual model towards a "translingual" one would entail, and why it matters. Language difference is a resource in the meaning-making described above, and thus in communication, a relationship that brings us back to our field's understanding of writing as inextricable from context and content rather than as transparent (communicative) window into meaning. As Horner et al. (2011a) argue, in a translingual model we need to redefine our understanding of fluency, proficiency, and competence, favoring strength in flexible negotiation and revision over strength in a single (apparently) stable practice (p. 307), the kind of multi-English flexibility Canagarajah (2006b) suggests is a deep resource. This project to engage with multiple languages in English composition is of course born out of Horner and Trimbur's (2002) initial call and further development by Canagarajah (2006a) and others, while the term of translingualism and its activist connotations appear to have originated with Venuti (1998), in the context of choosing what and how to translate in translation studies.

To date, the focus of U.S. translingual analyses has remained primarily on multiple Englishes (Brutt-Griffler, 2002; Canagarajah, 2006b; Meierkord, 2000; Rubdy & Saraceni, 2006; You, 2006), English as lingua franca (Canagarajah, 2006b; House, 1999), students operating within and across multiple languages in anglophone contexts (Horner & Trimbur, 2002; Lu, 2004; Matsuda, 2006; Silva, Leki, & Carson, 1997), and multilinguality (Heller, 2007; Kramsch, 2006; Lillis & Curry, 2006, 2010). This is understandable in the context of a national higher education system in which the dominant language of academic practice is

English, other than in language classrooms and departments. Parallel explorations of the resource afforded by multilingual mindsets and practices exist in other countries, and share theoretical perspectives, but the agenda is particular here in the United States: as English becomes a widely spread factor in international scholarly exchange and as our international student population grows, we grapple with the translingual question from that particular vantage point. A different informative set of concerns surfaces when we resituate our point of departure and consider the complicated nature of students writing in contexts in which the starting point is another language, subject to the same deep questioning about fragmentation, translation, and translinguality, albeit within different politico-ideological frames and research traditions dominating writing instruction.

Re-thinking the Cross-Cultural: A Study Reconsidered

The study I will report on in this section went through three developmental stages. It began as a traditional cross-cultural comparison of French and U.S. student writing, using both quantitative and qualitative measures. It then evolved, via sustained confrontation with theoretical frames from U.S. and French scholars. Those confrontations were themselves seeds of a translingual way of thinking. More recently, I have seen the study anew explicitly as a source for understanding some aspects of a translingual frame for composition work and for recognizing additional resources that both we and our students already have for engaging translingually.

Cross-Cultural Analysis Traditions

I began this major cross-national project as a traditional comparative study. For decades, monolingual understandings of language and reified features of cultural difference have dominated writing research discourses in many research traditions around the globe; the methods of analysis have, in effect, tended to support seeing languages and cultures as discrete boundaried entities we can compare and contrast (see for example many of the presentations at the biannual Indiana Center for Intercultural Communication conferences on written discourse and contrastive rhetoric; and, certainly, I recognize the groundwork accomplished by this international and interdisciplinary field (cf. Biber, 1991, 2006; Chafe, 1992; Connor, 1996; Kaplan, 1966, 2000)).

That contrastive rhetoric tradition of analysis has evolved more recently in the direction of what Connor, Nagelhout, and Rozycki (2008) are calling intercultural rhetoric:

> … dynamic models of cross-cultural research … extending to new genres, widening contextual research through historical and ethnographic inquiry, refining methodology, utilizing electronic corpora of texts, going beyond linguistic patterns to the study of other distinctive differences in writing,

and exploring contrasts even beyond writing, such as the differences in Web use between speakers of different languages.

(p. 4)

The shift is important to our broader understanding of language and culture as intersecting in writing, but still maintains a focus on differences and boundaries. For Pennycook (2008) and François (1998), this version of language use fails to account for internal heterogeneity, an essential aspect of its way of doing work.

Why Textual Analysis?

In this study, I focused on texts. This may seem to fly in the face of years of received wisdom regarding the U.S. "social" approaches to research on higher education writing, and may seem counterintuitive to what I've just posited about the problems with features-driven analysis. I do think that sustained research, including analysis of students' texts, dropped off the U.S. composition table for a time (see Bazerman, ch. 2 in this volume). Clearly, Bazerman and Prior's (2003) *What Writing Does and How It Does It* is based squarely on the idea that textual analysis provides insights we don't find without looking at text; Prior's (1998) work on laminated literate artifacts opens a universe of value. Taking this set of thoughts a step further, I would argue that the text is the trace of its own dialogic production; as Tardy (2006) has argued, the text, in a dialogic model, is not cut from its context. Texts do work in the world, and are thus dynamic. The text is social; the social is *in* the text. A polyphonic reading of a text offers insight into its constructed way of doing its work as text. This reading alone may never be enough, but at the same time, the rest without this is missing a key piece. The way Fairclough (2006) describes analysis of texts can illuminate the depth of the possibilities. He suggests that meaning-making comes from the interplay of producer–text–receiver, calling out interpretations from the language in use (p. 10). Text analysis is never restricted to linguistic units (though I would argue that, even if it is, we are still in the "social" in the Bakhtinian–Volosinovian sense; the words, shot through, are the social in linguistic and discursive action); it sees "texts in terms of the different discourses, genres, and styles they draw upon and articulate together" (p. 3). The textual ethnography proposed by Lillis (2008) similarly thrusts textual analysis into a different space, in which the ontological gap between text and context is narrowed (p. 373). Her work develops in particular the tools of indexicality and orientation in order to work across text–context (p. 376); Lillis' emphasis on the relational and mediational nature of the categories, in this kind of analysis, is the paradigm shifter.

The Study

The study I report here analyzed French university students' writing in relation to U.S. students' writing. The 250 student essays analyzed were roughly comparable in prompt and type, including a requirement to respond to a source or sources, and produced at the secondary/post-secondary threshold. I coded for patterns based on location of the thesis, features of coherence (deixis, connectors, external structure of the paragraphs), and markers of intertext.

I should note that the study was designed initially as a fairly straightforward contrastive analysis, using both quantitative and qualitative methods, not framed in the various deep ways evoked in the previous section. Already, however, this was not a traditional text-based study, in that the essays were studied in "textual context," a framing first described by Geisler (2003). Each text was studied in relation to the assignment prompt to which it responded and the readings with which it was supposed to work.

I identified, in the first approach, some clear contrasts (for a detailed report see C. Donahue, 2008; T. Donahue, 2008). The French students' essays showed statistically significant differences from the U.S. essays in terms of patterns of organization, placement of thesis, overall essay structure, and type/frequency of connector and deictic. But this work was not satisfying, for many of the reasons that have been detailed by others in the fields of composition and of contrastive rhetoric. I began to ask, given the significant differences in instructional purposes and practices in most French and U.S. institutions of higher education, how could any feature analysis of student work across two such different contexts be possible or useful?

Shifting Ground

In discussion with many French and U.S. scholars, I moved into a different phase of the analysis, one that confronted some of my assumptions and shifted the ground of the analysis. It now called on several research traditions and sets of literature. The U.S. field of composition and rhetoric (with specific reference to Bartholomae, 1985; Wall (1992); Bazerman, 1994; Bizzell, 1992; Geisler, 2003; Slevin, 2001) was cross-pollinated by the French field of functional linguistics (François, 1998; Gardin, 1990; Maingueneau, 1998). French functional linguistics, quite different from Australian systemic functional linguistics, explores language in use, its dynamic functionalities, and its open-ended contextual ways of doing work in the world (see also Fairclough (2009) on this kind of analytic approach). The specific methods included linguistic analysis of utterances to see how text is dialogic, and how text is shot through, interactive, heteroglossic, and semio-diverse (Bakhtin 1988). The work also drew on anglophone linguistics (Pratt, 1991; Lillis, 2008), francophone literary theory (Starobinski, 1999) and philosophy (Grize, 1996), and translingual (Canagarajah, 2010; Horner, 2010) and multilingual theoretical grounding. This encounter of "competing intellectual traditions" (Canagarajah, 2002, p. 67) was itself generative. The French research traditions I was bringing in are grounded in linguistics and didactics (a branch of education science); they are empirical and they explicitly resist "application" models. Composition theory, as

I was drawing on it, was focused on postmodern theorizing and critical analysis. Others depended on close reading, and still others on genre theory as developed in European readings of Bakhtin–Volosinov. As I negotiated, myself, among these traditions, each positioning itself as dominant—and "true"—I translated and transculturated, worked to create dialogue, and unlearned and relearned methods and their worldviews. The "givens" about knowledge as constructed collaboratively, discursively, and contextually, as summarized by Canagarajah (2002), were not the givens of colleagues reviewing my drafts and my study results.

I identified the units to be studied (utterances in discursive spaces). I used an overarching analytic tool drawn from linguist François' 1998 work: *reprise-modification* (literally, "re-taking-up-modifying as one interdependent event that is the essence of all discursive function ..., a way to operationalize and further develop ... dialogics as an analytic term, encompassing every textual feature from the broadest discourse to syntax to the single word, and in fact reaching beyond utterances to ways of being in the world" (T. Donahue, 2008). This tool serves as a meta-frame for the various locatable dynamic textual movements exposed in the analysis, and as a way of accounting for the work students' texts do in the institutional contexts of entering higher education.

I also used Pratt's (1991) literate arts in the contact zone as tools for understanding students' textual movements. As Canagarajah (2003) has pointed out, Pratt and others "have theorized that since colonialism we have had a situation where the clashing cultures have produced new literacies. These 'arts of the contact zone' often involve the different languages, ideologies, and literacies that competing communities have brought to intercultural engagement" (p. 157). These arts are particularly useful, in a different way, for capturing the resistance and the dynamics, the power relations in students' work. In particular, "transculturation," as a movement in which a speaker in a lesser position of power appropriates part of a dominant discourse and uses it back against the dominant group, is an effective analytic tool. Note that, again, this movement is not being studied as specific to working across languages; here, what I want to highlight is how a deeper understanding of writing within contexts can develop our understanding of translingual frames. I also adopted Swiss philosopher Grize's (1966) units of natural, "everyday" logic as analytic descriptors; these units allow us to parse students' texts in terms of the kinds of arguments they craft and the formal or informal structures they give them.

Specific units of reprise–modification studied thus included coherence (macro, meso, and micro), intertext, and subject positioning, in the contexts of the genre, the assignment, and the institution and cultural context in which the work is being done, as well as the readings to which it responds. This last component is key because it offers us a way to understand the relationship between student text and other texts. Each text was subdivided into these multiple isolated features, to be studied and then recomposed into the whole "reading." For a full report on this approach, see C. Donahue (2008) and T. Donahue (2008).

The study made three primary arguments within this broader framing: (1) *reprise–modification* is a powerful lens for understanding student work as an intersection between individual specificity and shared genericity, and enables a different understanding of textual coherence and intertextuality in any cultural context; (2) the deep reflection on students' text construction and negotiation these frames provide suggests that being a "first-year" student doing work on a given topic in a given genre might trump the cultural context, a finding that has ramifications for both cross-cultural analyses and student writing; and (3) new cross-cultural methodologies are necessary and can lead to cross-disciplinary and cross-methodological approaches that contribute to understanding translingual moves.

Specifically, using these tools, I could show that a text is dynamic; language in use is always "new," in the way Lu and Horner develop in their chapter in this volume (ch. 3): new in its *re-use of available resources*. Student writing in both France and the United States showed up as a weave of features that produced texts presenting coherent discursive positions as students engaged with university communities of practice. The negotiation in question is a textual manifestation of the kind of push–pull interaction described by Prior and Bilbro (2012) as part of dynamic enculturation in academic work.

Both the cross-cultural and the close reading analyses suggest that "academic writing" is a complicated, problematic notion. The average student writer's text in each context, *as witness to its own production*, is at a precarious point of negotiation and transition—uneasy, non-explicit, traced in layered genres, linguistic choices, displacements, literate arts: moving with and against given resources, adopting, bending, diverting available patterns and resources; reprise–modifying, playing, trying, appropriating, transculturating … The engagement is a negotiation, not an acculturation, in the monolingual texts of both countries. Whatever the intriguing different national–cultural characteristics, these other features are found *across* student work.

A Decade Later

As I began to hear and to learn about the term "translingual," I saw the underlying moves I had studied in the students' work as connected to the discussion. Translingualism, in my view, takes as normal the heterogeneity and the fluctuating character of languages and language practices within and between peoples, and the difficulties encountered and negotiated, emphasizing fluency in working with and across language differences. In this model, all language use is seen as requiring translation; multilingual and polyliterate approaches are expected. A readiness to adjust, an attitude of negotiation, the "metalinguistic, sociolinguistic, and attitudinal preparedness to negotiate differences even as they use their own dialects" (Canagarajah, 2006b, p. 593) are part of a necessary way of working.

The earlier study results suggested that the sophisticated linguistic and rhetorical attributes I found in student writing with this kind of analysis are some of the same attributes—fluidity, hybridity, particular kinds of agency, and a disposition towards negotiation of meanings and frames—that Canagarajah (2006b) or Horner, Lu, Royster, and Trimbur (2011) have highlighted in scholarship about how translingual texts work. Student writers in both cultural groups negotiated the discursive situation in similar ways, adapting to forms of accuracy and appropriateness (in Kramsch's 2006 terms), but also pushing back against them textually, testing the limits of university writing conventions, whether French or English.

Drawing Tentative Conclusions

There are many rich methods available to account for dynamic textual work. Significantly, they are not all used to study and understand multilingual writers or translingual moves—though they could be. Consider, for example, Lu's (1994) close, careful reading of student work to explore the ways in which students intentionally work against normalized or standard expressions as they negotiate nuances of meanings between different languages in which they are thinking and writing. Wall's (1992) push for adopting generous reading of all students' work supports this same analytic attention to student work, to students' choices and negotiating moves. Canagarajah's (2006b) methods are exemplified in his close reading of Geneva Smitherman (p. 603) or his careful analysis of the construction of Sri Lankan published articles (Canagarajah, 2002). Lillis' (2008) textual ethnography manages the complexity of text and context in interaction with methodical attention to textual features, talk around those texts, and talk methodologies that engage writers and researchers in longer sustained conversations. All of these methods represent a push for rich, thick understandings of text.

The kind of analysis described here nudges us outside of our areas of comfort, helping us to be willing to struggle productively with meaning. Major cultural differences can be recast at every turn by reframings in the complex contexts in which work is produced. We need more cross-disciplinary and cross-tradition pollination precisely because the translingual world of our students can be researched and we can best teach students in that world with methods that push us into the same spaces they are in. Our students may be more ready than we think for precisely this kind of work—potentially more ready than we are. They are already translingually disposed, already negotiating even when apparently "within" a particular institutional, social, and linguistic context. In some ways, we might consider that we are coming full circle. We want students to "strive for competence in a repertoire of codes and discourses" (Canagarajah, 2006b, p. 592). Rather than "simply joining a speech community, students should learn to shuttle between communities in contextually relevant ways" (p. 593), a shuttling that shares the negotiating flexibility uncovered in my study participants' discursive moves. What we saw as homogeneous monolingual student text moved to being seen as multilingual text, produced from shuttling across languages and contexts, to now imagining that within an apparently monolingual text this shuttling is also at work.

If the translingual project can be furthered by "the audacity of multilingual speakers to challenge the traditional language norms and standards of the 'native speaker'" (Canagarajah, 2006b, p. 589), it can also be furthered by the audacity of student writers challenging other norms and standards. Even in countries of high language standardization like France and the United States, we see with this particular cross-cultural analysis a deep heterogeneous negotiating style that leads us to broaden our parameters for the dispositional and practice-based changes we would like to see, if we want to tap students' already-in-action negotiating dispositions (Canagarajah, 2006b; Horner & Trimbur, 2002; Horner Lu, Royster, & Trimbur 2011).

As we begin to see all languages as also always in translation, we can begin to see our field's relationship to modern languages teaching and research as a resource for our research and teaching with multilingual students, or with "monolingual" students we hope to encourage to take risks and to play. Matsuda (2003) suggests that "second language writing is often considered to be a subfield of Teaching English to Speakers of Other Languages (TESOL) by default. This assumption … is limiting because it has tended to limit the scope of the field to L2 writing *in English*" (p. 172, emphasis mine). Indeed, in France the field of second-language writing has a deeply developed literature. We might grow the field by locating the crossovers, for example, to French teaching of French, as a "first" and as a "second" language.

We have new tools for analyzing the range and complexity of students' negotiating movements. The tools themselves *are drawn from cross-cultural contexts* and *allow students' linguistic–discursive negotiations to be captured* in multi-layered complex detail. The methods drawn from other traditions of analysis shaped by these cross-cultural analyses can, because of their own hybrid, fluid, dynamic nature, serve to further our research approaches in a new linguistic era in composition, partly because they push us into translingual spaces. Now, we certainly are hampered at the level of breadth of knowledge—only able to read the scholarship in languages we know—and our U.S. tangling with multilinguality has its own set of complications, different in other cultural and political landscapes—but how much more might we learn from these other theoretical discussions if we did have that access? What methods and approaches for reading student work in cross-cultural contexts offer the best insights? How might we move beyond comparison to complex treatments of student discourse in ways that illuminate both the work students do and the tools used to analyze that work, helping us to understand the dynamic construction of utterances in contexts? I believe these questions can help us to reconsider composition theory, composition studies, and comparative international work.

References

Bakhtin, M. M. (1988) *Speech genres and other late essays* (M Holquist & C. Emerson, Eds.; V. McGee, Trans.). Austin, TX: University of Texas.

Bartholomae, D. (1985). Inventing the university. In M. Rose (Ed.), *When a writer can't write: Studies in writer's block and other composing-process problems* (pp. 134–165). New York, NY: The Guilford Press.

Bazerman, C. (1994). *Constructing experience.* Carbondale, IL: Southern Illinois University Press.

Bazerman, C., & Prior, P. A. (2004) *What writing does and how it does it: An introduction to analyzing texts and textual practices.* Mahwah, NJ: Lawrence Erlbaum Associates.

Biber, D. (1991). *Variation across speech and writing.* Cambridge, UK: Cambridge University Press.

Biber, D. (2006). *University language: A corpus-based study of spoken and written registers.* Amsterdam, Netherlands: John Benjamins.

Bizzell, P. (1992). *Academic discourse and critical consciousness.* Pittsburgh, PA: University of Pittsburgh Press.

Brutt-Griffler, J. (2002). *World English: A study of its development.* Clevedon, UK: Multilingual Matters.

Canagarajah, A. S. (2002). *A geopolitics of academic writing.* Pittsburgh, PA: University of Pittsburgh Press.

Canagarajah, A. S. (2003). Practicing multiliteracies, in 'Changing currents in second language writing research: A colloquium.' *Journal of Second Language Writing, 12*(2), 151–179. doi:10.1016/S1060-3743(03)00016-X.

Canagarajah, A. S. (2006a). Negotiating the local in English as a lingua franca. *Annual Review of Applied Linguistics, 26,* 197–218. doi:10.1017/S0267190506000109.

Canagarajah, A. S. (2006b).The place of world Englishes in composition. *College Composition and Communication, 57*(4), 586–619.

Canagarajah, A. S. (2010). A rhetoric of shuttling between languages. In B. Horner, M. Z. Lu, and P. K. Matsuda (Eds.), *Cross-language relations in composition* (pp. 158–181), Carbondale, IL: Southern Illinois University Press.

Chafe, W. (1992). Information flow in speaking and writing. In P. Downing, S. D. Lima, & M. Noonan (Eds.), *The linguistics of literacy* (pp. 17–29). Philadelphia, PA: John Benjamins.

Connor (1996). *Contrastive rhetoric: Cross-cultural aspects of second-language writing.* Cambridge, UK: Cambridge University Press.

Connor, U., Nagelhout, E., & Rozycki, W. (Eds.). (2008). *Contrastive rhetoric: Reaching to intercultural rhetoric.* Amsterdam, Netherlands: John Benjamins.

Donahue, C. (2008). *Écrire à l'université: Analyse comparée, France–États-Unis.* Villeneuve-d'Ascq, France: Presses Universitaires du Septentrion.

Donahue, T. (2008). Cross-cultural analysis of student writing: Beyond discourses of difference. *Written Communication, 25*(3), 319–352.

Fairclough, N. (2006). *Language and globalization.* London, UK: Routledge.

Fairclough, N. (2009). *Analysing discourse: Textual analysis for social research.* London, UK: Routledge.

Fraiberg, S. & You, X. (2010, October). Re-assembling composition: Towards a multilingual–multimodal, transnational framework. Paper presented at the Watson Conference, Louisville, KY.

François, F. (1998). *Le discours et ses entours.* Paris, France: L'Harmattan.

Gardin, B. (1990). Engagement sociale et pratiques linguistiques. *La Linguistique, 26,* 107–128.

Geisler, C. (2003). *Analyzing streams of language: Twelve steps to the systematic coding of text, talk, and other verbal data.* New York, NY: Longman.

Grize, J. B. (1996). *Logique naturelle et communications.* Paris, France: Presses Universitaires De France.

Heller (2007). *Bilingualism: A social approach*. New York, NY: Palgrave Macmillan.

Horner, B. (2010). Introduction: From English-only to cross-language relations in composition. In B. Horner, M. Z. Lu, & P. K. Matsuda (Eds.), *Cross-language relations in composition* (pp. 1–20). Carbondale, IL: Southern Illinois University Press.

Horner, B., Lu, M., Royster, J. J., & Trimbur, J. (2011). Language difference in writing: Toward a translingual approach. *College English, 73*(3), 303–21.

Horner, B., NeCamp, S., & Donahue, C. (2011). Toward a multilingual composition scholarship: From English only to a translingual norm. *College Composition and Communication, 63*(2), 269–300.

Horner, B., & Trimbur, J. (2002). English only and U.S. college composition. *College Composition and Communication, 53*(4), 594–630. doi:10.2307/1512118.

House, J. (1999). Misunderstanding in intercultural communication: Interactions in English as a lingua franca and the myth of mutual intelligibility. In C. Gnutzmann (Ed.), *Teaching and learning English as a global language* (pp. 73–89). Tübingen, Germany: Stauffenburg Verlag.

Kaplan, R. B. (1966). Cultural thought patterns in inter-cultural education. *Language Learning, 16*(1–2), 1–20.

Kaplan, R. B. (2000). What in the world is contrastive rhetoric? In C. G. Panetta (Ed.), *Contrastive rhetoric revisited and redefined* (pp. vii–xix). Danbury, CT: Lawrence Erlbaum Associates.

Kramsch, C. (2006). The traffic in meaning. *Asia Pacific Journal of Education, 26*(1), 99–104. doi:10.1080/02188790600608091.

Leki, I. (2006). The legacy of first-year composition. In P. K. Matsuda, C. Ortmeier-Hooper, & X. You (Eds.), *The politics of second language writing: In search of the promised land* (pp. 59–74). West Lafayette, IN: Parlor.

Lillis, T. (2008). Ethnography as method, methodology, and "deep theorizing": Closing the gap between text and context in academic writing research. *Written Communication, 25*(3), 353–388. doi:10.1177/0741088308319229.

Lillis, T., & Curry, M. J. (2006). Professional academic writing by multilingual scholars: Interactions with literacy brokers in the production of English-medium texts. *Written Communication, 23*(1), 3–35.

Lillis, T. M., & Curry, M. J. (2010). *Academic writing in global context*. Abingdon, UK: Routledge.

Lu, M. Z. (1994). Professing multiculturalism: The politics of style in the contact zone. *CCC 45*(4), 442–458.

Lu, M. Z. (2004). An essay on the work of composition: Composing English against the order of fast capitalism. *College Composition and Communication, 56*(1),16–50. doi:10.2307/4140679.

Maingueneau, D. (1998). *Analyser les textes de la communication*. Paris, France: Dunod.

Matsuda, P. K. (1999). Composition studies and ESL writing. *College Composition and Communication, 50*(4), 699–721. doi:10.2307/358488.

Matsuda, P. K. (2003). Introduction, in "Changing currents in second language writing research: A colloquium." *Journal of Second Language Writing, 12*(2), 151–179. doi:10.1016/S1060-3743(03)00016-X.

Matsuda, P. K. (2006). The myth of linguistic homogeneity in U.S. college composition. *College English, 68*(6), 637–651.

Meierkord, C. (2000). Interpreting successful lingua franca interaction. *Linguistik, 5*(1), Retrieved from http://www.linguistik-online.com/1_00/MEIERKOR.HTM (accessed Nov. 15, 2012).

Pennycook, A. (2008). English as a language always in translation. *European Journal of English Studies, 12*(1), 33–47. doi:10.1080/13825570801900521.

Ortmeier-Hooper, C. (2008). English may be my second language, but I'm not "ESL." *College Composition and Communication, 59*(3), 389–419.

Pratt, M. L. (1991). Arts of the contact zone. *Profession, 91*, 33–40.

Prendergast, C. (2010). In praise of incomprehension. In B. Horner, M. Z. Lu, & P. K. Matsuda (Eds.), *Cross-language relations in composition* (pp. 230–235). Carbondale, IL: Southern Illinois University Press.

Prior, P. (1998). *Writing/disciplinarity: A sociohistoric account of literate activity in the academy.* Mahwah, NJ: Lawrence Erlbaum Associates.

Prior, P., & Bilbro, R. (2012). Academic enculturation: Developing literate practices and disciplinary Identities. In M. Castelló & C. Donahue (Eds.), *University writing: Selves and texts in academic societies.* Bingley, UK: Emerald Group.

Rubdy, R., & Saraceni, M. (2006). *English in the world: Global rules, global roles.* London, UK: Continuum.

Silva, T., Leki, I., & Carson, J. (1997). Broadening the perspective of mainstream composition studies: Some thoughts from the disciplinary margins. *Written Communication, 14*(3), 398–428.

Silva, T, J., & Matsuda, P. K (Eds.). (2001). *Landmark essays on ESL writing.* Mahwah, NJ: Hermagoras.

Slevin, J. F. (2001). *Introducing English: Essays in the intellectual work of composition.* Pittsburgh, PA: University of Pittsburgh Press.

Smith, K. (2011). What good is world literature? *College English, 73*(6), 585–603.

Starobinski, J. (1999). *L'oeil vivant.* Paris, France: Gallimard.

Tardy, C. (2006). Researching first and second language genre learning: A comparative review and a look ahead. *Journal of Second Language Writing, 15*(2), 79–101. doi:10.1016/j.jslw.2006.04.003.

Venuti, L. (1998). *The scandals of translation: Towards an ethics of difference.* London: Routledge.

Wall, S. (1992). Seeing the dancer in the dance. *Iowa English Bulletin, 40*, 69–86.

You, X. (2006). Globalization and the politics of teaching EFL writing. In P. K. Matsuda, C. Ortmeier-Hooper, & X. You (Eds.), *The politics of second language writing: In search of the promised land* (pp. 188–204). West Lafayette, IN: Parlor.

15

WRITING ACROSS LANGUAGES: DEVELOPING RHETORICAL ATTUNEMENT

Rebecca Lorimer

Much of the research that has set out to describe multilingual writers' resources focuses on writers' knowledge rather than their literate practices—what their literate resources are rather than how they are used. For example, sociologist Papastergiadis (2000) argues that "fissures within language and cultural identity" create a kind of "critical sensibility of innovation and improvisation" (p. 118), while Canagarajah (2002) suggests that multilingualism fosters "a curiosity towards the language, the ability to intuit linguistic rules from observation of actual usage, a metalinguistic awareness of the system behind languages" (p. 134) as well as the "patience, tolerance, and humility to negotiate the differences of interlocutors" (Canagarajah, 2006, p. 593). But descriptions of what multilingual writers know—their awareness that language difference is common, their sense that language can be improvised—often stop short of showing where these resources come from or how writers put them to use in specific moments of communication. Further, this focus can mistakenly suggest that multilingual writers' resources are fixed and stable, traveling directly from their home culture and language to the English-dominant United States as a static, fully formed repertoire of literate skills.

Instead, multilingual writers call on and create literate resources in the process of making-do, asserting themselves, or communicating on-the-fly in specific situations. This is a practice-based understanding of literate resources, one that Connor (2008) would call not "contrastive" rhetoric, but "intercultural" rhetoric, which describes the "cultural, social, and educational factors affecting a writing situation," and understands "the processes of writing as well as the historical background and context that affected the writing and the writer" (p. 304). She and other scholars (Baca, 2008; Bawarshi, 2010; Canagarajah, 2011; Cenoz & Gorter, 2011; Guerra, 2004; Horner, Lu, Royster, & Trimbur, 2011; Pennycook, 2010) are in pursuit of the "how" of multilingual writing: how multilingual writers use their languages to negotiate, create, and connect as they make meaning with others in socially and culturally infused situations. This chapter describes the shape of this experience, investigating not only how writing across languages creates a certain awareness or sensibility, but also how multilingual writers use this sensibility to take action with writing in their everyday lives.

The three brief accounts below show that this sensibility is inherently rhetorical. As multilingual writers use and create their literate resources in everyday practice, they develop an ear for difference, a practiced negotiation of meaning for effect, or what we might call "rhetorical attunement"—a way of acting with language that assumes linguistic multiplicity and invites the negotiation of meaning to accomplish communicative ends. By virtue of their daily experience with linguistic difference, the writers below are tuned toward the communicative predicaments of multilingual interaction. These predicaments are both idiosyncratic and ordinary, moments in which rhetorical strategies are practiced and often created. A rhetorical and practice-based framework shows us that these writers do not necessarily enter situations with an *a priori* sensibility that then dictates their writing activities, but instead come to understand language—become rhetorically attuned—across a lifetime of communicating across difference. The portraits of these three subjects derive from a study of 26 qualitative life history interviews conducted with multilingual immigrants over the course of a year. The interviews aimed to elicit the lived experiences of immigrants writing their way across languages by asking participants about their in- and out-of-school literacy memories, current literacy practices, and opinions about writing and communicating as multilingual individuals. Participants immigrated from 17 different countries and spoke 22 different languages, including English. Their class background, educational and work experience, and citizenship status varied widely: three came as students, 12 came with or to join their U.S.-employed husbands, one came for her own job, two were refugees, two immigrated under diversity "lottery" visas, and five did not share their reasons or status.

Sabohi

Sabohi, a school principal in the United States who speaks English, Urdu, Kashmiri, and Hindi regards language multiplicity as an unremarkable fact of life. She describes her former work in Pakistan for a Kashmiri television station with a shrug:

S   I would also present, which was not in English though, a program on the television that was in the native language. So I would do writing for that. I'd write my own script, what I wanted to say. And I always, it was in Kashmiri, but I wrote it in English.

R   So you wrote it out in English but you were presenting on TV in Kashmiri?

S   Yeah, I would jot, I'd note down that and then I would go along and just change.

R As you were speaking.
S As I was speaking, yeah.
R That is very brave.
S Yeah, that is very brave. [shrug]

On live TV, she was perfectly comfortable translating from what she had written in English on her script into Kashmiri in the moment she was speaking into
the camera. She explains that, occasionally, she asked her co-presenter for vocabulary help in Kashmiri, which is her third language and not the one in which
she feels most comfortable writing. She would note a rare Kashmiri word on the
script, but for the most part, what she read in English she fluently delivered in
Kashmiri into the camera.

Sabohi says this movement between languages was essential to her workplace,
and part of her everyday life in Pakistan. She explains, "You know that no, there
are other things, there are other people. You learn that early on in your life." She
says growing up she realized "okay this is Punjabi … this is Gujarathi, and this is
Hindi and this is this. And you try to communicate and you see, okay it's different." Because of this norm of multiplicity and difference, Sabohi knows that the
negotiation of meaning across multiple languages is not only a given, but a necessity in order to win over listening or reading audiences:

> When it comes to writing in mass communication, I have seen that in some
> newspapers, it is being done and it has been even effective to use different
> languages. Like when you are in India, it will definitely help you if you are
> communicating to the masses, what you are trying to get across to them
> if you use some Hindi words in there. And if you kept their culture, their
> beliefs, their traditions in mind, when you wrote that piece that you want
> to communicate them to, it will definitely help you to get across your point
> clearer than if you stick to, okay, literary Shakespearean English? No. I
> mean maybe few people have done masters in English or something they'll
> understand you, what about others? If you want to write to the masses you
> have to use the language they use, right? I mean even if that means there's
> mixing of a few, in school newsletter for example, I don't mind. … If you
> are able to add a few words, change a few words and still you are able to
> communicate, so what is the harm? So what if you don't protect it the way
> it is just because that is part of your identity and part of your culture you
> don't want it to be, um, contaminated, right?

Sabohi shows how she has carried a specific literacy practice—writing for a public audience—with her from Pakistan to her current job as a school principal in the
United States She slides between these settings as she makes her point, thinking
first of her writing experiences in Pakistan and ending with her school newsletter
writing in the United States As she describes the effect of this practice in both set-

tings, she reveals her developed sense of audience awareness, keeping an audience's "culture, their beliefs, their traditions in mind" to achieve a certain effect. In fact, Sabohi considers her audience at length, and it is this resource that she draws on to describe the rhetorical effectiveness of negotiation. She describes communicating to an audience for whom reading in only one language would not only be unnatural, but detrimental to communication. She knows that "mixing of a few" words from various languages is a way to extend a communicative hand to one's audience and show a willingness to work toward meaning-making together. From her lived experience writing across four languages in Pakistan and now writing to an audience in a school where at least seven or eight languages are spoken, Sabohi uses her discursive resources to improvise communication across varied traditions and values, and cultivate a distinct rhetorical attunement toward language multiplicity.

Further, Sabohi is attuned to the relationship of language and power. When she asks, "So what if you don't protect it the way it is just because that is part of your identity and part of your culture you don't want it to be contaminated, right?" she was extending an earlier thought about why individuals or institutions resist language mixing. Canagarajah (2002) notes that writing as a multilingual can "provide a critical detachment from dominant discourses" and Sabohi uses that detachment to recognize that there are high stakes in language maintenance, as well (p. 134). She cites India's move to revert cities back to their pre-colonial names, a move she says she understands as "people wanting to protect an identity and not keeping up altogether with the times." In other words, her attunement to "the times" is one of inevitable language change and an almost dismissive attitude toward colonial remnants of language practice. In other words, Sabohi's attunement is complex: in various turns she adapts to a widely diverse audience, dismisses the harm of language mixing, embraces language change, and recognizes a larger discursive system in which this communication plays out.

Yolanda

Yolanda, a Colombian veterinarian who now works in the United States as a bilingual science teacher, also assumes a norm of multiplicity and considers language negotiation a skill to be cultivated. In describing the language-mixing practices of her own multilingual students, Yolanda explains that she encouraged improvisation, negotiation, and cooperation in a manner that assumed language struggle would be present and normal:

> Sometimes I asked the kids when we're reading something scientific, "How do you think you say this?" And they say, "I don't know." ... They know I don't know how to say it, so I ask them, "How do you think? How would you say it?" And they find a way to say it, and I say "let's use it." And then I ask one of the kids that I know dad's a biology teacher or something: "Ask your dad and tell us the right way because we're using this way but

we don't know if it's right." [laughing] It would be nice to use the right way. Like me, hello I'm teaching biology and I don't know how to say the words we're writing. I mean, that's negative, but the thing is that I make it a comedy. It becomes a comedy for all of us, and then okay let's move on. ... And for kids that speak other languages you know, I have an accent, but look at me, I can do it, so go ahead. "But what if it's wrong?" Doesn't matter, look at me! You can say it wrong, you know. So I think I help the kids sometimes with that.

Yolanda carried this literacy practice—reading science writing in English—with her from the Colombian university where she had been trained as a veterinarian. Yolanda explains that at her college they rarely had access to Spanish-language translations of the scientific scholarly journal articles that were required reading. She had to work with classmates in groups to translate their reading into Spanish, or occasionally hire outside translators. Yolanda calls on these resources—collaborative meaning-making and accessing outside experts—in a new context in which she is not the student, but the teacher. As a teacher, she taps into her students' native-speaker knowledge and consults outside experts, as when she asked a student to consult his biologist dad on pronunciation. As a teacher, Yolanda continues to put into practice these linguistic resources to get through a text and, as she says, "use the words the right way."

The communicative event that invited Yolanda to call on these resources also allowed her to create resources for her students in that moment, showing them that language is up for negotiation. She models for her students a norm of language difference, fine tuning their ability to hear and understand accent. She has them laugh with her at the occasional comedy of reading and writing across languages and helps them, as she says, "move on" from certainty in a manner that evokes Firth's (1996) let-it-pass principle. Further, Yolanda practices negotiation in the specific rhetorical situation of her bilingual science classroom, encouraging students to use a provisional pronunciation—"let's use it"—and modeling how to negotiate these meanings until they get it right. Yolanda not only reveals her own attunement toward language in this context, but also attunes her students to the normalcy of language uncertainty: "'But what if it's wrong?' Doesn't matter, look at me!" Yolanda's linguistic and discursive resources prove to be particularly complex, indexing a quiet resistance to common classroom practices that treat multiple languages as separate and standard. Yolanda teaches her students the multilingual practices she has cultivated over a lifetime, continuing to foster her own as well as her students' rhetorical attunement.

Tashi

While Sabohi and Yolanda's experiences show how rhetorical attunement is cultivated in communicative exchanges of writer and reader or speaker and listener,

Tashi, a 24-year-old Tibetan nursing student from India, becomes attuned by constructing meaning on her own. During her years at an English-medium Indian boarding school for Tibetan orphans, she studied English-language newspapers and books in a self-sponsored practice of language analysis and exploration. She was motivated to begin such study when she realized that "Whatever you have in your brain can't be seen by other people. You just have to write it down and show them what you know." She explains that in Indian schools, "It's not like here, not like multiple choice, over there everything in essay. So you really need to express OUT all your brain." She felt that her grades were suffering because she couldn't express what she knew through writing in English. So she set out to learn how this was done. Tashi says she would collect books and newspapers and analyze "how they write … how they go about it."

> I just marked all the vocabularies and like and I point out the phrase, how they use it. And then I note how they uh … play with the words. And in contrast, and in literal meaning and in applied meaning. All those. This makes me know how to play around with the words and get the things done. And play around with the sentences. So yeah, then I really learned the skill of how to play around with the words and I really don't have to have a strict rule doing English.

If Tashi had been simply copying out grammatical patterns and mimicking them, or noting the organization of newspaper stories and following that structure herself, she would not seem to be negotiating meaning as she acquired more advanced levels of written English. But in fact she was specifically looking for how these writers "used" the vocabulary and phrases she marked, how these were used to make "literal" or "applied meanings," and how one might "play around" with sentences and words in English to "get the things done." Tashi's repeated use of "play" shows her acknowledgment that meaning is not fixed or static, but is up for negotiation. This is why she doesn't have "a strict rule doing English."

This practice of looking to textual models for the negotiation of meaning is one that Tashi continues in the United States She explains that, after entering nursing school in the United States, she continued this practice with her science textbooks in order to understand how science was composed differently. She also attempted to pass on this multilingual practice to a friend who was frustrated with her slow acquisition of written English:

> Then I was telling her, "You just have to take an essay and analyze how it is done. … And whenever you see a piece you wouldn't read for the content you will read for … how it's played around." So I was telling her. And once you get grip hold of it you can manipulate whatever you want to with the language … and you know how things going around and then you understand for yourself how it works.

Tashi's ability to access this resource and pass it on in the United States allows her to continue to play with and negotiate meaning in English, even after she has become a very proficient speaker and writer. Tashi exhibits what some scholars call "common multilingual traits," showing "a curiosity toward the language, [and] the ability to intuit linguistic rules from observation of actual usage" (Canagarajah, 2002, p. 134). Now that she feels she has a "grip" on English, she delights in manipulating it to accomplish "whatever [she] wants to with the language." But her willingness to work with language, to read for the playfulness of language at the word, sentence, or discourse level, shows how deeply Tashi is tuned to the natural negotiation of communicating across multiple languages.

Cultivating Rhetorical Attunement

These brief communicative moments from Sabohi, Yolanda, and Tashi's lives show how their literate resources developed over time, from ordinary, unpredictable, political, or emotional communicative experiences. While Sabohi, Yolanda, and Tashi share a common attunement toward difference and negotiation, they do so in specific ways informed by their own histories and changing life situations. In this way, their multilingual resources are in-process and situationally specific, what Blommaert (2010) calls the "truncated repertoires" that are "grounded in people's biographies and in the wider histories of the places where they were composed" (p. 24). Looking for moments of rhetorical attunement is one way to resist treating literate resources as stable and easily accessed knowledge, and instead account for the ongoing and often unstable practices that comprise multilingual writing.

And if we consider multilingual resources to be not discrete skills but practices informed by personal and cultural histories, then we need to rethink how to cultivate and assess these practices. If multilingual writers can nimbly negotiate language difference or create provisional meanings for the sake of communication, we need to focus less on naming and measuring what these writers know and instead investigate and facilitate what they already do. We might define proficiency not as a level of acquisition but as a stage in attunement, teaching for and assessing the relative success of language negotiation and play with specific audiences in certain situations. Fundamentally, we need to account for the depth and complexity of everyday multilingual practices and better understand how all writers act with multiple languages to navigate a larger discursive system.

References

Baca, D. (2008). *Mestiz@ scripts, digital migrations and the territories of writing*. New York, NY: Palgrave Macmillan.
Bawarshi, A. (2010). The challenges and possibilities of taking up multiple discursive resources in U.S. college composition. In B. Horner, M. Z. Lu, & P. K. Matsuda (Eds.),

Cross-language relations in composition (pp. 196–203). Carbondale, IL: Southern Illinois University Press.

Blommaert, J. (2010). *The sociolinguistics of globalization.* Cambridge, UK: Cambridge University Press.

Canagarajah, S. (2002). *Critical academic writing and multilingual students.* Ann Arbor, MI: University of Michigan Press.

Canagarajah, S. (2006). The place of world Englishes in composition: Pluralization continued. *College Composition and Communication, 57*(4), 586–619.

Canagarajah, S. (2011). Codemeshing in academic writing: Identifying teachable strategies of translanguaging. *The Modern Language Journal, 95*(3), 401–417. doi:10.1111/j.1540-4781.2011.01207.x.

Cenoz, J. & Gorter, D. (2011). Focus on multilingualism: A study of trilingual writing. *The Modern Language Journal, 95*(3), 356–369. doi:10.1111/j.1540-4781.2011.01206.x.

Connor, U. (2008). *Contrastive rhetoric: Reaching to intercultural rhetoric.* Philadelphia, PA: John Benjamins Publishing.

Firth, A. (1996). The discursive accomplishment of normality: On "lingua franca" English and conversation analysis. *Journal of Pragmatics, 26*(2), 237–259. doi:10.1016/0378-2166(96)00014-8.

Guerra, J. (2004). Putting literacy in its place: Nomadic consciousness and the practice of transcultural repositioning. In C. Guitierrez-Jones (Ed.), *Rebellious reading: The dynamics of Chicana/o cultural literacy* (pp. 19–37). University of California—Santa Barbara, CA: Chicano Studies Institute.

Horner, B., Lu, M., Royster, J., & Trimbur, J. (2011). Language difference in writing: Toward a translingual approach. *College English, 73*(3), 303–321.

Papastergiadis, N. (2000). *The turbulence of migration: globalization, deterritorialization, and hybridity.* Cambridge, UK: Blackwell Publishers.

Pennycook, A. (2010). *Language as a local practice.* New York, NY: Routledge.

16

RESEARCH ON MULTILINGUAL WRITERS IN THE DISCIPLINES: THE CASE OF BIOMEDICAL ENGINEERING

Mya Poe

In the last decade, Writing Across the Curriculum (WAC) scholars have become increasingly attuned to the needs of multilingual students across the curriculum (Johns, 2001; Zawacki, 2010). Yet, many WAC materials on assignment design, assessment, and peer review (Anson, 2002; Bean, 1996; Segall & Smart, 2005) remain aimed toward monolingual students. As a result, although WAC scholars have recognized the need to widen our perspective, we've done little to advance our research and teaching practices. Indeed, as Hall (2009) points out, the future of WAC in higher education is tied to our ability to address the needs of linguistically diverse students. Hall writes:

> The future of [Writing Across the Curriculum] ... is tied to the ways in which higher education will have to, willingly or unwillingly, evolve in the wake of globalization and in response to the increasing linguistic diversity of our student population.
>
> *(p. 34)*

But how exactly does WAC need to evolve? One way to answer that question is to ask how WAC research might evolve. In this chapter, I suggest how WAC scholarship with its rich tradition of naturalistic studies might contribute to our evolving conversation about multilingual writers across the curriculum (Frodesen, 2009; Johns, 2001; Wolfe-Quintero & Segade, 1999; Zamel, 1995). Drawing on findings from a multi-year study of a graduate student in biomedical engineering, I suggest how such findings might inform a research agenda on multilingual writers in the disciplines that goes beyond a focus on plagiarism or sentence-level concerns (Currie, 2006; Ferris & Roberts, 2006). My approach in proposing such an agenda aligns with Canagarajah's (2002a) theory of multilingualism in that there is always interaction and borrowing across cultures and communicative genres. In a multilingual framework, language difference is not a barrier to overcome but "a resource for producing meaning in writing, speaking, reading, and listening" (Horner, Lu, Royster, & Trimbur, 2011, p. 303). A multilingual perspective is especially valuable in studying the transnational contexts in which multilingual writers learn and work today. Such a perspective moves beyond contrastive studies, which although useful, too often rely on a binary approach to identity and writing that does not capture the dynamic process of learning to write in many communities of practice (Canagarajah, 2002a).

Because I am interested in the connection between disciplinary writing and professional practice, my work draws on notions of legitimate peripheral participation, "the process by which newcomers become part of a community of practice" (Lave & Wenger, 1991, p. 29). What is useful about Lave and Wenger's approach is that it is a social theory of learning. Learning is not acquisition of bits of knowledge or genres. Lave and Wenger write that, "conceiving of learning in terms of participation focuses attention on ways in which it is an evolving, continuously renewed set of relations" (1991, pp. 49–50). These relations are negotiated throughout a student's introduction to a disciplinary community and into full-fledged membership into that community. Through participation, apprentices learn to draw on various resources available to members of that community. Such strategies are relevant to multilingual writers as well as monolingual ones. Thus, by examining how multilingual writers in the disciplines draw on various linguistic resources in learning to write in their respective fields, we can better understand how individuals negotiate disciplinary participation.

The Changing Landscape of Writing Across the Curriculum Research

Research on writing in the disciplines has tended to follow one of three trajectories—research on the particular linguistic and textual practices used in disciplinary communication (Bazerman, 1988; Swales, 1990), research on the relationship between writing and learning (Britton, Burgess, Martin, McLeod, & Rosen, 1975 Emig, 1977), and studies on "the experiences and development of students involving writing in their disciplinary courses and of teachers as they have come to employ writing in their courses" (Bazerman et al., 2005, pp. 43–44).

One trajectory of research on writing—rhetorics of the disciplines—has been driven by the realization that we need to know about the forms, practices, and rhetorics of disciplinary communication (Lyne & Miller, 2009). Such work examines practices in individual disciplines, ranging from science to economics (Fahnestock, 2009; McClosky, 1985). In the natural sciences, for example, researchers have undertaken analysis of such topics as linguistic structures (Halliday & Martin, 1993; Hyland, 2004), scientific visuals (Baigrie, 1996; Lynch & Woolgar, 1990), knowledge claims made by scientists (Prelli, 1989), and the changing textual practices of scientific communication (Bazerman, 1988; Gross, Harmon, & Reidy, 2002). Such work has been important in providing detailed studies of how disciplinary knowledge is constructed through textual practices. Such research has been codified in textbooks and handbooks that offer students advice on writing in various disciplinary contexts (e.g., Porush, 1995; Swales & Freak, 2000).

Beyond research on disciplinary rhetorics, naturalistic studies in disciplinary and professional contexts have helped us understand how novices acquire disciplinary discourses and the connection between writing and learning. Drawing on theories such as socio-cultural theory (Prior, 2005), activity theory (Engeström, 1987; Russell, 1997), situated learning (Lave & Wegner, 1991), and North American genre theory (Miller, 1984), these studies have examined writing in secondary education contexts (Roth, Pozzer-Ardenghi, & Han, 2005), in college classroom and lab contexts (Berkenkotter, Huckin, & Ackerman, 1991; Haas, 1994), and in the workplace (Beaufort, 2008; Winsor, 1997, 2003). We have learned from these studies that development is neither linear nor consistent (Sommers & Saltz, 2004); mentoring and modeling are critical to development (Blakeslee, 2001); students must acquire genre knowledge, rhetorical knowledge, and process knowledge in addition to subject-area knowledge (Artemeva & Freedman, 2008; Beaufort, 2008; Patton, 2011); and that experts must be attuned to changing conventions in their fields (Lunsford, 2011).

In "Where Do Naturalistic Studies of WAC/WID Point?," Russell (2001) reviews naturalistic studies in the field and outlines four common factors that researchers find shape student learning:

1. The students' motives as they move through and beyond formal schooling, negotiating their future directions and commitments with those of the disciplines and professions that faculty and classrooms represent;
2. The identities that students (re)construct as they try on new ways with written words;
3. The pedagogical tools that faculty provide (or don't provide) students; and
4. The processes through which students learn to write and write to learn in formal schooling.

(p. 261)

As Russell points out, this group of studies supports the notion that learning occurs when students are offered a range of opportunities to model and practice the written activities of disciplinary communities. Focusing on motivation and identity reminds us that learning to write in a discipline is a deeply personal and social activity, not merely a set of textual practices, and that we ignore the social dimensions of disciplinary communication at the peril of helping students become better writers.

Research has suggested that the same factors are important for multilingual writers (for a review see Atkinson & Connor, 2008). For example, Tardy's (2009) portrait of four multilingual writers at a midwestern university shows how students develop genre knowledge in the disciplines through guided participation. As students like Chatri, a Thai PhD student in Electrical and Computer Engineering, moved further into lab-based research, he moved away from learning the isolated genres found in classroom contexts to learning the network of genres that operate within a discourse community. Tardy concludes that what allowed for Chatri's development as a writer was his "increased participation in the networks of research genres, a fluid movement among and across genres within this network, and the adoption of multiple roles and positions of agency within the network" (p. 246).

In *Writing Games: Multicultural Case Studies of Academic Literacy Practices in Higher Education*, Cassanave (2002) also writes of the importance of participation, flux, and identity in her research with multilingual writers at various stages in academic settings:

> People's identities as novices or experts and as more or less peripherally or centrally positioned change as their practices change or as they seek new playing fields. As their practices change, in other words, their understandings change (an intellectual or cognitive transition) and their roles change (a social and political transition). The result is that they come to see themselves and be seen in new ways.
>
> *(p. 256)*

Finally, Lillis and Curry (2006, 2010) in their research with a multilingual education and psychology faculty point to the importance of paying attention to the ways that globalization shapes disciplinary participation (see also Canagarajah, 2002b). As they explain, "the pressure to produce in English constitutes a significant dimension to multilingual scholars' lives" (Lillis & Curry, 2010, p. 4). They argue that notions of individual competence need to give way to a focus on academic text production as a networked activity in which participants must establish and maintain local as well as transnational connections. In examining the process of how multilingual scholars publish, Lillis and Curry advance the notion of "literacy brokers"—"a meta-category to refer to all the different kinds of direct intervention by different people, other than named authors, in the production of texts and to track what is actually involved" (2010, p. 88). Because brokers may hold quite powerful positions in the publishing process, they can exert enormous influence over the writing output of multilingual writers.

The work of Tardy, Cassanave, Lillis and Curry, and others point to productive directions for naturalistic studies of multilingual writers in WAC contexts. Following, I describe how an ongoing longitudinal case study of a Korean graduate student, Park, in biomedical engineering might contribute other insights for research. In examining the interplay of Park's experiences in a graduate seminar focused on writing in the disciplines and his experiences in his lab group, I argue that Park's writing development must not been viewed as the trajectory of an individual working within a scientific academic context but as multilingual writer who (1) could leverage his relationships with local and international collaborators to get his research in print, and (2) could draw on his increasing understanding of scientific grant genres to produce the materials necessary for his job application.

There are, of course, limitations to extracting too much from an individual case. However, I take the position that multiple, accumulated individual cases with their contradictions and inconsistencies can guide us as we advance a view of WAC that is inclusive of linguistic diversity. In the case described in this chapter, biomedical engineering is a useful site for such research because the notion of monocultural agents does not fit with the international activity of biomedical knowledge production and communicative practices. For example, U.S.-based researchers often must move beyond U.S. borders to gain access to resources such as clinical trial participants and stem cell lines. On the other hand, because of the government and industry investment in the United States in biomedical research, the United States is an attractive site for international scholars. For students like Park, a biomedical engineering degree from MIT means getting the best education in the field and obtaining a degree that has currency in the global job market.

Learning to Communicate in a Graduate Communication-Intensive Course

The basis for this case study is a multi-year collaboration with the Harvard-MIT Health Sciences Technology program (HST), a MD-PhD program. For five years I worked with a HST faculty member to develop instruction for first-year graduate students that linked to writing requirements for students' thesis proposals to classroom-based writing activities. Our goal in Frontiers in Biomedical Engineering and Physics (Frontiers) was to give first-year graduate students in the program an overview of the biomedical engineering field and guided support in grant writing. Specifically, we wanted students to learn the rhetorical, situated aspects of grant writing—scientific reviewers' expectations for grants, how grants were circulated and scored in the National Institutes of Health (NIH) review process, and how to present the ethos of a professional researcher by using certain rhetorical techniques that gave reviewers confidence in the researcher's approach.

Over the semester, students wrote a NIH R01 grant, which at 15 single-spaced pages, including aims, a literature review, discussion of preliminary data, and research plan, is a substantial task for a graduate student. If students had an existing research agenda, we encouraged them to write about their own research. Students who had not yet chosen a research area could write about a subject of their choice. At the end of the semester, students gave peer reviews based on the NIH peer-review format in which each grant receives an anonymous review from a primary and secondary reviewer and is scored by a team of experts in a "study section."

After several years of working with students, I wanted to know how well the course goals were being met in helping students learn disciplinary writing conventions. Using interviews with students, teachers, and teaching assistants, analysis of student writing and published materials, surveys, and direct participation, I followed several students through spring semester 2008 and then followed-up with those students in 2010. Through these interviews, I wanted to know how students were applying the rhetorical concepts taught in class, how outside forces such as students' mentors were shaping their learning, and students' identities were important in learning to write like a biomedical engineer. In what follows, I provide findings from one student, Park, a Korean graduate student.

Park: Writing in Classroom and Laboratory Contexts

When I first met Park in 2008 in Frontiers, he was a second-year graduate student working in an optics lab. For the Frontiers grant assignment, Park wrote about his Master's research on the membrane fluctuations of red blood cells in malaria patients. In malaria patients, the cell membrane becomes stiffer. Researchers have started to study these changes using optical techniques. Although Park was excited about his work, his mentor had encouraged him to leave behind the malaria research and focus on a different project related to leprosy. Yet, Park decided to write about his malaria research in Frontiers because he had data for the class assignment. The leprosy research was still too new to present.

Throughout the semester, Park worked on drafting and refining each section of his NIH grant application on membrane fluctuations in red blood cells. He had an excellent ability to generate text, use technical terminology correctly, and integrate the suggested content and rhetorical changes from the course teaching assistant and me. Although in many ways Park was an advanced writer, his prose still evidenced various errors, including subject–verb agreement and missing articles. Looking at Park's text, however, only provided a small window into his development as a scientific writer. Looking beyond specific "errors" in his texts to the contexts in which he was writing provided a richer story of his development as a writer.

In his lab group, Park had gotten the chance to work on various papers that were primarily focused on microscopy techniques. He found these writing activities helpful because he was learning about the scientific publishing process and getting to work closely with his mentor. Although some publishing opportunities were becoming available to him, he still had not gotten his mentor to take an interest in his work on the red blood cell characteristics of malaria. In spring of 2008, it seemed that Park's malaria research would be left abandoned.

The story was quite different when I talked to Park two years later. By May 2010, Park had not only defended his dissertation—which happened to be the red blood cell research on malaria—but also had secured a faculty position at a premier science and engineering university in Korea. He had published 16 scientific papers and had given an average of five talks per year since 2008.

This remarkable change in Park's professional trajectory had to do with the kinds of opportunities and access that had become available to him in his lab group. After I talked to him in 2008, Park was able to get help from a colleague to publish his research on malaria and red blood cells. His article was published in the *Proceedings of the National Academy of Science* (*PNAS*) and featured in the MIT news. The reception of *PNAS* article along with Park's grant application writing experiences in Frontiers got him noticed in the lab, and his mentor began directing more writing work his way, including grant applications. A second motivator in Park's professional development was the death of his mentor. With his mentor's death, Park's research support was uncertain. Another faculty member who worked with the group subsequently became Park's mentor and encouraged Park to complete his dissertation quickly because the lab's future was uncertain. And since Park had written extensively about his malaria research—for his Master's degree, for this Frontiers grant, and in various publications—his malaria research became the basis of his dissertation.

Park's professional progress was, in part, the result of his growing understanding of how to capitalize on peer networks for publishing. Working closely with his mentor for his first paper, Park then turned to international collaborators for subsequent papers, including researchers from Israel and Germany as well as U.S.-based researchers at the University of Illinois. Park explained the group's process for writing and revising: "we were separating the manuscript for all the people and I was getting the comment from everyone. That was very, very helpful to make that manuscript in good shape … we end up with 16 versions of the manuscript because every time you just send the manuscript back and forth." The group's process, thus, was one in which Park was able to position himself at the center of the publishing enterprise, working to draft the initial article and then synthesize comments. Park called this his "scientific networking community."

Another factor in Park's progress was his development of genre knowledge. From Frontiers, Park had gained a growing sense of how to shape his work to different audiences, and he started to aim his research at higher impact publications, i.e., those with broader audiences. In the most important application of genre knowledge, Park applied what he learned in Frontiers in his job search. Park used his research proposal from Frontiers as part of his job application materials. He explained that his ability to translate his research into a grant application impressed his Korean interviewers.

> I had a chance to have dinner with them and they were asking, how could you learn to write this way. I was to say that I learned from the course which is [Frontiers]. They said that was very unusual for the most graduate student because for post doc they could expect some post docs had a chance to write grant proposal in U.S. The Korean student is very unique, very rare case that I had the chance to write some kind of the unique and know the structures.
>
> (June 2010)

In the end, when I left Park in late 2010 he had achieved acceptance in the biomedical engineering community because of his ability to mobilize resources in the global contexts of biomedical research. By late 2011, his *PNAS* article had been cited more than 89 times in articles, reviews, and book chapters by researchers in the United States, Korea, Germany, England, France, Japan, Russia, Singapore, Israel, Australia, Austria, Portugal, China, Italy, India, and Canada.

An Agenda for Research on Multilingual Writers Across the Curriculum

So what can we learn from Park's story that might inform a research agenda for studying multilingual writers across the disciplines? As multiple scholars have pointed out (Johns, 2001; Leki, 1992), multilingual students are heterogeneous. Park is one case of a multilingual writer, but his case is a compelling portrait of a highly successful second-language writer whose writing development goes far beyond the mastery of one genre or fluency in Standard Edited English. His case provides three important points for research on multilingual writers.

First, Park's case reveals that in studying multilingual writers we must pay attention to the many dimensions involved in writing that go beyond surface-level features or the mastery of individual genres. Like Tardy (2009) in her study of four multilingual students, I began to see that Park's development as a writer was much more complex than could be captured by genre questions. Park's development as a writer was tied to the international context in which he wrote and the collaborators with whom who he worked in that space. Focusing only on Park's writing at the sentence or genre level would have not revealed these connections. Instead, a perspective on writing that looked beyond the MIT context revealed how Park was able to mobilize collaborators within and outside the United States These individuals actively composed and published with Park, who acted as a communication nexus. By tracing how multilingual writers draw on collaborative networks and the impact of those efforts via citation analysis, we may better understand the social–professional networks that are crucial in multilingual writing development.

Second, in addition to looking at networks of professional collaborators, it is important to specifically identify key individuals, such as mentors, who provide opportunities for multilingual writers. Mentors control access to official sites of publishing in the professional community. As Lave and Wegner (1991) write: "To become a full member of a community of practices requires access to a wide range of ongoing activity, old-timers, and other members of the community; and to information, resources, and opportunities for participation" (p. 101). Park's story points to the importance of giving multilingual writers access to community resources in order to gain proficiency with disciplinary discourses. WAC researchers have looked at some of these interactions (Blakeslee, 2001); newer research is beginning to examine the mentoring relationships of multilingual faculty members and monolingual graduate students, as well as multilingual faculty members and their multilingual graduate students. There are important insights to be learned from such studies in the myriad ways that linguistic identities intersect with writing development in the disciplines.

Finally, as Park's case shows, acceptance into a professional community and successful publication are just the beginning of a career as a multilingual scholar. For Park, who returned home to Korea to teach in English, publish in English, and run his lab in English, learning to write grants and getting published are but two of the challenges that lie ahead of him in his professional life. His continued writing development is tied to the many activities outside of publishing that are part of his normal work duties in a contemporary Korean university.

In the end, as Canagarajah and Jerskey (2009) point out, "it is counterproductive to treat all multilingual writers as unskilled in the language and subject them to grammar-level interventions when their linguistic and literacy experiences often provide considerable strengths to build on or where the mediated support of 'literacy brokers' ... can and should be resourced" (p. 477). Park's story underscores that learning to write in the disciplines for multilingual writers occurs in many locations, and we are remiss to ignore the powerful shaping role of spaces beyond classrooms, such as labs, where writing occurs. We are also remiss if we ignore mentors, literacy brokers, and the "scientific networking community" who help make writing happen (or not). Finally, through naturalistic studies of multilingual writers, we might come to understand how the cultural and linguistic diversity of individuals within disciplinary communities can shift community practices. Such a view of WAC is not content with understanding the reproduction of disciplinary knowledge but how individuals learn to manage, resist, reframe the communicative practices in their fields to support their own goals and purposes. Placing these concerns at the forefront of WAC research will help us better address the needs of linguistically diverse students across the curriculum.

References

Anson, C. (2002). *WAC casebook: Scenes for faculty reflection and program development*. New York, NY: Oxford University Press.

Artemeva, N., & Freedman, N. (2008). *Rhetorical genre studies and beyond*. Winnipeg, Canada: Inkshed Publications.

Atkinson, D., & Connor, U. (2008). Multilingual writing development. In C. Bazerman (Ed.), *Handbook of research on writing* (pp. 515–532). Mahwah, NJ: Lawrence Erlbaum Associates.

Baigrie, B. (1996). *Picturing knowledge: Historical and philosophical problems concerning the use of art in science*. Toronto, Canada: University of Toronto Press.

Bazerman, C. (1988). *Shaping written knowledge: The genre and activity of the experimental article in science*. Madison, WI: University of Wisconsin Press.

Bazerman, C., Little, J., Bethel, L., Chavkin, T., Fouquette, D., & Garufis, J. (2005). *Reference guide to writing across the curriculum*. West Lafayette, IN: Parlor Press.

Bean, J. (1996). *Engaging ideas: The professor's guide to integrating writing, critical thinking, and active learning in the classroom.* San Francisco, CA: Jossey-Bass Publishers.

Beaufort, A. (2008). Writing in the professions. In C. Bazerman (Ed.), *Handbook of research on writing* (pp. 221–236). Mahwah, NJ: Lawrence Erlbaum Associates.

Berkenkotter, C., Huckin, T., & Ackerman, J. (1991). The initiation of a graduate student into a writing research community. In C. Bazerman & J. Paradis (Eds.), *Textual dynamics of the professions: Historical and contemporary studies of writing in academic and other professional communities* (pp. 191–215). Madison, WI: University of Wisconsin Press.

Blakeslee, A. (2001). *Interacting with audiences: Social influences on the production of scientific writing.* Mahwah, NJ: Lawrence Erlbaum Associates.

Britton, J., Burgess, T., Martin, N, McLeod, A., & Rosen, H. (1975). *The development of writing abilities* (pp. 11–18). Urbana, IL: National Council of Teachers of English.

Canagarajah, S. (2002a). *Critical academic writing and multilingual students.* Ann Arbor, MI: University of Michigan Press.

Canagarajah, S. (2002b). *A geopolitics of academic writing.* Pittsburgh, PA: University of Pittsburgh Press.

Canagarajah, S., & Jerskey, M. (2009). Meeting the needs of advanced multilingual writers. In R. Beard, D. Myhill, J. Riley, & M. Nystrand (Eds.), *The SAGE handbook of writing development* (pp. 472–488). Thousand Oaks, CA: Sage.

Cassanave, C. (2002). *Writing games: Multicultural case studies of academic literacy practices in higher education.* Mahwah, NJ: Lawrence Erlbaum Associates.

Currie, P. (2006). Staying out of trouble: Apparent plagiarism and academic survival. In P. K. Matsuda, M. Cox, J. Jordan, & C. Ortmeier-Hooper (Eds.), *Second-language writing in the composition classroom* (pp. 364–379). Boston, MA: Bedford/St. Martin's.

Emig, J. (1977). Writing as a mode of learning. *College Composition and Communication, 28*(2), 122–128. doi:10.2307/356095.

Engeström, Y. (1987). *Learning by expanding: An activity–theoretical approach to developmental research.* Helsinki, Finland: Orienta-Konsultit. Retrieved from http://lchc.ucsd.edu/MCA/Paper/Engestrom/expanding/toc.htm (accessed 15 November 2012).

Fahnestock, J. (2009). The rhetoric of the natural sciences. In A. Lunsford, K. Wilson, & R. Eberly (Eds.), *The SAGE handbook of rhetorical studies* (pp. 175–196). Thousand Oaks, CA: Sage.

Ferris, D., & Roberts, B. (2006). Error feedback in L2 writing classes: How explicit does it need to be? In P. K. Matsuda, M. Cox, J. Jordan, & C. Ortmeier-Hooper (Eds.), *Second-language writing in the composition classroom* (pp. 380–402). Boston, MA: Bedford/St. Martin's.

Frodesen, J. (2009). The academic writing development of a generation 1.5 "latecomer." In M. Roberge, M. Siegal, & L. Harklau (Eds.), *Generation 1.5 in college composition: Teaching academic writing to U.S.-educated learners of ESL* (pp. 91–104). New York, NY: Routledge.

Gross, A., Harmon, J., & Reidy. M. (2002). *Communicating science: The scientific article from the 17th century to the present.* Oxford, UK: Oxford University Press.

Haas, C. (1994). Learning to read biology: One student's rhetorical development in college. *Written Communication, 11*, 43–84. doi:10.1177/0741088394011001004.

Hall, J. (2009). WAC/WID in the next America: Redefining professional identity in the age of the multilingual majority. *The WAC Journal, 20*, 33–49.

Halliday, M. & Martin, J. (1993). *Writing science: Literacy and discursive power.* Pittsburgh, PA: University of Pittsburgh Press.

Horner, B., Lu, M., Royster, J., & Trimbur, J. (2011). A translingual approach to language difference in writing. *College English, 73*(3), 303–321.

Hyland, K. (2004). *Disciplinary discourses: Social interactions in academic writing.* Ann Arbor, MI: University of Michigan Press.

Johns, A. (2001). ESL students and WAC programs: Varied populations and diverse needs. In S. McLeod, E. Miraglia, M. Soven, & C. Thaiss (Eds.), *WAC for the new millennium: Strategies for continuing Writing-Across-the-Curriculum programs* (pp. 141–164). Urbana, IL: National Council of Teachers of English.

Lave, J., & Wenger, E. (1991). *Situated learning: Legitimate peripheral participation.* Cambridge, UK: Cambridge University Press.

Leki, I. (1992). *Understanding ESL writers: A guide for teachers.* Portsmouth, NH: Boynton/ Cook Heinemann.

Lillis, T., & Curry, M. (2006). Professional academic writing by multilingual scholars: interactions with literacy brokers in the production of English-medium texts. *Written Communication, 23*(1), 3–35.

Lillis, T., & Curry, M. (2010). *Academic writing in a global context: The politics and practices of publishing in English.* London, UK: Routledge.

Lunsford, K. (2011). Professional development of postdoctoral scientists: Reports from advanced writing programs in Norway and the U.S. Paper presented at the Writing Research Across Borders conference, George Mason University, Fairfax, VA.

Lynch, M., & Woolgar, S. (1990). *Representation in scientific practice.* Cambridge, MA: MIT Press.

Lyne, J., & Miller, C. (2009). Introduction: rhetoric, disciplinarity, and fields of knowledge. In A. Lunsford, K. Wilson, & R. Eberly (Eds.), *The SAGE handbook of rhetorical studies* (pp. 167–174). Thousand Oaks, CA: Sage.

McClosky, D. (1985). *The rhetoric of economics.* Madison, WI: University of Wisconsin Press.

Miller, C. R. (1984). Genre as social action. *Quarterly Journal of Speech, 70*, 151–167. doi:10.1080/00335638409383686.

Patton, M. (2011). *Writing in the research university: A Darwinian study of WID with cases from civil engineer.* Cresskill, NJ: Hampton Press.

Porush, D. (1995). *A short guide to writing about biology.* New York, NY: Longman.

Prelli, L. (1989). *A rhetoric of science: Inventing scientific discourse.* Columbia, SC: University of South Carolina Press

Prior, P. (2005). A sociocultural theory of writing. In C. MacArthur, S. Graham, & J. Fitzgerald (Eds.). *The handbook of writing research* (pp. 54–66). New York, NY: Guilford Press.

Roth, W., Pozzer-Ardenghi, L., & Han, J.Y. (2005). *Critical graphicacy: Understanding visual representation practices in school science.* Dordrecht, Netherlands, Springer.

Russell, D. (1997). Rethinking genre in school and society: An activity theory analysis. *Written Communication, 14*, 504–39. doi:10.1177/0741088397014004004.

Russell, D. (2001). Where do the naturalistic studies of WAC/WID point? A research review. In S. McLeod, E. Miraglia, M. Soven, & C. Thaiss (Eds.), *WAC for the new millennium: Strategies for continuing writing across the curriculum programs* (pp. 259–298). Urbana, IL: National Council of Teachers of English.

Segall, M. & Smart, R. (2005). *Direct from the disciplines: Writing across the curriculum.* Portsmouth, NH: Boynton/Cook.

Sommers, N. and Saltz, L. (2004). The novice as expert. *College Composition and Communication, 56*(1), 124–149. doi:10.2307/4140684.

Swales, J. M. (1990). *Genre analysis: English in academic and research settings.* Cambridge, UK: Cambridge University Press.

Swales, J. M., & Freak, C. (2000). *English in today's research world: A writing guide.* Ann Arbor, MI: University of Michigan Press.

Tardy, C. (2009). *Building genre knowledge: Writing L2.* West Lafayette, IN: Parlor Press.

Winsor, D. (1997). *Writing like an engineer: A rhetorical education.* Mahwah, NJ: Lawrence Erlbaum Associates.

Winsor, D. (2003). *Writing power: Communication in an engineering center.* Albany, NY: State University of New York Albany Press.

Wolfe-Quintero, K., & Segade, G. (1999). University support for second-language writers across the curriculum. In L. Harklau, K. Losey, & M. Siegal (Eds.), *Generation 1.5 meets college composition: Issues in the teaching of writing to U.S.-educated learners of ESL* (pp. 191–210). Mahwah, NJ: Lawrence Erlbaum Associates.

Zamel, V. (1995). Strangers in academia: The experiences of faculty and ESL students across the curriculum. *College Composition and Communication, 46*(4), 506–521. doi:10.2307/358325.

Zawacki, T. (2010). Researching the local/writing the international: Developing culturally inclusive WAC programs and practices. Paper presented at the 10th International WAC Conference, Indiana University, Bloomington, IN.

17

Dated?

TRANSNATIONAL TRANSLINGUAL LITERACY SPONSORS AND GATEWAYS ON THE UNITED STATES–MEXICO BORDERLANDS

John Scenters-Zapico

> They saw the United States as a gateway to success and more opportunities. When I was a teenager, we already lived in El Paso, Texas and although the rent and bill were higher, they liked the United States. After 21 years of crossing the bridge everyday to take us to school, they enjoyed the United States.
>
> *(Menchu Rodriguez[1])*

Menchu's experience is not uncommon here on the United States–Mexico border, or, I suspect, in other impoverished regions of the country, where families purposively move to a big city because they have been told more opportunities exist at this new destination. Of course, moving a whole family is not an easy task and is not one taken lightly, but a family's awareness of more opportunities is the impetus to such decisions. As Menchu mentions, her family crossed the bridge from Juarez to El Paso everyday for 21 years, and, despite now living in El Paso, they still cross to shop and visit family in Juarez. The important piece of this movement is precisely this: Manchu's family, like the majority from the region, cross the international border on a weekly basis, and they traverse educational, linguistic, social and political experiences that intermix like the streams and rivers into the Rio Grande.

Once moved to a new place with more to offer, literacy seekers discover gateways in the form of schools, jobs, and resources. However, accessing community gateways is full of complex and myriad nuances. Based on a five-year ethnographic literacy study of and across the United States–Mexico border, this chapter will expand our definitions and understandings of two critical concepts: transnational and translingual literacy sponsors and gateways. The expansion of these terms is grounded in thousands of responses, and the new definitions will assist researchers studying translingual experiences of language users in the ecologies they inhabit. As Horner, Lu, Royster, and Trimbur (2011) have insisted, we need to view the practices of translingualers as resources (p. 300), and this, I further believe, includes those with whom they come into contact and the locations where the contact occurs. In transnational literacy niches such as the borderlands, we discover literacy encounters that expand our understanding of those who seek out literacy experiences, those who sponsor literacies, and the gateways where translingualers and sponsors converge.

In this chapter, I first review the traditional uses of the term "literacy sponsor" to capture the panorama of its current applications. With these definitions as a base, I then expand on sponsors in several important ways. My interviews with translingual language users and translingual sponsors contribute new understandings to sponsors and sponsorship forms useful to teachers and researchers examining language users from a 21st-century demographic. I then explore how "literacy gateways" have been traditionally defined. From here, based on the stories and responses from my research, gateways became more complex and nuanced for translingualers traversing international, national, social, economic, cultural, and linguistic borders. These two sections serve to open up nuances and shifts in the way we think, talk, and write about the converging spaces of translingual literacy practices in school settings and in communities.

Transnational Translingual Literacy Sponsors

A distinction exists between traditional and electronic literacy sponsors. We need to explore the differences in order to see how the two are intimately connected. The growth of our notion of sponsors comes directly from the variety and depth of responses I received, but first I will discuss how researchers have used "literacy sponsor."

The researcher who placed the notion of traditional literacy sponsors on the academic map is Brandt. Her work on literacy sponsors investigates how and why participants of traditional literacy and their sponsors interact as they acquire and offer literacy opportunities. It is important to note that her subjects all write and respond in one language. She explores these traditional literacy sponsors in several ways and in a variety of publications. In "Sponsors of Literacy" (Brandt, 1998), she defines sponsors as "any agents, local or distant, concrete or abstract, who enable, support, teach, model, as well as recruit, regulate, suppress, or withhold literacy—and gain advantage by it in some way" (p. 167).

Importantly, this research yielded insights into the types of individuals who served as sponsors, such as "older relatives, teachers, priests, supervisors, military officers, editors, influential authors" (Brandt, 1998, p. 167). In *Literacy in American Lives* (Brandt, 2001), she makes even clearer the power, especially economic, that sponsors have over literacy learners (pp. 166–167). In "Literacy Learning and Economic Change" (Brandt, 1999), she describes sponsors as "any agents, local or distant, concrete or abstract, who provide, enhance, or deny opportunities for literacy learning and gain advantage by it in some way" (p. 376). In "Drafting

US Literacy" (Brandt, 2004), she expands on the political and societal underpinnings that literacy, illiteracy, and sponsors serve in society (p. 487). Finally, in "At Last: Losing Literacy" (Brandt, 2005) she echoes the powerful role that sponsors partake in and distribute to participants of literacy (p. 310). Brandt's corpus of ethnographic and theoretical research has been a pillar in how we view and study literacy and literacy sponsors. Key is the focused role that sponsors exercise with and over traditional literacy participants.

While Brandt's work primarily focuses on 20th-century traditional English only literacy narratives, Selfe and Hawisher's (2004) work picks up the thread in the 21st century and immerses us in a digital world, one full of changing literacy experiences, yet they are also English only. Their equally influential work in digital realms looks at the role of sponsors, yet brings in technology: "Individuals who gain access to technology through the standard gateways of school, home, and increasingly the Internet also frequently network with those who may serve as literacy sponsors" (p. 166; see also Hawisher, Selfe, Guo, & Liu, 2006, p. 633). Importantly, moreover, they introduce the Chinese term, *guanxi*, to extend Brandt's notion of sponsors: "The Chinese term *guanxi*, then, serves to extend Brandt's explanation of literacy sponsorship—providing a more complex, concrete, and global perspective on how such relationships function in an increasingly networked world" (Hawisher et al., 2006, p. 634; see also Selfe & Hawisher, 2004, pp. 37, 56, 181 for additional definitions of sponsors). This is a first instance in the literature of sponsors and how another language (culture) can enrich another and be inserted in the text (although *guanxi* itself is transliterated).

The work on sponsors these researchers spearheaded is important because it gives us tools in how we analyze the interactions of sponsor and sponsored. Taking their research to the United States –Mexico borderlands, I am studying how transnational translingual language practices cross, intersect, and confront each other in the contexts of using multiple languages in multiple settings. As Horner et al. (2011) argue, such insights on actual practices and interactions become resources (p. 300).

With the transnational translingual participants making up my study, I found that in order to understand the complex interactions I had never seen or read about in our scholarship, I needed to separate traditional and electronic literacy and the forms of sponsorship into two initial forms, as shown in Figure 17.1. However, the diagram also shows where the two forms have points in common as well.

In Figure 17.1 there are several attributes I would like to draw your attention to because they add many new insights to our understandings of sponsorship, and because they represent responses shared by literacy learners seeking and receiving assistance for multiple types of literacies (traditional English, Spanish, and Spanglish; digital literacies in English, Spanish, and Spanglish).

First, the two largest circles, traditional and electronic literacy sponsorship forms, separate the two dominant classes of literacy sponsorship from each other. Understanding that many readers are uncomfortable with dichotomies, I believe the initial distinction is important in order to appreciate the differences as much

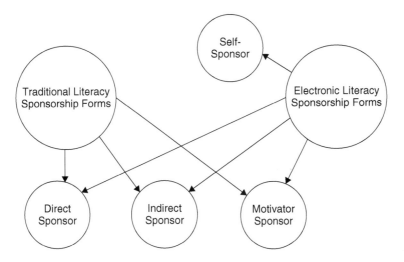

FIGURE 17.1 Traditional and electronic literacy forms of sponsorship

as the commonalities between the two. Further, Figure 17.1 reveals, at this point, not who, but *how* sponsors operate. The three lowermost circles—direct sponsors, indirect sponsors, and motivator sponsors—are the ways that sponsors entered into participants' lives. These three forms of sponsorship determine how literacy learners are affected. The topmost small bubble, Self-Sponsors, is also revealing because it is the one quality that electronic literacy learners have that traditional literacy learners do not. These four forms require further elaboration; moreover, they are original to the experiences of transliterate learners.

Indirect Sponsors

Indirect sponsors occupy an important role in literacy development here on the United States–Mexico border and came to light in this research and have not been mentioned by other researchers to date. I believe the following forms of new sponsorship came to light because of the nature of this border's history of intermixing languages and cultures. With both traditional and electronic literacies, the literacy learners in my study revealed that indirect literacy sponsors purchase or supply such items as books, comics, and newspapers, or computers, digital cameras, and software. Indirect sponsors typically do not actively engage in teaching literacy skills—traditional or electronic—to those they assist. However, without indirect sponsors, many literacy learners would not have such items available, resulting in either an extreme of no literacy learning, in slow or stagnated literacy growth, or in literacy learners having to seek out places where they can use and learn new literacies. Indirect sponsors fill an important role in electronic literacy development. Most of the literacy learners indicated that someone other than themselves purchased their electronic items; significantly these indirect sponsors neither teach them how to use these items nor how to communicate their ideas to others with them.

Direct Sponsors

Direct traditional literacy sponsors are involved in directly teaching the literacy learners to read or in discussing what the content of the textual items means. Similarly, direct electronic literacy sponsors actively teach literacy learners how to use and communicate with electronic technologies, but with electronic literacies, direct sponsors tend not to be the persons who purchase the technology, that is, they are not typically indirect sponsors; this distinction has not been observed in other research to date.

Motivator Sponsors

Another newly observed sponsorship form to surface from this research is from a mid-sized bubble from the bottom row: motivator sponsors. These sponsors serve an in-between role outside of direct and indirect sponsor, and function based on the status of the economy. With electronic literacy, these sponsors literally push family members or close friends who had been laid off or underemployed to go to school to learn an electronic literacy that would, ideally, serve to advance the literacy learner to a better paying job. For example, Alicia Rodriguez's daughter pushed her to find a better job than the one she had:

> Her daughter pushed her to attend a business college, where she would have her first contact with computers in 2005 at fifty-six years old. The daughter's motive for encouraging her mother was economic: "I was encouraged by my daughter to get a better job." Alicia responded to her daughter's encouragement and successfully learned new electronic literacies.
>
> (Scenters-Zapico, 2010, p. 21)

Self-Sponsorship

The last form in this category seems obvious, yet because of its prevalence has not been noted or discussed in the literature on literacy sponsorship forms: electronic literacy self-sponsorship. Hawisher, Selfe, Moraski, and Pearson (2004) point out why this might be:

> Our professional radar is tuned so narrowly to the bandwidth of print and the alphabetic—to school-based and workplace writing—that we miss a great deal of the more interesting and engaging self-sponsored reading and composing students do on their own time. These activities, these values remain generally invisible to us. And because we often miss such activities,

[handwritten margin note: But students are aware of them]

our instructional practices and values, our interests, and the texts we read and compose may be moving further and further away from those that students consider important.

(p. 676)

I found that literacy learners self-sponsored, that is, taught themselves their own electronic literacies more than others sponsored them. Self-sponsorship, to my knowledge, never occurs with traditional literacy, that is, we never learn to read and write without the assistance of others. With electronic literacies, literacy learners overwhelmingly are involved in the process of teaching themselves. While my research did not seek out possible reasons for this form of sponsorship, it does raise a whole new realm of questions about the ways multiple language users and transcultural border crossers self-sponsor with technology. Do they learn from trial and error? Do they use online video tutorials and, if so, in what (preferred) language and cultural setting?

Another new form surfaced from direct, indirect, self-, and motivator sponsorship roles, and this involved how sponsors actually interact and affect literacy learners. This form adds another dimension to our notion of translingualism because it evokes rhetorical motives that electronic literacy sponsors enact (Horner et al., 2011, p. 301, also are interested in the rhetorical nature of how translinguals negotiate in their day-to-day interactions).

An important notion I learned from interacting with the literacy learners in this study is that literacy sponsors cannot be considered homogeneous bodies acting in one consistent fashion. Instead, sponsors interact in varying degrees of physical, psychological, and financial manners (Figure 17.2). Sponsors take on *physical* roles because they allow access to a computer or software at a concrete location. They hold the key of access for literacy learners.

Literacy learners indicated this happens in the home, when a family member allows or does not allow a family member to use an electronic tool. It transpires in the workplace when an employer decides to allocate, or not, new hardware or software, and who is not taught particular systems. It happens in other places, such as schools or friends' homes. The *financial* role is what sponsors deem they

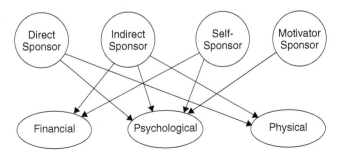

FIGURE 17.2 Financial, psychological, and physical forms of sponsorship

can afford, what a sponsor believes is a worthy investment, or what an employer thinks employees need to be competitive.

Important questions surface from these observations. How do transliterates negotiate (rhetorically persuade) for the things they need to succeed? How are transliterates perceived in some spaces like school or work and given access to the tools to compete and succeed? Do their language skills help or hinder this process?

In the *psychological* realm, sponsorship can be motivational or destructive. This is another experience that has not been noted in other studies on literacy learning. Because one individual's words or actions can cause a lifetime of positive or negative effects on an individual, this may be by far the most important sponsorship subcategory for translingual scholarship because it keys in on how language users are affected by being branded inferior thinkers, speakers, and writers. I came to call these psychologically positive and negative events micro-tear zones. These were outcomes that surfaced in responses time and time again and ranged from how a sponsor showed patience with a literacy learner in attempting to use a piece of technology, simple phrases like "good work" or "bad work," being called lazy, or by having peers laugh at a learner for using a transliterate term, e.g., "*ya finishiamos.*" At the psychological plane, one person, word, or instant can produce an enduring constructive or destructive transformation for learners.

Who exactly are the individuals that literacy learners listed as the various sponsors with their varying roles? Figure 17.3 shows the people who literacy learners indicated as sponsoring them.

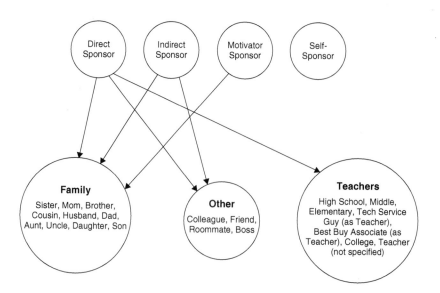

FIGURE 17.3   The sponsors

Family and Others (Friends)

Literacy learners indicated that family (171 responses) and friends (128 responses) sponsored them a total of 299 times in various ways (Figure 17.4). As might be expected, family and friends occupy an important role in teaching literacy learners electronic literacies, but this also means that they must search for these sponsors in locations other than their own home or school. As one literacy learner insightfully commented, "With technology in my home I have more time and am more inclined to experiment and learn more than if I have to go out and find technology places."

Teachers

Teachers serve a vital role in translinguals' literacy learning lives. These literacy learners stated that teachers assisted them an electronic literacy 245 times. Figure 17.4 shows the percentage breakdown of all sponsorship categories based on all 889 assists.

Self-Sponsorship

This category came initially as a surprise. It is common to read of instances of participants of literacies' experiences teaching themselves electronic literacies but hard data have been difficult to come by. The participants of literacies' assists and stories suggest that they learn electronic literacies from a variety of electronic literacy sponsors. However, overwhelmingly, literacy learners self-sponsored/ assisted at 345 times. The next section seeks to answer the question "Where are all these literacy learners and sponsors interacting?"

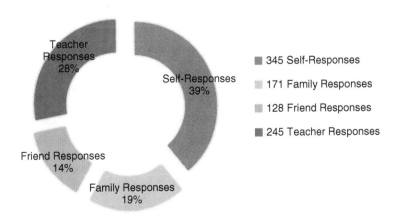

FIGURE 17.4 Summary of all sponsor assists

Electronic Literacy Gateways

Hawisher and Selfe (2006) pay careful attention to technology gateways, the places where literacy learning occurs. Literacy gateways are important to study, so we can better understand the roles they serve in facilitating literacy learning. They found that, "Schools, homes, and increasingly the Internet itself are primary gateways through which people gain access to digital literacies" (p. 633). Moreover, they characterize technology gateways as sites and occasions for acquiring digital literacies that vary across peoples' experiences and the times and circumstances in which they grow up.

My own view of technology gateways is similar. They are physical, ecological locations, such as the structures for our homes or offices where literacy tools are available. As importantly, *awareness* of technology gateways is critical. Based on literacy learners' responses about literacy gateways from my research, new ways of seeing them opened up. I struggled to attempt to order these places into categories that would be useful for making sense of both gateway forms and how sponsors traverse these demarcated zones. I arrived at three broad locations: school gateways, cubbyhole gateways, and other gateways (Figure 17.5).

Hawisher et al. (2004) discovered that literacy learners most often learn electronic literacies outside of the classroom (p. 644). My literacy learners' results corroborate their assertion that translingual literacy learners infrequently learned from teachers, but they did learn at schools!

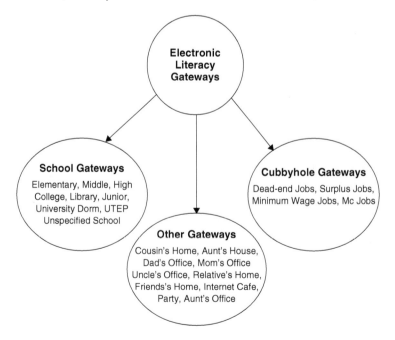

FIGURE 17.5 Electronic literacy gateways

Based on 773 responses about literacy learners' gateway experiences, I found the following. First, 347 responses indicated that schools are significant gateways for translingual literacy learners. While Selfe and Hawisher (2004) found that homes were a less-used gateway, 326 responses from my study indicate translinguals had learned some form of electronic literacy at home. Other categories, such as work, indicated 39 literacy learners had learned at these locations (see Figure 17.6 for breakdown by percent).

My literacy learners' own stories characterize the complexities they face in learning and practicing electronic literacies. The following three examples from two countries and, at times, both countries, disclose the challenges transnational translinguals deal with every day. Menchu Rodriguez shares her experience of accessing technology in Mexico and the United States:

> The money was a big issue that made it hard to develop electronic literacy. There were classes that taught you how to use computers, but some were expensive. Since we were young we were not too interested in using a computer at home. Also, at that time there were few schools that had access to computers and this made it harder for people to become electronic literate. Here in the United States it is easier to develop electronic literacy because starting from grade school there is access to computers.

In Mexico, Jesus Real felt that "since we did not have the money to buy a computer we had to go the library and used it there but since we would not be little angels all the time sometimes we were prohibited to go to the library in a while." While Gloria Fernandez felt, "Here in the United States was easier to find a computer because the schools will provide them to students."

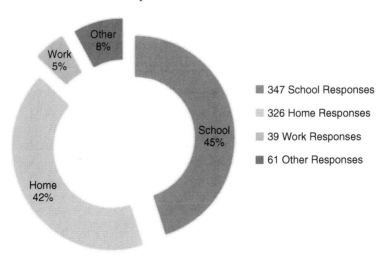

FIGURE 17.6   Summary of all gateway data

One site literacy learners indicated as a gateway, I labeled "Other" because of the variety this group makes up. More often than not these places were in a family member's, relative's, or friend's home, or office. Literacy learners used these places, not in a job-related sense, but as places where they could get their hands on technology. For example, Manuel Licón also sees accessing computers elsewhere (not home) as normal: "Since my cousin had a computer it was just a matter of going over to his house." Later he saw access at school as ordinary: "Once I started middle school access to a computer was relatively easy because I could go to the computer lab and have access to one there." In the case of the translinguals participating in this study—some who see English as their first language, some Spanish, and some Spanglish—these places are important for communities that do not have the means to own their own technologies. The lesson we can grasp here is that access to technology is important for development, and for translingual learners to learn the many changing literacies that are expected of them in mainstream society.

At the time of interviewing literacy learners, I found that the way on-the-job literacy is defined determines the type of responses literacy learners shared. While only five percent of translinguals said they learn electronic literacies at the workplace, it became clear that many thought what they learned did not count as literacy in the unvalued minimum-wage market. However, and importantly, what has surfaced is: (1) they did learn electronic literacies, and (2) they gained self-confidence from what they learned. This pattern became another new discovery in where and how the translingual literacy learners picked up new literacy skills. I came to call these spaces "cubbyhole gateways." These are jobs ranging from a store clerk who uses a cash register, to a secretary using a computer for the first time. While viewed as low-prestige, dead-end jobs, they serve an important role because they make literacy learners aware that they can learn to work with technology and achieve more than they or society has given them credit for.

The gateway forms discussed in this section reveal that many manifestations of new, unstudied gateways exist in translingual communities. Since gateways are where literacy learners access technology, it is important for educators to think beyond normal access points and to broadcast that there are many other places and means to access technology. At the same time, we need to understand the additional challenges and burdens literacy learners are under as they seek out these gateways. Last, with the digital divide in mind, we need to recognize that more affluent electronic literacy learners likely will not have to seek out gateways in the ways less affluent ones must, and as a result they will most likely have different experiences.

Conclusion

In literacy and language research, two frequently used concepts are sponsors and gateways. These terms have served as tools to help researchers better understand how literacy learners interact with those who grant access to or teach them desired literacies, as well as a way to study the locations where such learning takes place. From the information collected from my five-year ethnographic study, I initially set out with traditional concepts of sponsor and gateway to see how, on the international border of the United States–Mexico, transnational translinguals (those who frequently cross an international border and who use multiple language and linguistic forms in each country) have transeducational experiences and transcultural interactions. The new information from this project is revealing.

At the conclusion of my data collection, I discovered that several new ways of thinking about these interactions had revealed themselves, and they had not been talked about or documented in any research. I was challenged with these freshly revealed interactions because I was on unfamiliar ground. As I looked for themed experiences from these out-of-the-box stories, however, they became more and more apparent.

For teachers and researchers studying translingualism, this discussion of the learning experiences of transnational translinguals should prove useful in the growing resources of translingual experiences. The cross-pollination of schooling, work, family, languages, and social experiences in this international setting has created unique hybrid forms of learning. The fusion of forms of sponsorships and gateways are invaluable for understanding the evolving 21st-century demographics of language use, learning, access, and experiences.

Outside of this border, these expanded concepts are important for teachers and researchers working with populations that represent the changing demographics of the United States. When we think of sponsors, we now need to understand that translingual individuals will have multiple sponsors in the various language forms they regularly use. This means that how they are sponsored will have a variety of pedagogies that are both complex and rich beyond mainstream discussions of sponsorship. Moreover, translingual individuals also will have different places and means of accessing locations where they learn. When we are mindful of these learning experiences, we can more effectively draw from these learning encounters in order to teach our students the evolving communicative demands they need in society today (for similar a point see Canagarajah, 2006).

Seeing the multiplicity of newly observed ways that transnational and translingual populations from the United States–Mexico border of Juarez and El Paso interact provides much data and stories for future research. I believe these new and expanded understandings of literacy sponsorships and gateways can guide us as we proceed at this historical juncture in attempting to redefine how we teach learners who bring rich ways of learning that are intermixed and hybridized, showing they have adapted and evolved in new social and educational landscapes. More importantly, they can reveal some effective best practices that such learners and teachers can share with us as we redefine and redesign our learning pedagogies and spaces.

Note

1 All participants of literacy signed Internal Review Board approved consent forms; they are identified by pseudonyms.

References

Brandt, D. (1998). Sponsors of literacy. *College Composition and Communication, 49*(2), 165–185. doi:10.2307/358929.

Brandt, D. (1999). Literacy learning and economic change. *Harvard Educational Review, 69*(4), 373–394.

Brandt, D. (2001). *Literacy in American lives.* Cambridge, UK: Cambridge University Press.

Brandt, D. (2004). Drafting U.S. literacy. *College English,* 66 (5), 485–502. doi:10.2307/4140731.

Brandt, D. (2005). At last: Losing literacy. *Research in the Teaching of English,* 39(3), 305–310.

Canagarajah, A. S. (2006). The place of world Englishes in composition: Pluralization continued. *College Composition and Communication, 57*(4), 586–619.

Hawisher, G. E., & Selfe, C. L. (2006). Globalization and agency: Designing and redesigning the literacies of cyberspace. *College English, 68*(6), 619–636.

Hawisher, G. E., Selfe, C. L., Guo, Y. H., & Liu, L. (2006). Globalization and agency: Designing and redesigning the literacies of cyberspace. *College English, 68*(6), p. 619–636. doi:10.2307/25472179.

Hawisher, G. E., Selfe, C. L., Moraski, B., & Pearson, M. (2004). Becoming literate in the information age: Cultural ecologies and the literacies of technology. *College Composition and Communication,* 55 (4), 642–692. doi:10.2307/4140666.

Horner, B., Lu, M., Royster, J. J., & Trimbur, J. (2011). Language difference in writing: Toward a translingual approach. *College English, 73*(3), 303–321.

Scenters-Zapico, J. T. (2010). *Generaciones' narratives: The pursuit and practice of traditional and electronic literacies on the U.S.–Mexico borderlands.* Retrieved from http://ccdigital-press.org/ebooks-and-projects/generaciones (accessed 15 November 2012).

Selfe, C. L., & Hawisher, G. E. (Eds.). (2004). *Literate lives in the information age: Narratives of literacy from the United States.* Mahwah, NJ: Erlbaum.

PART V

Pedagogical Applications

18

LITERACY BROKERS IN THE CONTACT ZONE, YEAR 1: THE CROWDED SAFE HOUSE

Maria Jerskey

Literacy Brokers: From the Periphery to the Center

The imperative to publish in English and the inequities and challenges subsequently faced by multilingual scholars writing from outer and expanding circles of English (Kachru, 1986) have been extensively documented and theorized (e.g., Belcher, 2007; Braine, 2005; Canagarajah, 2002; Flowerdew, 2008, Flowerdew & Li, 2009; Lillis & Curry, 2010). We know that it can take these multilingual scholars twice as long to write in English as it does in their home language and that they routinely feel the sting of rejection and the strong preference that more prestigious academic journals have for "accomplished English academic writing" (Curry & Lillis, 2004, p. 678). As such, multilingual scholars face considerable discrimination and stigma for perceptions of their English-language proficiency (Flowerdew, 2008). Interventions to address these inequities range from mentoring periphery scholars into center-based academic discourses and research article genres, to transforming publishing practices that favor scholar writers from the center over those of the periphery (Canagarajah, 2002, p. 158).

In their longitudinal text-based study on the academic text production of scholars working in expanding circle countries in Europe, Lillis and Curry (2010) illustrate how different kinds of literacy brokers—behind-the-scene mediators instrumental in shaping multilingual scholars' texts as they move to completion (or not)—"orient to texts and knowledges" and "impact on specific shifts and changes to texts" (p. 87). They identify two categories of literacy brokers: *language brokers* and *academic brokers* (p. 93). *Language brokers*, providing formal English language support, are (most often paid) translators and proofreaders as well as English-language specialists—teachers and tutors of English. (Informal *language brokers*, such as friends, spouses or other family members, provide serendipitous

English-language support.) *Academic brokers* are professional academics working within universities and research institutes and are subcategorized further as *general academics* who are not necessarily from the same discipline as the scholar writer; *disciplinary experts* who have the same disciplinary background as the writer; and *subdisciplinary specialists* from the same specialty area.

Whether *language* or *academic brokers*, literacy brokers influence the production of academic knowledge in powerful and important ways that multilingual scholars both welcome and resist. While they may edit and proofread for inner-circle English-language preferences, they may also shift and change writers' original intentions, particularly since *academic brokers* can also include journal editors and other "gate keepers" who have the power to reframe and demote scholars' new contributions to knowledge to mere confirmations of existing knowledge (Lillis & Curry, 2010, p. 114). Among other implications, Lillis and Curry's study challenges editors of English-medium academic journals and books to be more inclusive of and sensitive to multilingual scholars by intentionally steering the role of literacy brokers to shape and influence texts in ways that respect and retain multilingual scholars' claims and perspectives. By working with *language brokers*, scholar writers could begin to negotiate more effectively a voice that represents their own values and interests favorably and carve out for themselves a space for their own voice in the dominant discourse (Canagarajah, 2004, p. 268). Examples include mentoring international scholars into the reviewing process of English-medium academic journals (Lillis, Magyar, & Robinson-Pant, 2010) and accommodating an approach to scholarship that might differ from anglophone-center conventions (Canagarajah, 2010).

Of course multilingual scholars writing from anglophone centers—the inner circle—also face challenges. Even with easier access to prime resources like English-language journals and native English speakers, many multilingual scholars find writing in English to be a tremendous struggle often accompanied by high emotional and time cost, and requiring large reserves of perseverance.[1] Thus, another way to equitably steer the role of literacy brokers would be to develop and cultivate a community of literacy brokers in local, inner-circle settings.

Behind the Scenes of the Literacy Brokers Program

The idea of intentionally steering the role of literacy brokers to shape and influence texts in ways that respect and retain multilingual scholars' voices and intentions resonated in me as a multilingual writing scholar and teacher committed to designing writing programs and materials that address the needs of an increasingly complex and heterogeneous U.S. population of multilingual student writers. Shifting a perception of language difference-as-deficit to language difference-as-resource has meant challenging tacit (and some would argue, irrelevant) language policies that uphold standards of monolingual English in a world that is increasingly multilingual and in which non-native speakers of English outnumber native speakers three to one (Graddol, 1999).

Perhaps by making visible the range of writing practices of an increasingly multilingual faculty, we could extend Horner and Trimbur's (2002) call to "resist thinking of identifying students and our teaching in terms of fixed categories of language, language ability, and social identity" (p. 622) to resist identifying ourselves and our own writing in terms of the same fixed categories. That way as we envision "a multilingual and polyliterate orientation to writing" (Canagarajah, 2006, p. 587) we could move institutionally toward a *translingual* approach to writing (Horner, Lu, Royster, & Trimbur, 2011) in which multiple languages are employed strategically, intentionally, and contextually rather than accessed as discrete, separate systems for discrete, separate audiences. In other words, making visible and legitimate literacy brokers' behind-the-scenes practices of negotiating linguistic and disciplinary conventions would not only support multilingual scholars as they moved their writing toward publication, but also play a role in cultivating a college's writing culture into the image of its actual writers.

This is particularly relevant to linguistically diverse locales such as the City University of New York (CUNY), the largest urban university in the United States, where the diverse student population is a celebrated point of pride. The university's website declares that students across CUNY "trac[e] their ancestries to 205 countries" (City University of New York, n.d.).[2] When I directed the writing center at CUNY's Baruch College, its website prominently showcased (and still does) its recognition "as the most ethnically diverse campus in the nation by both U.S. News & World Report and the Princeton Review more times than any other college in the United States" (Diversity, n.d.). And the first thing you notice when you enter the main building at CUNY's LaGuardia Community College (where I currently hold a faculty position) is its lengthy Hall of Flags: "presented as a gift by the United Nations to celebrate LaGuardia's diversity, [it] represents the nationalities of every student that has ever registered for a class at the school" (Hall of Flags, n.d.). In spite of our students' rich linguistic resources, these bragging rights have not translated well into the writing instruction culture at CUNY. A myth of linguistic homogeneity (Matsuda, 2006) holds both students and faculty to monolingual English norms and suppresses important linguistic strategies that culturally and linguistically diverse students could practice and share with a culturally and linguistically diverse faculty.

Writers Navigating Contact Zones, Constructing Safe Houses

Pratt (1991) conceptualizes contact zones as "social spaces where cultures meet, clash, and grapple with each other, often in contexts of highly asymmetrical relations of power" (p. 33). Safe houses offer respites from these dynamic but hostile contact zones, providing instead "social and intellectual spaces where groups can constitute themselves as horizontal, homogeneous, sovereign communities with high degrees of trust, shared understandings, temporary protection from legacies of oppression" (p. 40). The contact zone and safe house metaphors allow language and literacy support programs to cultivate empowering, alternative narratives. In the writing center at Baruch, for example, we resisted a monolithic perception of "English as a Second Language (ESL)," which recognized students' language difference as deficits to be filled. Breaking ESL down into a more realistic matrix of students' language and literacy experiences—the resources their language differences provided—allowed us to tease out nuanced approaches in addressing their learning needs. Transforming through our interventions the stigma that accompanied the label ESL (or even "non-native") into a valued status of "multilingual" became a central tenet of our pedagogy (see Jerskey, 2011). Many of our consultants—graduate students and adjunct faculty who also taught composition or writing intensive courses—were multilingual users of English themselves. They too were in the process of negotiating the demands of academic writing in English while tutoring mono- and multilingual students. The community of practice in our writing center—one in which language difference was perceived as the norm rather than an aberration—provided a safe house within the college's larger contact zone. But students weren't the only ones who needed a safe house.

Multilingual faculty members at Baruch routinely asked me if they were eligible to have the writing center's consultants "check grammar" on their research articles. They faced the same pressures (and fears) as their students in producing error-free, academic-"sounding" texts, and it made sense that they, like their students, would need a space to become more sure of themselves as writers in English. With the writing center's limited resources allocated to student support, I could only offer a list of consultants who privately earned up to $75/hour editing and proofreading their projects. On their own time, these consultants made up an invisible crowd of literacy brokers at Baruch not unlike those Lillis and Curry (2010) describe in their study. I often wondered what it would be like to legitimize and make visible their practices—an opportunity I had once I moved to CUNY's LaGuardia Community College.

Multilinguals at LaGuardia

LaGuardia's students come from more than 160 countries and speak 127 languages (Office of Institutional Research, 2011). It's more difficult to cite demographics of its exceptionally diverse faculty since neither Human Resources nor Institutional Research collect data on the faculty's linguistic backgrounds or home countries, so I surveyed faculty and staff members (a considerable number of staff also teach at the college). Out of the 250 respondents, 93 percent reported using languages other than English. The respondents came from 44 home countries across Africa, Asia, the Caribbean, Europe, and North and South America, speak 34 first languages and more than 75 second and third languages. While I have yet to tease out perceptions of their individual language proficiencies, I extrapolate from this sample that our culturally and linguistically diverse population of students have counterparts in the faculty who teach them. Monolinguals are a minority on our campus.

I marvel at the linguistic competencies that so many of the multilingual faculty members exhibit at LaGuardia. Impressive publication records and important leadership roles at the college validate their English-language mastery. But I also observe those who struggle to write in English and to cultivate, as a consequence, their presence as active members of the college's faculty. Grammatical and spelling errors, lapses in fluency in email correspondence, PowerPoint presentations, and hand-outs at college-wide committee meetings and faculty development seminars betray their challenges. And yet, while I've worked at campuses where grammatical correctness is a blood sport and the presence of a typo inspires profound shame, language differences at LaGuardia —which elsewhere might be perceived as error—seems to be tolerated. Is it because people are unsure how to broach the subject, afraid that they might embarrass the writer? Or are people willing in certain circumstances to favor intelligibility over correctness? If so, what happens when perceived errors inhibit intelligibility? What support is in place to negotiate the differences? Could the Literacy Brokers Program provide a safe house for faculty members to negotiate their language options?

Implementing the Literacy Brokers Program: Challenges and Surprises

When I proposed to develop the Literacy Brokers Program to the Vice President of Academic Affairs, I pointed out that few, if any, successful academic writers—monolingual or multilingual—write alone. Editors, reviewers, academic peers, and English-speaking friends and colleagues are present behind the scenes of any published academic text. Rather than struggling alone to learn the rhetorical moves and expectations of English-medium journals, the Literacy Brokers Program would—I hoped—cultivate a proactive and community-based approach to an individual's text production.

I received teaching release-time to coordinate the program during the 2010–2011 academic year and planned to recruit seven to ten faculty members to participate in five, 90-minute workshops during the fall and spring semesters. The goals were (1) to move writing projects toward completion, (2) to actively elicit support from literacy brokers, and (3) to begin cultivating a community of literacy brokers on campus. *Language brokers* would come from faculty in my department, which houses the ESL Academic Writing Program. Based on the kind of academic support they might want, the participants themselves could determine who their *academic brokers* would be. For example, they might work with disciplinary experts in their departments (or advisors if they were in doctoral programs), but they would also work with me and each other to fine tune and identify the support they'd need.

During the 2010 fall semester, nine participants from five academic departments and a range of linguistic backgrounds signed up to participate.[3] Their writing projects included three research articles, a dissertation chapter, a conference proceedings, two grant proposals, a conference paper, and a research essay for a doctoral course. During the workshops we considered each text's intended audience, purpose, and form; we looked at grammar and language at both sentence and word-choice levels; and we discussed writing behaviors around carving out time to write during the semester, how and when to elicit literacy brokers' support, and how to approach journal editors or advisors. Of the nine writers, all of whom had grown up outside the United States, eight had completed or were in the process of completing their scholarly work in the United States and had written most, if not all, of their scholarly work in English. They were familiar with reading and writing for English-medium journals and had intuitively, if not explicitly, established individual networks of literacy brokers to support their writing. Their eagerness to participate in the program suggested their recognition of yet another resource available to them. The other participant, "Hamid," a faculty member in the Natural Sciences Department, had completed his scholarly work in his home country in the Middle East before immigrating to the United States. While he was familiar with the genre of research articles he needed to write and even phrases in English specific to his discipline, he struggled more than the others to produce fluent sentences in English. However, he was clearly accustomed to seeking out and accepting English-language support and deftly evaluated, as did the other participants, whether suggested edits truly reflected his intentions.

Attrition set in over the fall semester as teaching and committee obligations competed with participants' time to write. As participants dwindled down to three or four at a time, feedback became less predictable, and cultivating a network of literacy brokers more challenging. I tried to compensate by meeting individually with those participants who wanted to complete their projects by fixed deadlines, concerned that the program would fall apart before it had gotten going. Certainly, I knew to expect this. Writing-support programs can sound and look great on paper, but anyone who's run one knows they fray at the edges. They get battered by the realities of time crunches and people looking for shortcuts (like those who wanted to drop off their drafts with me to be edited because they didn't have time to attend the workshops). They also can take a while to earn credibility beyond their mission statements and attract writers who will engage and benefit.

I wondered why the faculty members I had predicted would participate— those who clearly struggled with English—expressed no interest. Perhaps they were unavailable during the scheduled workshops or they had no time during the semester to write. Or perhaps they were resisting the support. Eventually a few did contact me—after their department chairs "urged" participation. Their publication records might have been satisfactory (publishing scholarly articles and books in languages other than English can count toward tenure at LaGuardia), but there was concern that the grammatical errors or lapses in fluency in their departmental texts (e.g., peer observations, committee memos and minutes, etc.) and their classroom instructional materials were affecting their performance.

Students at LaGuardia evaluate their teachers' performance—including English proficiency—using the Student Instructional Rating Survey (SIRS). Untenured faculty members whose scores fall below the national community college average are at risk of non-reappointment. Faculty members could seek accent-reduction support from a communications professor on campus; the Literacy Brokers Program appeared to be an analog to address their "written" accent. Unhappy and mortified, these colleagues approached me privately to see if we might work in my office. I had flashbacks of truculent students showing up at the writing center with a red-marked, low-graded paper in hand because they were required to show proof that they had had their writing "fixed." I was concerned that the Literacy Brokers Program might develop similar stigmatizing associations.

At the same time, there was unanticipated interest in the program: To begin with faculty members who had had non-scholarly, professional careers as nurses, engineers, or accountants before joining LaGuardia's faculty asked if they could participate as they were unsure how to approach the kinds of academic writing they were expected to publish. The catch was that this cohort "spoke English fluently" and wondered if they were still eligible. Another small group included non-faculty administrators from a range of linguistic backgrounds who wondered if they could participate even if they weren't faculty. (I discovered that some members of the professional staff are required to publish for promotion.) Another cohort included faculty who wanted to write about teaching practices in their disciplines but were unfamiliar with the scholarship of teaching and learning (SoTL). (SoTL is highly valued at LaGuardia, and publications count favorably at promotion and tenure reviews.) Finally, an experienced academic journal editor on campus volunteered to be a *literacy broker* but also expressed interest in writing and publishing herself; she wanted the motivation and intellectual stimulation that a community of peer writers would provide. Complicating all of this was that, within these groups, there were faculty and staff members who spoke non-standard varieties of English—including African American Vernacular and Caribbean Creoles.

It seemed that the Literacy Brokers Program felt stigmatizing to some and exclusive to others. At first I was protective of the program's boundaries and concerned that accommodating these interested parties would shift its focus; I resisted what seemed like incursions. But, perhaps, I reflected, the categories "multilingual writers" and "literacy brokers" needed to be more fluid and dialogic to account for the range of writers on campus, their concerns and needs, but also their strengths as language users and writers; perhaps the program needed to offer a larger cadre of participants the opportunity to share their expertise and benefit from the expertise of others—to grow in their roles as both writers *and* literacy brokers. Wouldn't this be a more inclusive way to cultivate a local network of literacy brokers? In order to allow that to happen, I needed to open the door of the safe house and meet the writers who came in.

I explored scholarship on academic-based writing circles and found their use has been instrumental in fostering the research development of university faculty (Lee & Boud, 2003). Their studies have shown, for example, that when writing is "seen as a starting point, rather than an endpoint, of the research process," university staff and faculty have been able to reposition themselves as "active scholarly writers within a peer-learning framework" (p. 198). For the spring semester, I supplemented the writing workshops' emphasis on literacy-broker-supported text production with a peer-learning/writing circle framework. I offered the bi-weekly writing circle to anyone who wanted to participate—faculty and staff, multilingual and monolingual. This brought a rich representation of writers and would-be literacy brokers from academic departments and administrative units, working on an array of writing projects.

The writing circle served to unveil and promote a range of writing practices as it helped to collapse dichotomies between those who needed support from those who offered it. *Language brokers* and *academic brokers* participated as writers and were joined by *institutional brokers* whose institutional memory of LaGuardia provided rich feedback for those writing about the college. Two administrators, for example, who were writing articles about their student-support initiatives helped each other unpack and broaden what had been internal reports and assessments into descriptive analyses for publications on higher education. Another faculty participant wondered if the instructional materials she had developed for her adult continuing education ESL course might be considered for publication as a textbook. I was able to put her into contact with two publishers I know from my own experience of publishing textbooks on writing. Yet another faculty member was in the process of developing an online application that would collect, collate, and make available college-level lesson plans across disciplines. Could we resource *technology brokers* on campus to help writers design Web 2.0 texts?

When conversations turned to the stigma and shame of those multilingual faculty members who had been told to attend because of their grammar errors, the writing circle also offered opportunities for them to showcase their savvy strategies. One such faculty member had successfully published articles in top-tier English-medium journals by co-authoring research articles with native speakers of English. Familiar with the rhetorical moves others' research articles needed to take, he offered invaluable advice and encouragement. And sharing his expertise made him more receptive to the English-language support the writing circle could provide to fine tune his instructional materials.

Conclusion: The Crowded Safe House

There is something both hopeful and ironic about a crowded safe house. How long before its walls collapse and writers from a host of language and literacy backgrounds redraw the lines of the larger contact zone? During its first year, the Literacy Brokers Program began with an intention to adapt and make visible and legitimate behind-the-scenes strategies used by multilingual scholars on the periphery here in an Anglophone center. In the process of creating a safe house on campus for multilingual scholar writers, we may have alienated the very people we meant to support, while attracting others we hadn't imagined would be interested. These are important lessons: As writing teachers and program designers, we try to make writing into this special place—but it's special in different ways for different people. For some, it's the short bus that "special kids" have to ride to school—it's stigmatizing because it labels their deficiency. For others, it's the special privilege some people get to have, but that they themselves feel excluded from: They didn't get the invitation. Perhaps they wonder why they always get left off the guest list as if they're too average to merit the invite. This special place needs to be re-imagined as an enabling writer's space, where we destigmatize and make accessible (not exclusive) the exciting, intellectual, creative work of writing. Then we can begin to mitigate some of the enormous pressure we all feel to write and publish; we can also imbue writing with some of the spirit it should have but so often loses in academic settings because the pressure is so much in the fore.

Notes

1   See, for example, the first-person narrative accounts of second-language users in discussing their "struggles and successes along the path to language learning" in Belcher and Connor (2001, p. 2).
2   This is a significant feat, since the U.S. State Department recognizes only 195 independent states and the United Nations 193.
3   In order to protect their anonymity, I do not reveal participants' academic departments, linguistic backgrounds, or home countries. Instead, I use pseudonyms and provide composite backgrounds.

References

Belcher, D. (2007). Seeking acceptance in an English-only research world. *Journal of Second Language Writing, 16*(1), 1–22. doi:10.1016/j.jslw.2006.12.001.

Belcher, D., & Connor, U. (Eds.)> (2001). *Reflections on multiliterate lives.* Clevedon, UK: Multilingual Matters.

Braine, G. (2005). The challenge of academic publishing: A Hong Kong perspective. *TESOL Quarterly, 39*(4), 707–716. doi:10.2307/3588528.

Canagarajah, A. S. (2002). *A geopolitics of academic writing.* Pittsburgh, PA: University of Pittsburgh Press.

Canagarajah, A. S. (2004). Multilingual writers and the struggle for voice in academic discourse. In A. Pavlenko & A. Blackledge (Eds.), *Negotiation of identities in multilingual contexts* (pp. 266–289). Clevedon, UK: Multilingual Matters.

Canagarajah, A. S. (2006). Toward a writing pedagogy of shuttling between languages: Learning from multilingual writers. *College English, 68*(6), 589–604. doi:10.2307/25472177.

Canagarajah, A. S. (2010). Internationalizing knowledge construction and dissemination. *Modern Language Journal, 94*(4), 661–664. doi:10.1111/j.1540-4781.2010.01105.x.

City University of New York. (n.d.). *The student body.* Retrieved from http://www.cuny.edu/about.html (accessed Nov. 15, 2012).

Curry, M. J. & Lillis, T. (2004) Multilingual scholars and the imperative to publish in English: Negotiating interests, demands, and rewards. *TESOL Quarterly, 38*(4), 663–688. doi:10.2307/3588284.

Diversity @ Baruch. (n.d.) retrieved from http://www.baruch.cuny.edu/diversity (accessed Nov. 15, 2012).

Flowerdew, J. (2008). Scholarly writers who use English as an additional language: What can Goffman's "Stigma" tell us? *Journal of English for Academic Purposes, 7*, 77–86. doi:10.1016/j.jeap.2008.03.002.

Flowerdew, J., & Li, Y. (2009). The globalization of scholarship: Studying Chinese scholars writing for international publication. In R. M. Manchón (Ed.), *Writing in foreign language contexts: Learning, teaching, and research* (pp. 156–182). Bristol, UK: Multilingual Matters.

Graddol, D. (1999). The decline of the native speaker. *AILA Review, 13*, 57–68.

Hall of Flags (n.d.). Retrieved from http://www.lagcc.cuny.edu/virtual_tour/m-building/hall_of_flags.htm (accessed Nov. 15, 2012).

Horner, B., Lu, M. Z., Royster, J. J., & Trimbur, J. (2011). Language difference in writing: Toward a translingual approach. *College English, 73*(3), 303–321.

Horner, B., & Trimbur, J. (2002). English only and U.S. college composition. *College Composition and Communication, 53*(4), 594–630. doi:10.2307/1512118.

Jerskey, M. (2011). The fortunate gardener: Cultivating a writing center. In J. Summerfield & C. Smith (Eds.), *Making teaching and learning matter: Transformative spaces in higher education* (pp. 73–93). New York, NY: Springer.

Kachru, B. (1986). *The alchemy of English: The spread, functions and models of non-native Englishes.* Oxford, UK: Pergamon.

Lee, A. & Boud, D. (2003). Writing groups, change and academic identity: Research development as local practice. *Studies in Higher Education, 28*(2), 187–200. doi:10.1080/0307507032000058109.

Lillis, T., & Curry, M. J. (2010). *Writing in a global context: The politics and practices of publishing in English.* New York, NY: Routledge.

Lillis, T., Magyar, A., & Robinson-Pant, A. (2010). An international journal's attempts to address inequalities in academic publishing: Developing a writing for publication programme. *Compare: A Journal of Comparative and International Education, 40*(6), 781–800. doi:10.1080/03057925.2010.523250.

Matsuda, P. K. (2006). The myth of linguistic homogeneity in U.S. college composition. *College English, 68*(6), 637–51. doi:10.2307/25472180.

Office of Institutional Research, LaGuardia Community College. (2011). *2011 Institutional Profile.* Retrieved from http://www.lagcc.cuny.edu/uploadedFiles/Main_Site/Content/IT/IR/docs/2011factbook.pdf (accessed Nov. 15, 2012).

Pratt, M. L. (1991). Arts of the contact zone. *Profession, 91*, 33–40.

19

MOVING OUT OF THE MONOLINGUAL COMFORT ZONE AND INTO THE MULTILINGUAL WORLD: AN EXERCISE FOR THE WRITING CLASSROOM

Joleen Hanson

Approaching writing as translingual practice appreciates and builds upon the rhetorical resources of multilingual students. However, it also requires us to expand our expectations of students who self-identify as monolingual. Many students enter college believing that reading or writing in a language other than English is both unnecessary and too difficult. They may falsely perceive their environment as "English only" due to self-segregation and to what Bawarshi (2010) has pointed to as "learned inclinations" that can prevent them from noticing the languages and varieties of English that they do encounter (p. 198). This chapter describes an exercise designed to help self-identified monolingual students learn strategies for moving out of their monolingual comfort zone and into negotiating language difference in a multilingual world.

The presumption of English-language homogeneity in the midst of actual linguistic diversity in academia is not new, and it is a view often held not only by students, but also by faculty and administrators. Horner and Trimbur (2002) point out that one result of the assumed "inevitability" of English monolingualism in higher education is the belief that English-language learners have a problem, but students who can only function in English do not (p. 617). The exercise described here makes the opposite assumption: that writing teachers need to help all students, but particularly those who function only in English, to gain fluency in working across language differences in all features of written language (Horner, Lu, Royster, & Trimbur, 2011, p. 312).

Not only does a multilingual orientation more accurately reflect the linguistic reality within the academic community, it is also consistent with "connected" online culture. College students today expect to find everything from information to entertainment to friendship on the Internet, and as Danet and Herring (2007) argue, "the Internet is a multilingual domain" (p. 28). Though English may currently be the most widely used language on the Internet and concerns have been raised about the Internet being a means of extending the dominance of English worldwide, nevertheless the Internet and connected technologies at the same time offer opportunities for language preservation and for greater cross-language interaction. For example, the Google Translate Toolkit offers speakers of endangered languages a means of preserving their language (Helft, 2010). Translation technology combined with online social-networking practices can create powerful opportunities for language learning as well as cross-language dissemination of knowledge and viewpoints.

The application of translation technology outside of academia suggests that its thoughtful, strategic use may deserve a place in the writing classroom as well. While online translators do not provide uniformly reliable translations, they can help students to negotiate language barriers rather than to simply ignore content presented in languages other than English. In fact, the limitations of online translators may foster critical thinking because students realize that they cannot rely on the translator alone in order to comprehend a text. As the discussion that follows will show, students using an online translator for Internet research drew on the knowledge they had of other languages, visual rhetoric, and their knowledge of Web genres to help them to extract meaning from non-English-language websites.

The Exercise: Internet Research in Languages Other Than English

Students in two sections of first-year composition completed an Internet research exercise while working on a researched argument essay. The exercise was introduced after students had chosen research topics and refined relevant search terms. Students used Google Translate to translate the search terms, and then paste the terms into a web browser to find non-English-language websites related to their research topic. To select a website to review from the list generated by the search engine, students could use their understanding of the language, if any, and the knowledge that the domain name in the URL can be an indicator of the reliability of the information provided in the page (e.g., .edu, .gov, .org)

Before inserting any text from the non-English language website in Google Translator, students were asked to observe the page's organization, graphics, and text in order to see how much they could learn about it. Once they had written their deductions about the web page content, they could use Google Translator to help them identify the topic of the page and to determine if their initial deductions were on target. Students carried out the search, observation, and translation twice, once with a familiar non-English language—perhaps one they used at home or had studied in school—and once with a less familiar language.

Purpose

The exercise was designed with two main purposes. First, as a research exercise it would provide students with information or perspectives about their research topics that might not be available on English-language websites. The exercise was intended to challenge the expectation that all relevant, useful information would always be available in English. A second purpose was to engage students in negotiating language difference and to uproot the notion that a native-like fluency in another language is needed in order to use it.

Evaluation

I used pre- and post-exercise surveys to evaluate student response to the exercise. The surveys focused on whether guided practice using an online translator would increase students' willingness to seek information from non-English language websites. The surveys also included questions about students' language backgrounds and how they might already be using online translators. The surveys and the exercise were completed within one 85-minute class period.

Participants

All 40 participants were enrolled in the second semester of the first-year composition sequence at a four-year, polytechnic campus of a state university system in the Upper Midwest. Students represented a range of majors, though the programs and course offerings at this institution focus on applied arts and sciences. No major is offered in English or in any other language. Only one student reported that she used a language other than English at home (Italian).

As in any university community, language differences exist among the students, faculty, and staff on this campus. The student population draws heavily from family farms and small regional high schools in the Upper Midwest where successive waves of immigration have occurred. The most recent wave brought families from Laos and from Mexico who speak varying dialects of Hmong and of Spanish, respectively. Other families who send students to the institution are descendants of earlier immigrants whose heritage languages come from Northern and Eastern Europe, languages such as English, German, Norwegian, Swedish, and Polish. A small number of students have roots in nearby Native American communities. In addition, the polytechnic campus programs attract some students from larger cities who use urban varieties of English. Finally, the university also recruits a small but increasing number of international students, many of whom are multilingual. Nevertheless, language diversity is practically invisible in our classrooms where the linguistic environment is "English only."

Student Response to the Exercise

As summarized in Table 19.1, more than half of the students reported that they had
not previously viewed web pages in languages other than English. Among those who
had viewed non-English web pages, foreign-language homework assignments were
the most common reason for doing so. A few students named other purposes, such
as to follow French Canadian hockey, find song lyrics, or explore fashion design.

The majority of the students had experience using an online translator, most
often to help with foreign-language homework. Three students reported using an
online translator in order to communicate with friends via email, Facebook, or in
person. Only nine students said they had never used an online translator at all.

Completion of the Exercise   *Because ...? How did they choose?*

When working with a relatively familiar language, 26 students were able to correctly identify the topic of the non-English web page before translating any text.
Only four students reported that they did not correctly identify the topic of the
web page in a familiar language. The remaining ten students felt that their first
impression of the topic was "close" or partially correct. When working with a less
familiar language, the success rate was similar, as shown in Table 19.2.

Strategies for Negotiating Language Difference

Students reported using different strategies to interpret the non-English websites
before entering any text into Google Translate. They examined visual elements

TABLE 19.1 Frequency of Viewing Non-English Web Pages

Number of responses	Response category
24	Never
14	Rarely
2	Sometimes
0	Often
40	All responses

TABLE 19.2 Success in Identifying the Topic of Non-English Language Websites

	Familiar language n = 40	Less familiar language n = 33
Identification of website topic was correct	26 students (65%)	18 students (55%)
Identification of website topic was incorrect, but similar	10 students (25%)	10 students (30%)
Identification of website topic was entirely incorrect	4 students (10%)	5 students (15%)

and drew on language knowledge, topic knowledge, and genre knowledge to help them identify a web page's content.

When working with a familiar language, students often understood key words or whole sections of text. Students also noted that, even when viewing less familiar languages, they could find recognizable borrowed words or cognates. A student who had studied Spanish explained, "I can't really read Spanish all that well, but I can understand certain phrases and words and that really helps me form an understanding of what they are trying to tell me without getting every last detail."

When the language was not familiar, students found that their knowledge of their research topic could help them correctly identify the nature of the web page content. They might be able to recognize key dates, events, or names of people or places. For example, a student noted, "I think this paragraph is about airports because [of] the words Heathrow and Singapore …" Another student whose topic was the 2011 tsunami in Japan explained, "… many of the Spanish words are similar to those in English. The words like 'precaution and 8.9 grados' give it away."

In addition, familiarity with websites and with conventional ways of presenting numerical data helped students glean meaning from websites even when the language was incomprehensible to them. A student observed, "I could see a picture of hockey players and they had a place for statistics. I was on a page that was directly about one team." After using Google Translate, he confirmed his identification stating, "[it] was a recap of the game that the team had played earlier. I had assumed that it was a team website. Overall the website is very similar to a USA website …"

A student who tried out his search terms in Chinese noted, "I could not understand this website at all, but it looks like it could be news headlines." After using Google Translate, he confirmed that it was indeed an online newspaper. Likewise, another student was able to recognize a newspaper format in a French-language page. He wrote, "The first web page I found seemed to be an online newspaper source … The graphics look like the title symbol at the top of a newspaper."

Student Evaluation of the Exercise

Overall, students differed in their assessment of the difficulty and usefulness of the exercise, but positive comments (24) outnumbered the negative ones (12). Negative remarks focused on the difficulty of the task, or the belief that everything the student would need to know would be available in English. Examples of students' negative comments about the exercise include:

- I found better web pages when I just used English.
- I think I would have an easier time and find enough information in English.
- I didn't find anything that wasn't already posted in English.

The positive responses, on the other hand, focused on the new information or viewpoints obtained from web pages in other languages. Examples of students' positive comments about the exercise include:

- I found a lot of useful information about my topic.
- I found it helpful to look at things in different languages; there is a greater amount of resources available this way.
- I could get a different perspective on the topic I am writing about.
- I find trying to read a different language interesting and challenging.

Assessment of the Exercise: Change in Student Attitudes

The pre- and post- exercise surveys indicated that the exercise increased students' willingness to seek information from non-English-language web pages. On the pre-exercise survey, 28 students (70 percent) said that they were not at all likely to seek information from non-English language web pages. After the exercise, that number was reduced by half. The majority of the students moved from being "not at all likely" to seek information from a non-English language website to being at least "somewhat likely" to do so.

As shown in Table 19.3, comparing individual answers to the pre- and post-exercise surveys showed that 28 students (70 percent) were more willing to seek information from non-English language websites after the exercise than they were before it. Seven students gave exactly the same answers on the pre- and post-exercise surveys, with six repeating "not at all likely" and one repeating "somewhat likely."

TABLE 19.3 Change in Individual Answers to the Pre- and Post-Exercise Survey Question: How Likely Are You to Seek Information from Non-English Language Web Pages?

Number of students n = 40	Post-exercise survey response compared to pre-exercise survey	
	Academic research	*Any non-academic purpose*
16	More likely	More likely
8	More likely	No change
4	No change	More likely
2	Less likely	More likely
7	No change	No change
1	Less likely	No change
2	Less likely	Less likely
	Summary by purpose	
	24 More likely	22 More likely
	11 No change	16 No change
	5 Less likely	2 Less likely

In the post-exercise survey, only eight students (20 percent) said that they were "not at all likely" to seek information from websites in other languages for *both* academic research and non-academic purposes. Of these, seven had not correctly identified the topic of at least one of the non-English-language websites they viewed. This lack of success with the exercise may also have affected their willingness to seek out non-English-language web pages in the future.

Implications for Teaching

The exercise moved students beyond a monolingual approach to gathering information online. Most students realized that they could get some meaning out of web pages written in languages other than English, and they became more willing to try to do so in the future. The exercise opened an avenue of research and linguistic interaction for them.

Extending the exercise to require incorporating a quotation from a non-English-language website into the researched argument essay could enhance students' critical reading skills and their ability to integrate sources into their own writing. Howard and Jamieson (2011) have shown that students at a range of institutions cut and paste quotations into their academic writing without fully understanding the meaning of what they are quoting. When the language is English, students may feel that they can paste in a quotation and rely on the reader to make sense of the quote, even if it does not fully make sense to the student writer. When quoting from a source text in a less familiar language, students would be more likely to recognize the need to precede the quote with a brief statement about the source and to follow the quote with an explanation in their own words of how the quote fits into their argument. Likewise, if students cannot easily scan the text for a quotable line to paste into their paper, they may pay attention to other "readable" features of a website, such as the type of URL.

The exercise affirms the resources of multilingual students without exacerbating their sense of being different. Other approaches to working against monolingualist assumptions of linguistic homogeneity might involve highlighting the language differences that exist among students in a classroom. Yet, in settings where monolingualist assumptions prevail, language difference can be subtle and socially marked. As a result, students may resist moving away from an "English only" orientation when doing so entails immediate social risks, such as identifying themselves as multilingual or revealing their use of stigmatized language varieties. While uprooting the view that some language varieties are "substandard" is a central objective of a translingual approach to writing instruction, exercises that engage students in negotiating language difference without requiring the vulnerability of self-disclosure can provide a less threatening way to begin the journey out of the monolingual comfort zone. The classroom exercise described here invites students to negotiate a wide language difference, which places users of different varieties of English on a relatively equal footing.

In addition to engaging students in negotiating meaning across language difference, the exercise also promotes a range of skills that are typically reinforced in first-year writing courses: narrowing a research question, identifying useful search terms, and evaluating online sources. It could be expanded to include effectively incorporating research data and the views of other writers into the student's own argument. Changing the way we think about the nature of language and of language users can enhance and strengthen our existing writing pedagogy.

References

Bawarshi, A. (2010). The challenges and possibilities of taking up multiple discursive resources in U.S. college composition. In B. Horner, M. Z. Lu, & P. K. Matsuda (Eds.), *Cross-language relations in composition* (pp. 196–203). Carbondale, IL: Southern Illinois University Press.

Danet, B., & Herring, S.C. (2007). Introduction. In B. Danet & S. C. Herring (Eds.), *The multilingual Internet: Language, culture, and communication online* (pp. 3–39). Oxford, UK: Oxford University Press.

Helft, M. (2010, March 9). Google's tool-kit for translator helps feed its machine. *New York Times*. Retrieved from http://bits.blogs.nytimes.com/2010/03/09/googles-tool-kit-for-translators-helps-feed-its-machine (accessed 15 November 2012).

Horner, B., Lu, M. Z., Royster, J. J., & Trimbur, J. (2011). Language difference in writing: Towards a translingual approach. *College English, 73*(3), 303–321.

Horner, B., & Trimbur, J. (2002). English only and U.S. college composition. *College Composition and Communication, 53*(4), 594–630. doi:10.2307/1512118.

Howard, R. M., & Jamieson, S. (2011, April). *The citation project: Results of a 15-college study of students' use of sources.* Paper presented at the annual Conference on College Composition and Communication, Atlanta, GA.

20

WHEN "SECOND" COMES FIRST—हिंदी TO THE EYE? SOCIOLINGUISTIC HYBRIDITY IN PROFESSIONAL WRITING

Anita Pandey

Introduction

Growing interest in translingualism in predominantly monolingual societies (Canagarajah, 2002; 2006; 2007; Horner, Lu, Royster, & Trimbur 2011) evidences increased contact between monolinguals and multilinguals. The increased use of (e)written communication has undoubtedly contributed to code-mixing or code-meshing (Bamgboṣe, 2001), and the emergence of linguistically mobile, hybrid identities (Pandey, 2011).

Apart from becoming an increasingly important mode of communication, writing—much of it translingual or *bilingually flavored*—is more globally involving and complex today (Kamil, Pearson, Moje, & Afflerbach, 2010). How so? Individuals from different parts of the globe can engage with each other relatively easily, and technology enables multiparty and multimodal discourse (and one can participate without necessarily contributing to e-exchanges). More and more bilinguals and/or bidialectals are communicating with each other and with monolinguals through email, text messaging, and other forms of electronic communication. These are more readily available, and more time- and cost-efficient than face-to-face communication, phone contact, and even snail mail. Indeed, technology has created viable translingual (e-)communities that cut across language and geography. However, our ability to decode translingual (e-)writing, and bridge linguistic divides lags behind.

An understanding of Indian writing—much of it translingual—is, therefore, critical. This chapter aims to enhance pedagogical understanding of (e-)writing. It does so by (1) identifying noteworthy research gaps in the field, (2) illustrating how literacy practices differ across contexts, and (3) outlining a discourse framework, STEPS, that is linguistically comprehensive and readily applicable. STEPS stands for *Structure, Theme(s), Etiquette, Purpose,* and *Style.* Its value in enhancing communication across languages, and in yielding more meaningful and comparable corpora (Moreno, 2008) is also outlined.

"Second" First? Examples of Translingual Writing

Today, many "second-language" writers of English are, in fact, English dominant. A growing number are literate in English (Pandey, 2011), yet fluent in more than one language and/or dialect. Translinguality accommodates linguistic diversity. One need not be a multilingual in the traditional sense to create and/or participate in translingual exchanges. Translinguals, individuals who traverse codes, include *comprehensive* or all-around bilinguals; passive, or *partial bilinguals,*[1] who merely understand but rarely speak and/or read/write; *fluent bilinguals*, conversant with just listening and speaking; and *functional bilinguals*, who know enough of a variety to elicit a smile or break the ice.

Just as one's "second language" could technically be one's first in some areas (e.g., writing), word order is not fixed in some languages. For example, while we might expect *Hindi* to be written in the same (letter) order in the Devanagari script, this is not the case for many Hindi words. Short vowels are either implied (i.e., absent, as in Arabic) or, when orthographically present, placed to the left of the consonant that they follow, and read second. In short, you read the consonants first in words like हिंदी (i.e., Hindi). The English letter sequence spells *Ihndi.* Interestingly, the word *Hindi* only contains a hint of the "*n*" sound, so only half an *n* is used in Devanagari, by way of the dot on top.[2] As is characteristic of Hindi, and the mother language, Sanskrit, the line across the top indicates letter-sound blending (i.e., a word). Arguably this bidirectionality and/or multidirectionality is reflected in the writing of many multilinguals. Some engage in one-shot messaging, a relatively complex phenomenon for monolinguals, whose writing tends to be overtly purpose delineated.

That many words are multipurpose is reflected in the brevity of the writing; much is implied. An example from a conference organizer in south India follows, in Excerpt 1:

Excerpt 1
Dear Sir/Madam,

Thank <u>U</u> for your kind response. Kindly send your paper on or before 15.3.2008, <u>then only</u> we can include <u>ur</u> paper in the proceedings. Looking forward your reply.

Thank <u>U</u>
Organizing secretary

This economical, text-like email contains the following translanguage features:

1. Spelling pronunciations (i.e., phonetic spellings).
2. <u>then only</u>: from Hindi <u>thabhee</u> = <u>thab</u> (then) + <u>-hee</u> = emphasis particle.
3. Acronyms like *ur* (vs. <u>your</u>) and *U* which reflect the writer's preference for e-speed (since online access can be unreliable) and orality, yet these are likely to be misread as attempts at informality.

Excerpt 2 is an email inquiry from an Indian publisher in New Delhi to a U.S.-based editor of Indian descent. Observe how the sender does not thank the recipient. This is because expressions of gratitude (like apologies and even acknowledgments of thanks) are considered distancing and formal in this context. So Indian writing sometimes sounds abrasive or obsequious (Pandey, 2011).

> **Excerpt 2**
> Hi dear,
>
> Trust this finds you <u>fit as ever</u>. It's been 2 days since I sent you the drafts of all the papers with <u>updations</u>. Have you forwarded them to the respective contributors? Dear send me Frank's address and I <u>shall do the needful</u>.

In this excerpt, the casual Americanism <u>Hi</u> replaces the more formal <u>Dear</u>. Cowie (2007) reports that younger call-center employees in India frequently mix American and Indian English. Indianisms are underlined and include <u>fit as ever</u> (i.e., healthy), <u>updations,</u> and <u>the needful</u>. The last line might be unclear to some. *Please* is generally considered overly formal among fellow Indians, so this writer uses "Dear" instead. *Needful* is another Indian English term, a direct translation from "zaroori," Urdu for something that needs prompt attention. Notice how the request is phrased—indirectly and using *shall* (vs. *will*). Such *translanguage(d) English* is common in this type of writing. Pandey (2011) observes that transdialectal English constitutes a fourth circle of *hybrid English* that needs to be added to Kachru's three circles of World Englishes.

While some might argue that the more frequent and immediate exchanges that technology affords us in our more interconnected world likely accelerate our learning curve as professional communicators seeking to understand diverse discourse, this is not necessarily the case. If it were, then mere exposure to different varieties would ensure acquisition of strategic know-how in our global village, and guarantee that all participants could accurately decode the messages intended. Hence the need to develop appropriate pedagogical strategies.

Putting First "Second"

For too long, *intercultural rhetoric* (IR) has persisted with the increasingly inapplicable "first" language (L1) versus "second" language (L2) dichotomy, despite the increased use of *indigenized* and *hybrid* varieties in professional exchanges, and noteworthy changes in corporate relationships (i.e., more outer-circle employers). Additionally, the so-called "native-speaker" writing—an elusive construct and increasingly infrequent—tends to be the default *measure* (see Connor, 1996).

Some IR studies assume that one is most competent in the language one acquired "first," and that age and/or sequence of language acquisition and linguistic competence are correlated. These are questionable assertions. In the case of a bilingual, identifying one's first language, second language, and more often than not, one's first and "second" first languages, is especially challenging. The so-called "second" language (L2) is actually the *first*, primary, or only written medium of communication for a growing number.[3] In the absence of a comprehensive framework of analysis that effectively contextualizes corpora, these L1–L2 accounts tend to be binary, oversimplistic, and norm based.

Differences between participants' discourse are overwhelmingly viewed as "interference" from the first language (L1) when, in fact, the boundaries between language(s) and/or culture(s) are often indistinct, and communication is not necessarily limited to two language varieties. Moreover, all too often, "interference" is viewed as cultural. Arguably, unlike *language*, "culture" is a relatively vague construct.

Unfortunately, so-called "second-language" writing is usually portrayed as second rate by many Western scholars. Much of such writing employs *indigenized language varieties* (e.g., Indian English). Yet these legitimate dialects that embody vital cultural differences still struggle for recognition (see Canagarajah, 2007; Kachru, 2005; Pandey & Pandey, 1993). Globalization, through outsourcing and increased contact across linguistic contexts, might hasten their recognition, but this remains to be seen.

Unlike in the United States, English is one of two official languages in India (Kachru, 2005), and the medium of instruction in most schools. The fast-expanding pool of participants trained in Indian schools—few of whom are technically "second-language" English users—and the multimodal means of interaction available today necessitate changes in our conceptualization of international communication.

To address a few more limitations in the IR model, not all participants use primarily or solely claim-supportive argumentative language (Kelly & Bazerman, 2003), unlike what the term "rhetoric" in IR suggests. Furthermore, not all involve interactions between two distinct cultures and/or parties, unlike what the prefix in "*inter*cultural" suggests. Multiparty exchanges are increasingly common (Pandey, 2005).

Furthermore, U.S. writing conventions are still the most widely discussed, despite the proliferation of international organizations. Papers that do not conform to U.S. and/or British writing conventions are readily dismissed as "disorganized," "longwinded," and/or "unclear" (Pandey, 2010), making it hard for those not trained in this *literacy tradition* to be taken seriously, and often too, to get published in English-language venues (see Canagarajah, 2002). This situation is common in other areas of professional writing also, and every effort must be made to develop a better understanding. First, familiarity with common American English expressions, as well as with U.S. writing conventions—which require a thesis spelled out early on, chronologically supported, and reiterated throughout—cannot be assumed. Second, unlike what many writing resources recommend (Chaney & Martin, 2007; Locker, 2006), the chronological/Toulmin model of writing is unlikely to guarantee success in all parts of the world (see Campbell, 1998). For these and other reasons, the term *translingual discourse*[4] is preferable.

A Handy Framework: Capturing Breadth and Depth

The absence of a globally applicable and multidimensional framework of analysis that provides a comprehensive understanding of translingual discourse across linguistic levels is one of the research gaps this chapter aims to fill. Effectively decoding translingual writing requires a systematic approach and framework, as outlined below.

Most IR studies (see Connor, 1996) employ a vertical framework. Non-standard dialects are consistently placed below Standard equivalents, and differences in writing are essentially viewed as deviations from the norm, namely, American, and British English. Structural differences are highlighted, and the reader's interpretation is not consistently considered, rendering this model inapplicable to outer-circle settings (see Pandey, 1998), which have developed their own brand of English. A more robust and cross-contextual discourse framework is, therefore, in order, particularly one grounded in linguistics.

The *World Englishes* framework (Kachru, 2005), in contrast, is a horizontal one that places language varieties side by side—not one on top of the other. Its three dimensions (*acceptability*, *comprehensibility*, and *intelligibility*) emphasize discourse/pragmatic distinctiveness and listener/reader involvement, yet it is not as easily applicable.

Fairclough's (2001, 2006) and van Dijk's (2008, 2009) *critical discourse analysis* (CDA) frameworks, and Suárez and Moreno's (2008) tend to be nebulous and unidimensional (i.e., the recipient's interpretations are rarely considered). For instance, as if CDA isn't complex enough, Fairclough (2006) uses "a version of CDA embedded within a 'cultural' approach to political economy" (p. 6). Variable interpretations of key constructs, for instance, *cultural*, *textual*, *contextual*, and *ideological* components of discourse—each of which could have variable linguistic indicators (e.g., phonological, morpho-lexical, syntactic, and pragmatic) could yield different analyses. Identifying the boundaries between these constructs is just as challenging. One could argue that both the textual and contextual spheres have ideological dimensions. Indeed, we should be interested in "closing the gap between text and context" (Lillis, 2008, p. 388), but not only in academic writing. Professional exchanges are more commonplace, and just as decisive.

Move analysis (Chang & Swales, 1999; Connor, 2000; Swales, 1990) is inapplicable to all writing. *Rhetorical moves* are open to interpretation and are not always sequential. Online, for instance, links could be introductory moves in any part of the discourse (opening, middle, and/or end). E-discourse is, therefore, not as easily divisible into distinct moves. A certain element of subjectivity is unavoidable when one employs these frameworks. Hence, they are closer to guidelines than easy-to-apply frameworks.

Therefore, a more comprehensive framework is needed. STEPS offers a step-by-step analysis of discourse. It captures the range and breadth of variation in discourse, including multilingual discourse.

STEPS and Application

STEPS draws on the World Englishes' paradigm, and *conversation analysis* (CA) (see Sacks, Schegloff, & Jefferson, 1974), since writing, like verbal exchanges, prompts turn-taking. Most email, for instance, requires a response (like a speaker-selected turn). Accurate analyses of written exchanges therefore necessitate a focus on all parties' contributions, including what preceded or pre-empted a piece of writing. Figure 20.1 is a visual representation of core components of STEPS, followed by examples of applications to professional (e)writing.

As noted, in this framework, variations in writing are attributable to differences in STEPS, namely, structure, theme(s), etiquette, purpose, and style. STEPS requires examining both language structure and usage elements, and *text* and *context* are connected. The result is enhanced *mutual intelligibility*. One of the biggest plus points of a linguistic approach is the fact that language is construed as a significant medium—so all languages are accommodated and analyzable, including hybrids. Linguistic domains subsumed under each category are identified in square brackets below.

The first "S" in STEPS stands for *structure*, which refers to format. This includes sequence[5] (as, for instance, in the case of a poem vs. a memo/email message vs. a formal letter vs. a report vs. a proposal), as well as word, sentence, and discourse choice, mechanics or punctuation, capitalization, and spelling conventions; and the physical layout of each section. *Structure* could vary across context (geographic, sociolinguistic) and genre. [Primary linguistic focus: discourse.]

FIGURE 20.1   STEPS: Structure, Theme(s), Etiquette, Participants/Purpose, and Style

The "T" stands for *theme(s)*, and refers to the content or focus, both the stated content, and the implied meaning(s). Not all information supplied is expected by all recipients. [Primary linguistic focus: semantics, which cuts across linguistic levels—phonology, morphology, syntax, and discourse.]

The "E" in STEPS refers to writing *etiquette* or expectations that guide participants' language (verbal, written, nonverbal) and content. These are usually tied to operant sociolinguistic and pragmatic conventions. Differences in writing etiquette account for directly goodwill-oriented language versus writing that might be interpreted as (potentially) rude.

Etiquette focuses primarily on discourse/pragmatic features. These include (1) organization of information (e.g., chronological purpose identification) and (2) language employed. In increasing order of size, the latter include numbers and associated sounds (phonemes and tone), affixes, words, phrases, sentences, and discourse units (e.g., saluting and thanking, as well as expected register or language-specific writing acts—like speech acts—associated with openings and closings).

Etiquette, being convention-based, also accounts for whether or not a writer sends a cover letter alongside a CV and/or references the prompt that initiated the writing (for instance, a posted or word-of-mouth job opening, a question or a request), or the outcomes or next steps. [Primary linguistic focus: sociolinguistics and pragmatics.]

"P" stands for *participants* and their *purpose*, both the sender's/writer's and the recipient's, in this dynamic framework, where discourse is assumed to be inter-action-oriented (i.e., designed to elicit a response, even if the objective is primarily appreciation, as in the case of literature). Proper interpretation requires dialog with the recipient and/or informants knowledgeable in the sociolinguistic and discourse practices in use in the context in question. The term *context* is preferred (i.e., to *culture*), as it is more tangible, yet fluid enough to cover geography and physical setting.[Primary linguistic focus: sociolinguistics and pragmatics.]

The final "S" stands for *style*, individual and contextual. Some of these components overlap, as is to be expected. For instance, there's a fine line between *etiquette* and *style*; both are, to some extent, the product of pragmatic norms. *Etiquette* is contextually expected (behavior), while *style* could be distinctive. *Context* is an integral ingredient, subsumed in each component of STEPS.

Applying STEPS

Translinguality is evident in Indian CVs (see Pandey, 2010) and cover letters (see Excerpt 3). I will apply STEPS to Indian job application correspondence below. Interpretations of the cover letter are based on an interview with the author.

Excerpt 3: An e-response to an advert
Hi Anita Pandey mam

I am from India I have done Masters degree M.A. in Applied Linguistics from University of Hyderbad (CALTS—Centre for applied linguistics and translation studies) India also have worked as a Linguist Editor in IIIT, Hyderabad (International Institute of Information Technology) And currently teaching Mandarin(Chinese) in an M.B.A institution since last 2 and ½ years as a visiting faculty also at present I am working in an IT firm in Mumbai as a Globlization Engineer. Here I would like to work in your institute and I am very much interested to work with here enclosed is my cv please find the attachment and let me know the reply.

Regards
Nitu

Structure

The length and layout (two-sentence single paragraph), the punctuation (i.e., listing of the candidate's relevant work experience in run-on mode that emphasizes her multiple qualifications) and mechanics mirror the orality and structure of spoken Hindi.

Theme(s)

Most Indians prefer spoken to written discourse, so the content (i.e., implied purpose and summary of Indian-standards-based qualifications using Indian English) supersedes format considerations. Hence the minimal attention paid to punctuation and mechanics, including capitalization and paragraphing.

Etiquette

The reader's use of *Hi* (a hallmark of American English) and the recipient's full name signal her familiarity with U.S. culture and spoken American English address norms which have quickly been adopted by the call-center world of which India is a leader. The *mam* reflects Indian politeness. Also, the writer mentions just her qualifications and work experience. No mention is made of her skills, a key measure of success in the United States, nor what she will do for the institution in question. This information has to be inferred. It is not until the end that she mentions her desire to work at the addressee's institution. Even then, the position she is interested in is unspecified. From an Indian perspective, mention of her qualifications and experience(s) is sufficient for the reader to determine how and in what capacity her services could best be utilized. Supporting her candidacy and outlining her potential responsibilities, apart from being redundant, could be considered signs of an aggressive individual. In a language and culture where humility and obedience are prized, such information could, in fact, hurt her chances of being hired. That the writer provides just her first name is also noteworthy. In contrast, in both verbal and written Hindi (as in most Indian languages), use of the recipient's first name is considered rude.

Purpose

The writer's purpose is only communicated at the end, a purposeful move, and in her words, "typical in spoken Hindi." She first seeks to establish common ground by connecting with the reader on some level. Otherwise, as she observed "My letter may not get enough attention." The first line serves as a bridge to a professional relationship, as the writer assumes the reader is also Indian. She therefore opens by identifying her nationality. In her view, her being Indian is an added qualification and, to some in this trust-oriented culture, more persuasive than training and relevant work experience alone. She is essentially saying: I am a fellow Indian so you can count on me. The reason she appeals to a (presumably) shared identity is because Hindi last names like Pandey (from *Pundit*/teacher) mirror nationality, caste (Brahmin), and more.

Style

The speech-like qualities of Excerpt 3 can best be explained by the fact that spoken Hindi closely resembles the written version (stylistically and phonetically). The writer confirmed that she attempted to recreate Hindi discourse in English. The wording, organization, and purpose could easily be misconstrued, since this example meshes at least two languages (Hindi and English). For instance, "mam" is a politeness marker which would stand alone in British English but, in this case, is conjoined with the addressee's name, as is the Hindi honorific "-ji," yielding both formality and (cultural) familiarity. The text in Excerpt 3 might be considered disorganized. Its brevity, its mix of formality and informality, and the absence of conventional inner-circle English leave-taking and politeness devices (e.g., Thank you), might be viewed by those unfamiliar with Indian languages as vague and curt.

Directions for Future Research and Conclusion

Individuals, languages, and cultures are more mobile today and in transition, so more interactions elude classification along cultural lines. While Englishization, and Hindization (among other processes) mirror the kinds of changes in progress, to concentrate on increasingly defunct L1-to-L2 interference (vs. purposeful linguistic extension) yields an incomplete picture. The onus of understanding rests squarely on all sides. In short, we must learn (about) other language varieties and research the parameters and impact of language contact in individual writing acts (on analogy with *speech acts*, a linguistics term that captures the interactivity of conversation). To this end, contextualized studies of translingual writing and reading *acts* (another term proposed) are in order.

As illustrated, to enhance mutual intelligibility, we would do well to research both writer and reader perspectives (Hyland, 2001). Since technology is both a globalizer and a vital medium for global contact (see Aggarwal, 2007), success today necessitates three skills, namely:

1. translingual competence or *functional bilingualism*,
2. familiarity with World Englishes (Kachru, 2005), and
3. a working knowledge of linguistics or the ins-and-outs of language, the foundation of STEPS.

The first requires knowledge of contextually appropriate reading and writing practices. Bilingualism, or even *functional bilingualism*, is the ability to perform key communicative functions in the recipient's primary language. A functional bilingual aims to come across like a *bilingual*. Indeed, *strategic literacy* is required for success in today's global economy (Kamil, Mosenthal, Pearson, & Barr, 2000). Familiarity with variable writing and reading styles and preferences, as well as with different brands of English, helps minimize misunderstanding and ensure a competitive edge.

STEPS, a linguistically comprehensive framework of analysis, was outlined. STEPS could enhance global communication, since it captures translanguaging (i.e., writing across languages and linguistic levels). It could also serve as a blueprint for more semantically full automation and more sociolinguistically representative corpus analyses than the predominantly keyword taggers available (Biber, Conrad, & Reppen, 1998).

Today we must be familiar with diverse content (phonetic, lexico-semantic, discourse/pragmatic) and form conventions. Learning about differences in writing practices and acquainting ourselves with the distinctive features of résumés and other key documents employed in the global marketplace is essential.

We also need to expand our definition of "audience." It would help to have access to a preliminary list of words and expressions frequently employed in different linguistic contexts. For example, students might be interested in knowing that meetings are sometimes "preponed" (i.e., moved up) in India. The term "rescheduling" in contrast, requires moving a meeting to a later date. It helps to know that many words are decoded differently. Additional questions worth investigating include: Are writing acts negotiated and negotiable? Does reading impact writing? If so, how? A focus on reader and writer expectations is highly recommended, since *identity* is at a crossroads for many, and constantly being reconstituted.

As noted, reading and writing are key skills and likely to become more important (Kamil et al., 2000). Developing writing fluidity or *writing accommodation* skills is one way to increase students' marketability. One of the easiest ways to meet the needs of different audiences is by varying our (e)language to appeal to different audiences.

A working knowledge of linguistics is, therefore, highly recommended. As demonstrated, linguistics provides us with a sharper lens through which to process translingual discourse. It helps us become more astute at using and examining language as a global navigational system. So in this global race, "Who or what is first, and/or second?" you might ask. The answer depends on the language(s) in question. Written Hindi, as we saw, is a multidirectional language; short vowels appear to the left, long ones to the right, and still others, like long /oo/ (as in the word *Hindu*, हिंदू) are straddled at the bottom (see the comma-like symbol pointing southeast). In short, it is time we stopped reading and writing from just left to right. We need to look up and down, as well as to the east and west. Translinguality, like progress, is multidirectional.

Notes

1   Researchers are hard pressed to answer questions like "What's the minimum skill one needs in each language to be considered a bilingual?"
2   A full *n* would look like न as in the word <u>nana</u>/नाना (paternal grandfather). In this word, the Hindi spelling matches the English equivalent (i.e., four full letters).
3   This is generally the case with reading, as well.
4   *Discourse* encompasses multiple modes of expression. Moreover, e-writing is less conventionalized (e.g., email, text messaging), and more fluid and multidirectional in orientation today.
5   Since most assume that a linear piece starts with the main idea, a piece of discourse could be linear or considered chronological, as long as it's organized in line with one's expectations.

References

Aggarwal, R. (2007). Technology and international business: What should we know and teach? *AIG Insights*, 7(1), 8–14.

Bamgboṣe, A. (2001). World Englishes and globalization. *World Englishes*, 20(3), 357–364. doi:10.1111/1467-971X.t01-1-00220.

Biber, D., Conrad, S., & Reppen, R. (1998). *Corpus linguistics: Investigating language structure and use.* Cambridge, UK: Cambridge University Press.

Campbell, C. (1998). Rhetorical ethos: A bridge between high-context and low-context cultures? In Niemeier, S., Campbell, C., & Dirven, R. (Eds.), *The cultural context in business communication* (pp. 31–48). Philadelphia, PA: John Benjamins.

Canagarajah, A. S. (2002) Multilingual writers and the academic community: Towards a critical relationship. *Journal of English for Academic Purposes*, 1, 29–44. doi:10.1016/S1475-1585(02)00007-3.

Canagarajah, A. S. (2006). The place of world Englishes in composition: Pluralization continued. *College Composition and Communication*, 57(4), 586–619.

Canagarajah, A. S. (2007). Lingua franca English, multilingual communities, and language acquisition. *Modern Language Journal, 91*, 923–939. doi:10.1111/j.1540-4781.2007.00678.x.

Chaney, L. H., & Martin, J. S. (2007). *Intercultural business communication* (4th ed.). Upper Saddle River, NJ: Prentice Hall.

Chang, Y., & Swales, J. (1999). Informal elements in English academic writing: Threats or opportunities for advanced non-native speakers? In C. Candlin & K. Hyland (Eds.), *Writing: Texts, processes and practices* (pp. 145–167). London, UK: Longman.

Connor, U. (1996). *Contrastive rhetoric: Cross-cultural aspects of second language writing.* Cambridge, UK: Cambridge University Press.

Connor, U. (2000). Variation in rhetorical moves in grant proposals of US humanists and scientists. *Text, 20*(1), 1–28. doi:10.1515/text.1.2000.20.1.1.

Cowie, C. (2007). The accents of outsourcing: The meanings of "neutral" in the Indian call centre industry. *World Englishes, 26*(3), 316–330. doi:10.1111/j.1467-971X.2007.00511.x.

Fairclough, N. (2001). *Language and power.* New York, NY: Longman.

Fairclough, N. (2006). *Language and globalization.* New York, NY: Routledge.

Horner, B., Lu, M. Z., Royster J. J., & Trimbur, J. (2011). Language difference in writing: Toward a translingual approach. *College English, 73*(3), 303–321.

Hyland, K. (2001). Bringing in the reader: Addressee features in academic articles. *Written Communication, 18*(4), 549–574. doi:10.1177/0741088301018004005.

Kachru, B. B. (2005). *Asian Englishes beyond the canon.* Hong Kong: Hong Kong University Press.

Kamil, M., Mosenthal, P., Pearson, D., & Barr, R. (2000). *Handbook of reading research* (Vol. 3). Mahwah, NJ: Lawrence Erlbaum Associates.

Kamil, M., Pearson, D., Moje, E., & Afflerbach, P. (Eds.). (2010). *Handbook of reading research* (Vol. 4). New York, NY: Routledge.

Kelly, G., & Bazerman, C. (2003). How students argue scientific claims: A rhetorical semantic analysis. *Applied Linguistics, 24*(1), 28–55. doi:10.1093/applin/24.1.28.

Lillis, T. (2008). Ethnography as method, methodology, and "deep theorizing": Closing the gap between text and context in academic writing research. *Written Communication, 25*(3), 353–388. doi:10.1177/0741088308319229.

Locker, K. (2006). *Business and administrative communication* (7th ed). New York, NY: McGraw-Hill.

Moreno, A. I. (2008). The importance of comparable corpora for cross-cultural studies. In U. Connor, E. R. Nagelhout, & W. V. Rozycki (Eds.), *Contrastive rhetoric: Reaching to intercultural rhetoric* (pp. 25–41). Philadelphia, PA: John Benjamins.

Pandey, A. (1998). Code alteration and Englishization across cultures: Cyclic differences. In E. Thumboo (Ed.), *The three circles of English* (pp. 142–170). Singapore: University of Singapore Press.

Pandey, A. (2005). A cyber stepshow: E-discourse and literacy at an HBCU. *Critical Inquiry in Language Studies, 2*(1), 35–69. doi:10.1207/s15427595cils0201_3.

Pandey, A. (2010, July). "Hi Ma'am": Distinctive features of Indian business documents, and the STEPS framework." Paper presented at the 16th Conference of the International Association for World Englishes, Vancouver, BC, Canada.

Pandey, A. (2011). Introduction. *International Journal of Communication, 21*(1), 1–4.

Pandey, A., & Pandey, A. (1993). Nigerian English today. *World Englishes, 12*(3): 401–414.

Sacks, H., Schegloff, E. A., & Jefferson, G. (1974). A simplest systematics for the organization of turn-taking for conversation. *Language, 50*, 696–735. doi:10.2307/412243.

Suárez, T. L., & Moreno A. I. (2008). The rhetorical structure of literary academic book reviews: An English–Spanish cross-linguistic approach. In U. Connor, E. Nagelhout, & W. Rozycki (Eds.), *Contrastive rhetoric: Reaching to intercultural rhetoric* (pp. 147–168). Amsterdam, Netherlands: John Benjamins.

Swales, J. M. (1990). *Genre analysis: English in academic and research settings.* Cambridge, UK: Cambridge University Press.

Van Dijk, T. (2008). *Discourse and context. A sociocognitive approach.* Cambridge, UK: Cambridge University Press.

Van Dijk, T. (2009). *Society and discourse. How social contexts influence text and talk.* Cambridge, UK: Cambridge University Press.

21

"AND YEA I'M VENTING, BUT HEY I'M WRITING ISN'T I": A TRANSLINGUAL APPROACH TO ERROR IN A MULTILINGUAL CONTEXT

Aimee Krall-Lanoue

Using a translingual approach to reading student error in writing requires a detraining of teaching practices. Instead of attempting to understand what students mean in their writing when we encounter "error," we must focus on the text, not what a student "meant to do." We often direct students to do this in their own writing, but we rarely take seriously the same advice.

In his discussion of multilingual speakers communicating with others who speak a different language, Canagarajah (2009) writes, "they don't resort to adopting a common medium ... nor do they pressure each other to adopt the language belonging to one of them. They stick to their linguistic peculiarities and negotiate intelligibility through their difference" (p. 18). They negotiate with the "ungrammatical" or "unintelligible," and these phrases, items, and structures become "shared resources" (p. 18). This is the strategy I suggest teachers use when reading student writing from a translingual approach. Instead of questioning students about what they meant to write and how to conform to written conventions, we might "negotiate intelligibility" through difference. Using difference as a shared resource rather than a problem to be eliminated, a stain to be cleansed out of writing, demands that students take an active role in their understanding of writing. It also reminds teachers to act as engaged readers and not simply experts of rules and conventions. In the following examples I demonstrate how teachers might use this strategy with student writing when they encounter three common types of error: tense, incorrect word choice, and sentence boundary issues.

Although this strategy works more easily with some kinds of errors than others, it is productive nonetheless. It also works to train and retrain students and teachers to read critically. Again, it is important to recognize that this is not a comprehensive method for editing writing; instead it creates pedagogical situations for discussing difference in writing. The following samples were taken from four basic writing students' journals from the fall of 2010 at a small, private, urban Midwestern college. The writing here is representative of much of what composition instructors see, regardless of the distinction between basic or mainstream writing courses.

In fact, because these students were all native English speakers, the process of reading I outline here is applicable to all students in a composition course. Although these students might only speak and write in one language and be classified as monolingual, they all use varieties of English, particularly nondominant and less privileged versions. As others have argued, though, it is less about what English they use and more about how they use it. In the case of these students, it is their language differences which offer rich insight into the ways we might rethink error.

Tense

In many ways, tense issues are one of the easiest to work with when using a translingual approach to reading error. It becomes automatic for an instructor to cross out or circle the wrong tense of a verb, but here I suggest accepting the tense as intentional. For example, one student, Josh, wrote the following in his journal:

> To understand the language that I never could learn so I can write. I'm still learning more and more each day in the English language. I learn a lot this year about my writing. I gain the experience I need to be able to write a paper, but I make the small mistakes. I finally able to recognize the mistakes better than what I use too. I learned that you need to give a 110% to learn anything and remember it. I gain a lot of this in English 095 this year and English 096.

One of the predominant problems an instructor might notice when reading this example is the shift between how Josh understands what he learned throughout the semester and how he understands his current position in relation to language. He writes, "I gain the experience I need to be able to write a paper" and "I gain a lot of this in English 095 this year and in English 096." Typically an instructor would circle or rewrite the word *gain* and replace it with *gained*. It is something that already happened in the past. However, if we defer that understanding and resist editing Josh's sentences, we might see a more complex way Josh feels about his learning. Perhaps, for Josh, the experience he has gained is not something entirely in the past but is something that is still happening at the time of the writing. As he writes in the second sentence from this excerpt, "I'm still learning more each day." He continues this thought, then, by writing, "I learn a lot this year about my writing."

One could certainly argue that if Josh meant to describe his learning as ongoing, he should have written "I am learning a lot this year about my writing."

The purpose in using a translingual approach, though, isn't simply to correct the writing here and edit out difference. Instead it is to negotiate meaning. My strategy for dealing with Josh's writing is to talk with him about how I understood exactly what he wrote—that is, because he uses the present tense of *learn* it seems like learning is ongoing, but because he's also writing about events that happened in the past, the process of learning could be over. This is a conversation that attempts to negotiate what exactly Josh wants to say, has started to say, continues to say, and may say about his learning experiences in the course. Now maybe Josh wanted to say that it was something that he learned in the past, and using the past tense would be more appropriate. But, that is what the discussion is about. Regardless of what might be more appropriate or correct, the significance of a translingual reading is that it opens up a conversation for talking about reading, language choices, and making meaning.

We see something similar in the following example from Connie, who wrote in this excerpt about an experience with her ex-husband: "I knew he felt bad but I want him to feel worse." In a traditional reading of this sentence, we would probably cross out the *want* and replace it with *wanted* because the situation she describes happened in the past. However, if we read it as it is written, we might understand that although the situation occurred in the past, she continues to want him to feel bad about it—the feelings she has are not finished. As a reader, I am not sure if this is what she means to say here and how I should understand the sentence. This is a site for a conversation about how I understand what she has written and what she thinks about that understanding. Again, she might want to change the tense of *want*, or she might not. But that is exactly what a negotiation of meaning is about. In both of these cases of verb tense "error," what arises out of a discussion may in fact be more important than what will eventually end up in the draft. And, this negotiation offers the possibility of becoming a shared resource for thinking and writing about events and feelings that may or may not be in the past.

Incorrect Word

With the overwhelming use of Microsoft Word in the composing process today, instructors would agree that we see a far greater number of what appear to be incorrect words—words that simply do not make sense within the context of the sentence or ideas presented. Often these are words that Microsoft Word suggests to a writer when a word is misspelled. Sometimes the intended word seems obvious to the instructor; other times it creates a whole host of interesting, confusing, and comic meanings. For example, Josh wrote in another journal, "This hole week over all stunk, I never had the hang to hang with my family nor with any of my true friends." In the second part of the sentence, it appears that he might have repeated the word *hang* and meant to say something else in one of those places. But we could, perhaps, think of the first use of *hang* as in having "the hang of" doing something, knowing how to do something. If we read the second half of the sentence in that way, Josh is saying something about his relationship with his family and maybe a current tension. Or, it might be the same word accidentally repeated. But, a conversation with Josh about this sentence opens up a space for negotiating meaning. Likewise, the beginning of Josh's sentence opens up an interesting way of thinking about his week if we read *hole* as indeed hole and not *whole*. In this case, it is not the entire week but something missing or incomplete in his week, a gap in his week. The usual response as a teacher would be to circle or cross out *hole* and state "wrong word" or rewrite *whole*. But, in that scenario an opportunity is missed to talk about how we read and make meaning out of language.

In the following example from Connie's journal, we see a common mistake of using a homonym. She writes of taking care of her children, "I started to understand peace of mind is far more important then my simple worries." If we think she is comparing two things, then she has an error: she should write "far more important *than* my simple worries." But, if she wants to put these two things in order, first think about peace of mind and next think about simple worries, *then* might be the appropriate word.

Another example, is found in Tyler's journal when he writes, "The overview of my weak Monday was one of my tired days." We might understand him here to be talking about the overview of his *week*, but when we read it as it is, he is writing about a particularly puny day, Monday. Here it is a *weak* Monday. In these examples, I am not suggesting that there are not eventual corrections that must be made. If Tyler is writing about Monday, there is still confusion in the construction of the sentence. Regardless of how we negotiate the meaning, there will still need to be changes that help to make that meaning clear. But, that isn't really the purpose of a translingual approach. It is about negotiating language difference and creating shared resources, not editing student writing.

Sentence Boundaries

The previous example from Tyler's journal leads me to the final type of error in my study. If we discuss the previous sentence with Tyler, work through the word issue, and finally determine that he wants to write *week* instead of *weak*, a new "error" emerges because "The overview of my week" is not a complete sentence. Instead of rephrasing this, adding sentence boundaries in the form of a period or comma and conjunction, and then creating an independent or clearly subordinate clause to match the second part, we might discuss with Tyler our uncertainty and negotiate the sentence together. We might talk about how the clauses might or might not work together and why, as a reader, I am unclear about where the paragraph is going or what exactly he is thinking. These sentences might provide a common resource for us to talk about how sentences work as units of meaning.

Connie offers a different kind of sentence boundary error when she writes the following, "It so weird to me because despite how I felt at that time. This man is still to me God's gift to Earth." The perceptive reader might see that Connie attempts to work through and correct what she sees as a run-on sentence. Instead of a comma, though, she puts a period and creates one sentence that is incomplete and a second that is complete but seems to fit more effectively with the first. If we focus on that first sentence, though, we can have a conversation with Connie about the key word in her sentence *because*. It is this *because* that lets us know that she has more to say, that she wants to say something about how she felt at the time. A teacher might automatically assume that that is the direction Connie is heading, but discussing it with Connie creates a space to talk about reading expectations. A discussion would most likely lead both of us to see that the second sentence must be connected to the first. But, more importantly, the discussion has transformed correction into negotiation.

In my final example of sentence boundary issues, we see Eddie combining multiple independent clauses together in one sentence and not separating them with punctuation and coordinating conjunctions. He writes,

> So later on in that day she had called my mom and asked her and they found out that I lied and I was in even more trouble. We have to realize just because it would be easier to lie then tell the truth and face the consequences telling the truth is what we need to do.

This is primarily a problem of not separating the independent clauses with punctuation.

Instead of simply correcting these sentences for Eddie, though, we might consider negotiating the potential meanings of the sentences. Often when I read sentences like these out loud to students, they hear the confusion. When I explain why I am reading the sentence in a particular way, they can understand the confusion. For example, in reading Eddie's last sentence, I might illustrate how I understand the sentence by emphasizing the word order and action, which suggests that it is the "consequences telling the truth" and not us who accepts the consequences when we tell the truth. Through a conversation with Eddie about these sentences, though, I can help to create a resource for talking about sentence boundaries and meaning that goes beyond teaching punctuation rules. These are the kinds of conversations that we must have for students to see themselves as writers who can negotiate with language to fit their own needs and interests.

Error, Inquiry, and Interrogation

To return to part of the title of this chapter, "And yea I'm venting, but hey I'm writing isn't I," when using a translingual approach to reading student writing, what initially appears as error is really only difference—difference in expectations, difference in language use, and difference in relation to genre. Tyler, the student who wrote the above sentence, made unconventional choices in what he wrote. His sentence shows a different relationship to class, language, and literacy than teachers of writing expect from their students. But, it also shows a complex way of viewing his relationship to learning and his teacher: he understands that he isn't writing exactly what's expected of him but that if the goal is simply to write, then he is meeting that goal.

According to Horner, Lu, Royster, and Trimbur (2011), "A translingual approach proclaims that writers can, do, and must negotiate standardized rules in light of the contexts of specific instances of writing" (p. 305). This student writer tests those rules and attempts to negotiate what is permissible in his academic writing. If writers negotiate, however, so must readers and teachers. While many teachers may argue that a translingual approach is difficult or, perhaps, even impossible for so-called monolingual teachers and students, Horner et al. (2011) call us to recognize what is most useful and significant about this approach:

> While increasing one's linguistic resources is always beneficial, taking a translingual approach is not about the number of languages, or language varieties, one can claim to know. Rather, it is about the disposition of openness and inquiry that people take toward language and language differences.
>
> *(p. 311)*

By not marking Tyler's sentence as incorrect, by not crossing out the *yea* and *isn't*, I am negotiating with the rules and my own expectations for writing. Tyler would not write this kind of sentence for another audience or in another genre because he understands that there are different expectations.

In "Multilingual strategies of negotiating English," Canagarajah (2009) describes what non-native English users do when they speak to one another and offers a powerful and useful redefinition of the word *error* that can apply to native speakers' Englishes and shift writing pedagogy. *Error* is not miscommunication; it is not breaking a rule. Instead *error* is those items one or both members of the interaction refuse to negotiate—that is, it is when one or more speakers, writers, or readers refuse to engage, participate. This is the only true way an *error* can occur.

We might think about this as akin to retraining our "learned inclinations" as Bawarshi (2010) describes. It is our learned inclinations as teachers to cross out, rewrite, edit, even flinch when we see "errors" in student writing. As we have seen through a reading of my students' writing, a way of interrogating those inclinations is to redefine *error* and negotiate with students about the meaning they are making in their writing; it is to defer judgment and to read what is exactly on the paper, as it is, without assuming we know their intentions. If we believe that language is not fixed or static and that it is shifting according to the needs, desires, and interests of users, we must also ask ourselves and our students to critically and intensely read what is on the page rather than what ought to be on the page.

References

Bawarshi, A. (2010). The challenges and possibilities of taking up multiple discursive resources in U.S. college composition. In B. Horner, M. Z. Lu, & P. K. Matsuda (Eds.), *Cross-language relations in composition* (pp. 196–203). Carbondale, IL: Southern Illinois University Press.

Canagarajah, S. (2009). Multilingual strategies of negotiating English: From conversation to writing. *JAC: A Journal of Composition Theory, 29*, 18–48.

Horner, B., Lu, M.-Z., Royster, J. J., & Trimbur, J. (2011). Opinion: Language difference in writing: Toward a translingual approach. *College English, 29*, 303–321.

22

AFTERWORD: REFLECTIONS FROM THE GROUND FLOOR

Dorothy Worden

The introduction to this volume starts with a question: What does "trans" do to language? In one sense, the answer is, "Nothing." People go on using language as they always have, drawing from all their communicative resources, negotiating between and across languages to communicate. A new term and a new approach do nothing to change this. But what if we change the question slightly, asking not what "trans" does to language, but what it does to us as literacy scholars and teachers? What happens then? The chapters in this volume have begun to answer this question in exciting ways. Their answers, I believe, share some important themes that cast light on the ongoing trajectory of a translingual approach to literacy.

Before reflecting on these themes, however, I feel compelled to reflect on my own position as a writing scholar and teacher. In one sense, I am keenly aware that I am an odd choice to sum up a book of such scope. Afterwords, as a genre, are typically reserved for the most senior of scholars. Yet in another sense I believe that perhaps I, as a writing teacher and budding writing researcher, am uniquely suited to the task of interpreting the import of this book. After all, as Paul Kei Matsuda notes in his chapter, the current resurgence of interest in language issues in composition is one that has captured the interest of both established and novice scholars, a mixture that is even reflected in the backgrounds of this volume's contributors. Furthermore, it is novice scholars and classroom teachers who will be called on to develop a translingual approach from a collection of intriguing theoretical notions into the complete and nuanced research agendas and pedagogical approaches the authors of this volume envision. As a result of my position within the field, my reflections on the work done in this volume and my suggestions for future developments take on, for me at least, a greater sense of urgency. I am not, after all, surveying the state of the field from a scholarly penthouse, but from the ground floor. Penthouse reflections help us make sense of new approaches in one way. Ground floor reflections help us make sense of them in a different way. With that caveat, I offer my reflections from the ground floor.

From here, it seems to me that one effect of questioning the separation between languages that has been a feature of our field for so long is that other separations naturally come under scrutiny. Or, to put it more positively, reconnecting languages leads us to reconnect other ideas and practices that we have previously considered as independent subfields. This process of reconnecting is expressed in many different ways throughout the chapters in this book. These chapters work to re-forge connections within and between various scholarly traditions.

One such connection is made between various areas of focus within the study of rhetoric. In particular, the chapters by LuMing Mao, Morris Young, and Jon Reyhner work to reconnect indigenous rhetoric with other rhetorical traditions. From a translingual perspective, they argue, indigenous rhetoric cannot be understood in isolation, but must be recognized as mobile rhetorical practices, always emergent and always in conversation with other discourses. This reconnection of rhetorical traditions is valuable in that it more closely reflects the reality of all rhetorical practice and encourages us to avoid essentializing rhetorical practices, especially non-Western rhetorical practices. Still, vigilance is needed as we proceed in these lines of research. Ellen Cushman's chapter highlights the danger of connecting rhetorical traditions from a one-sided perspective. While her research clearly demonstrates that the Cherokee writing system developed in connection to and resistance against English literacy, that connection does not imply that Cherokee can be understood or taught solely from an English point of reference. Attempting to so understand it limits the accuracy of research and the efficacy of teaching. The question of how to research connections between distinct language practices in a balanced way, one that avoids the trap of forcing the framework of one practice onto another practice, is one that we will do well to address in our future research.

In addition to connecting different rhetorical traditions, a translingual approach also encourages us to question distinctions between established categories of language users and language practices. Joleen Hanson, for example, asks us to reconsider the usefulness of the distinction between monolingual and multilingual students, noting that even those students who self-identify as monolingual posses a variety of strategies for negotiating language difference, strategies that writing teachers can help them to develop. Aimee Krall-Lanoue demonstrates the negotiability of what is an "error" in student writing, and calls into question whether such a term is accurate or useful. Maria Jerskey shows how the boundaries between literacy brokers and literacy learners can break down in the midst of real language practices. Min-Zhan Lu and Bruce Horner likewise demonstrate that a recognizably code-meshed paper and the most conventional of student essays are not actually so very different. Both are exercises in writers' agency as they recontextualize language forms. This questioning of these categories is useful as it asks us to consider anew which of our conceptualizations of language and literacy are accurate and beneficial for us as language researchers and teachers. But here I must urge restraint, especially for myself and my colleagues on the ground floor. Deconstructing the old is exciting and it is often a necessary step, but we should never stop with deconstruction, nor should we be too quick to reject the terms and concepts we have inherited. Rather than tearing it all down and starting from scratch (which leads to the kind of problems Matsuda outlines in his chapter) I suggest that we heed Lu and Horner's chapter and recognize that recontextualizing an old term is just as much an agentive act as replacing it, and both can be used in productive ways.

Additionally, as the title of this book suggests, a translingual approach leads us to redraw connections between community practices and classroom activity. Many of the chapters work to forge these connections, drawing on the language practices of Lebanese cab drivers (Ayash), Kenyan hiphop artists (Milu), the World Social Forum (Wible), and Indian business people (Pandey) to develop new insights and strategies for writing pedagogy. Together, these chapters demonstrate that what happens in the world can help us understand and improve what happens in our classrooms.

Yet we must not be too quick to declare the end of linguistic barriers. A translingual approach holds that language resources are fluid, but such resources are still used in specific contexts, and these contexts are not always so open. Charles Bazerman makes this point well, highlighting the impact of diverse networks of communication on literacy practices and knowledge production. Though processes of globalization have rendered nation states and traditionally defined languages as less important among these networks, we must not neglect the overall impact of these complex contexts. To ignore the power and impact of such contexts leaves us open to serious scholarly and pedagogical pitfalls. Vershawn Ashanti Young and Vivette Milson-Whyte remind us that, though a translingual approach holds that languages are ideological constructions, language ideologies still have a very real impact. Linguistic discrimination carries on, despite our new theories, limiting which language resources are deemed legitimate in which contexts.

Adopting a translingual approach also has an impact on the way we do language research. If language resources are understood as fluid, it only makes sense that our methods for researching them must become equally flexible. It may lead us to expand categories and constructs from existing methodologies, as it did in the chapters by Rebecca Lorimer and John Scenters-Zapico. A translingual approach may also encourage us to move beyond the boundaries of our own disciplinary traditions to find both theories and methodologies to explain what we see in our data. Paul Kei Matsuda advocates rich forms of such cross-disciplinary research as we move forward, and the chapters by Mya Poe and Christiane Donahue demonstrate the benefits of moving beyond disciplinary boundaries in writing research.

The chapters in this volume represent an important step in reimagining writing research and teaching from a translingual perspective. Yet there remains much work to be done, perhaps especially for those of us on the ground floor. For one, a great deal of research into what people actually do in translingual communication is needed. The title of this volume spells out the goal: to connect communities and classrooms, but we cannot connect what we do not understand. Descriptive studies may not always be the most valued in our field, but they provide a crucial empirical basis that is necessary for meaningful pedagogical innovation. Furthermore, this research must not revert to simple tallies of the languages used in a given instance of communication. Such a methodology still sees languages as separate and pre-existing entities. Instead, we need research that examines writer's attitudes, knowledge, and strategies as they emerge in specific acts of writing. As we move forward, we must also work to make our fields more widely and deeply cross-disciplinary. Paul Kei Matsuda provides a strong explanation of the need for such forms of cross-disciplinarity. Such cross-disciplinary research allows us to both enlarge and refine our understandings of how translingual writing works. Finally, future research must strive to take writing classrooms seriously as places of knowledge creation, not just knowledge reception. While translingual writing has already demonstrated its value as theoretical and research concept, its value as an *instructional approach* remains largely untested. For me, the classroom is always the ultimate ground floor perspective, and it is here that the ideas proposed and explored in this book will be tested, refined, and developed. The studies and perspectives included in this volume promise that such ground floor research will be fruitful indeed.

LIST OF CONTRIBUTORS

Nancy Bou Ayash
University of Louisville

Charles Bazerman
University of California Santa Barbara

A. Suresh Canagarajah
The Pennsylvania State University

Ellen Cushman
Michigan State University

Christiane Donahue
Dartmouth College

Joleen Hanson
University of Wisconsin, Stout

Bruce Horner
University of Louisville

Maria Jerskey
LaGuardia Community College

Aimee Krall-Lanoue
Concordia University, Chicago

Rebecca Lorimer
University of Massachusetts, Amherst

Min-Zhan Lu
University of Louisville

LuMing Mao
Miami University

Paul Kei Matsuda
Arizona State University

Vivette Milson-Whyte
The University of the West Indies, Mona

Esther Milu
Michigan State University

Anita Pandey
Morgan State University

Mya Poe
The Pennsylvania State University

Jon Reyhner
Northern Arizona University

John Scenters-Zapico
University of Texas, El Paso

Scott Wible
University of Maryland

Dorothy Worden
The Pennsylvania State University

Morris Young
University of Wisconsin, Madison

Vershawn Ashanti Young
University of Kentucky

INDEX

García, O. 108
Geisler, C. 154
generational boundaries 75–6
genre 22, 155, 176
Giddens, A. 27, 31
Gilmore, P. 73, 77
Githinji, P. 106
global citizenship 41, 42, 43, 150
global hiphop 104–5; *see also* Kenyan
  hiphop
globalization 15–17, 77, 130; of
  English 19–20
Gómez de García, J. et al. 75, 79
Google Translate Toolkit 208
grammar 30, 31, 33, 110
Grize, J. B. 155
guanxi 184
guided participation 173

habitus 5, 52
Haboud, M. 75
Hall, D. L. 50
Hall, J. 170
Harvard-MIT Health Sciences
  Technology program (HST) 174
Haswell, R. 21
Hawai'i 63–8
Hawaiian language immersion schools 75
Hawisher, G. E. et al. 184, 186, 190, 191
Helft, M. 208
heritage languages 16, 17; Asian
  Americans 72–3
Herring, S. C. 207
higher education *see* universities
Hill, R. 78–9
Hindi 216–17, 221–3, 225, 225n2
hiphop *see* African American hiphop;
  global hiphop; Kenyan hiphop
Hoang, H. 68
hole hole bushi 63–8
Holm, A. 76
Holm, W. 76
Holmes, R. B. 85
Hopi 72, 75, 76
Horner, B. et al. 26, 35n1, 54, 93, 96,
  117, 121, 123, 131, 151, 157, 171,
  182–3, 184, 199, 207, 233
House, D. 74–5
Howard, R. M. 213
HST (Harvard-MIT Health Sciences
  Technology program) 174
Hu Jintao 55n2
hybrid academic writing 130

hybrid English 217
hybrid texts 3

Ibrahim, A. 104–5
identity 78–80, 108–9
immigration 16, 17
imperialism 14, 15, 16, 115–16
India 167, 218; *see also* e-writing
Indian Self Determination Act (1972) 84
indigenized language varieties 218
indigenous languages: and colonialism 71–
  2, 73–6; language preservation 93
indigenous rhetoric 49, 51, 52–3, 54, 55n1
institutional brokers 204
intelligibility 219, 220, 224, 228
intercultural rhetoric (IR) 152–3, 162,
  217–19
International Reading Association
  (IRA) 145n1
International Society for the Advancement
  of Writing Research 21
International Symposium on Genre
  Studies (SIGET) 22
Internet 207–8; *see also* monolingual
  students in the writing classroom
IR *see* intercultural rhetoric
IRA (International Reading
  Association) 145n1
Irujo Ametzaga, X. I. 74
Irvine, P. 120
Isaacs, M 116
Isocrates 39, 46

Jaffe, A. 75
Jamaicans and Jamaican Creole (JC) 119–
  20; *see also* code-meshing in U.S.
  classrooms
Jamieson, S. 213
Japanese and Japanese Americans: Hawai'i:
  hole hole bushi 64–8; World War II
  internment camps 60, 68
Jerskey, M. 178
Johnson-Eilola, J. 88
Johnson O'Malley Program 91

Kabotie, F. 72
Kachru, B. B. 119, 120, 217, 219
Kellman, S. G. 108
Kenya African National Union
  (KANU) 107
Kenyan hiphop 104–11;
  Bantuization 106, 107; linguistic
  situation 105; Sheng as translingual

of exercise 211–12; assessment: change
in attitudes 212–13; implications for
teaching 213–14
monolingualism 3
Mooney, J. 85, 87, 89–90
Moreno, A. I. 219
Morgan, M. J. 92
Morris, M. 120
motivator sponsors 186
Mountford, R. 59–60, 67
move analysis 220
Muchiri, M. et al. 125
multilingual writers 170–8; agenda
for research 177–8; biomedical
engineering 173–7; guided
participation 173; learning to
communicate 174–5; mentors 177;
naturalistic studies 172–3; Park:
classroom and laboratory contexts 175–
7; rhetorics of the disciplines 171–2;
WAC writing research 171–4,
177–8; Writing Across the Curriculum
(WAC) 170; see also writing across
languages
multilingualism 77, 93, 162, 170–1; and
English 15, 19–20; at LaGuardia 200–1
mutual intelligibility 220, 224

nation states: cultural nationalism 49; and
literate activity systems 15–17; and
rhetorical education 39–40
National Council of Teachers of English
(NCTE) 21, 132, 141, 145n1
National Institutes of Health (NIH) 174
National Rainbow Coalition (NARC,
Kenya) 107
National Writing Project 23
Native Americans see American Indians
"native-speaker" writing 218
Navajo 74–5, 76
Neal, L. 66
negotiation of meaning see error: a
translingual approach
Nelson, C. 119
Nero, S. J. 120
New Zealand 73, 75, 78–9
Nicholas, S. E. 75, 76
Nyairo, J. 107

Ogechi, N. 106
Ogunde, J. 107
Okihiro, G. 64–5, 68n1
Omi, M. 49

Omoniyi, T. 108–9
orthography 110
Ortmeier-Hooper, C. 150

Pakistan 163–5
Pandey, A. 217, 218
Panos Institute West Africa (PIWA) 43–4
Papastergiadis, N. 162
Parsons-Yazzie, E. 76
partial bilingualism 216
participation 171, 173
pedagogy 7–8
peer learning 204
Penn State Rhetoric and Composition
Conference 128, 134–5
Pennycook, A. 30, 31, 96, 97, 98, 101,
151, 153
persuasion 6
Pickering, J. 94n2
PIWA (Panos Institute West Africa) 43–4
place 6
Pollard, V. 120
polysynthetic languages 76, 89
Powell, J. W. 78
Pratt, M. L. 155, 199–200
prestige boundaries 73–4
Prior, P. 153, 156

Quichua 75

Rastafarianism 106
Ratcliffe, K. 5
recontextualization 6, 30–1, 33
religious boundaries 71–2, 78
reprise–modification 155–6
research 7, 18, 19; see also writing
research
Reyhner, J. 91, 93
Reynolds, N. 66
rhetoric 5–6; indigenous rhetoric 49, 51,
52–3, 54, 55n1; intercultural rhetoric
(IR) 152–3, 162, 217–19; see also Asian
Americans
rhetorical attunement 5, 163, 165, 166–7,
168
rhetorical education 39–46; African Social
Forum communication strategy 44–5;
discourse theory of citizenship 40–1;
and global citizenship 41; and the
nation state 39–40; World Social
Forum 41–3
rhetorical listening 5, 68
rhetorical moves 220